013977

Language and Globalization

Series Editors: **Sue Wright**, University of Portsmouth, UK and **Helen Kelly-Holmes**, University of Limerick, Ireland.

In the context of current political and social developments, where the national group is not so clearly defined and delineated, the state language not so clearly dominant in every domain, and cross-border flows and transfers affect more than a small elite, new patterns of language use will develop. The series aims to provide a framework for reporting on and analysing the linguistic outcomes of globalization and localization.

Titles include:

David Block
MULTILINGUAL IDENTITIES IN A GLOBAL CITY
London Stories

Jenny Carl and Patrick Stevenson (*editors*)
LANGUAGE, DISCOURSE AND IDENTITY IN CENTRAL EUROPE
The German Language in a Multilingual Space

Diarmait Mac Giolla Chríost
LANGUAGE AND THE CITY

Julian Edge (*editor*)
(RE)LOCATING TESOL IN AN AGE OF EMPIRE

Aleksandra Galasińska and Michał Krzyżanowski (*editors*)
DISCOURSE AND TRANSFORMATION IN CENTRAL AND EASTERN EUROPE

Roxy Harris
NEW ETHNICITIES AND LANGUAGE USE

Jane Jackson
INTERCULTURAL JOURNEYS
From Study to Residence Abroad

Helen Kelly-Holmes and Gerlinde Mautner (*editors*)
LANGUAGE AND THE MARKET

Clare Mar-Molinero and Patrick Stevenson (*editors*)
LANGUAGE IDEOLOGIES, POLICIES AND PRACTICES
Language and the Future of Europe

Clare Mar-Molinero and Miranda Stewart (*editors*)
GLOBALIZATION AND LANGUAGE IN THE SPANISH-SPEAKING WORLD
Macro and Micro Perspectives

Ulrike Hanna Meinhof and Dariusz Galasinski
THE LANGUAGE OF BELONGING

Richard C. M. Mole (*editor*)
DISCURSIVE CONSTRUCTIONS OF IDENTITY IN EUROPEAN POLITICS

Leigh Oakes and Jane Warren
LANGUAGE, CITIZENSHIP AND IDENTITY IN QUEBEC

Christina Slade and Martina Möllering (*editors*)
FROM MIGRANT TO CITIZEN: TESTING LANGUAGE, TESTING CULTURE

Colin Williams
LINGUISTIC MINORITIES IN DEMOCRATIC CONTEXT

Forthcoming titles:

John Edwards
CHALLENGES IN THE SOCIAL LIFE OF LANGUAGE

Mario Saraceni
THE RELOCATION OF ENGLISH

Language and Globalization
Series Standing Order ISBN 978–1–4039–9731–9 Hardback
978–1–4039–9732–6 Paperback
(*outside North America only*)

You can receive future titles in this series as they are published by placing a standing order. Please contact your bookseller or, in case of difficulty, write to us at the address below with your name and address, the title of the series and the ISBN quoted above.

Customer Services Department, Macmillan Distribution Ltd, Houndmills, Basingstoke, Hampshire RG21 6XS, England

From Migrant to Citizen

Testing Language, Testing Culture

Edited by

Christina Slade
City University, London, United Kingdom

and

Martina Möllering
Macquarie University, Australia

First published 2010 by
PALGRAVE MACMILLAN

Palgrave Macmillan in the UK is an imprint of Macmillan Publishers Limited,
registered in England, company number 785998, of Houndmills, Basingstoke,
Hampshire RG21 6XS.

Palgrave Macmillan in the US is a division of St Martin's Press LLC,
175 Fifth Avenue, New York, NY 10010.

Palgrave Macmillan is the global academic imprint of the above companies
and has companies and representatives throughout the world.

Palgrave® and Macmillan® are registered trademarks in the United States,
the United Kingdom, Europe and other countries.

ISBN-13: 978–0–230–57633–9 hardback

This book is printed on paper suitable for recycling and made from fully
managed and sustained forest sources. Logging, pulping and manufacturing
processes are expected to conform to the environmental regulations of the
country of origin.

A catalogue record for this book is available from the British Library.

Library of Congress Cataloging-in-Publication Data
From migrant to citizen : testing language, testing culture /
    edited by Christina Slade, Martina Mollering.
        p.   cm. — (Language and globalization)
    ISBN 978–0–230–57633–9 (hardback)
    1. Language and languages—Ability testing. 2. Language policy.
    3. Immigrants—Language. 4. Immigrants—Cultural assimilation.
    5. Citizenship—Australia. 6. Citizenship.
    I. Slade, Christina. II. Möllering, Martina.
    P53.F75 2010
    407.6—dc22   2010004787

10   9   8   7   6   5   4   3   2   1
19 18 17 16 15 14 13 12 11 10

Printed and bound in Great Britain by
CPI Antony Rowe, Chippenham and Eastbourne

Contents

Part III Citizenship Tests Under Revision: Philosophical Implications and Popular Attitudes

List of Tables and Figures

Tables

Figures

Foreword

Christina Slade and Martina Möllering

The issues of citizenship and migration are shared between classical countries of immigration and those nations of Western Europe for whom immigration is largely a post-war phenomenon. The political context of the early twenty-first century has seen a shift in debates about citizenship testing across the nations we examine, reflecting a shift in the role of the nation state, in the understanding of national values and a transformation of both the concepts and practices of the multicultural state. All too often, the various debates about citizenship testing remain isolated. Linguists discuss the level and complexity of language skills required by national tests; cultural theorists examine the underpinnings of the supposed national cultural knowledge that is tested; and others describe how those tested interpret the process. Historians describe the precursors and earlier forms of tests for citizenship and the historical factors influencing their introduction. Lawyers look to the constitutionality of tests; political theorists and philosophers examine the understanding of the relationship between the individual and the state that is presupposed by such tests; and sociologists describe their impact.

This book brings such diverse discourses together, aiming to identify forms of reasoning about citizenship that survive disciplinary divides. Through close attention to the Australian case in the wake of the proposal to introduce citizenship testing in 2006, and its re-emergence after the Woolcott Report in 2008, we aim to chart the historical background, the global context and the philosophical underpinnings of the turn to testing. While bureaucrats develop and politicians impose citizenship tests, as academic lawyers, linguists and historians it is for us to debate the detail of tests; and as philosophers, sociologists and cultural theorists to look to the preconditions for such tests to emerge.

The book is divided into three parts: in the first part, the political debate on citizenship testing is set in the context of Australia's history of citizenship. In the second part, we analyse the proliferation of new tests for citizenship. Finally, we turn to the philosophical debates about identity, values and nation and the implications both for Australia and for the wider international community.

Part I: Citizenship in Australia: From Empire to Multicultural State and Back

This part provides an overview of citizenship testing in Australia. It begins with Christina Slade's 'Shifting Landscapes of Citizenship'. In the case studies presented in the book, drawing together apparently disparate local debates, Slade sees a broad similarity of approach by different nation states. While this may be a consequence of direct modelling (such as the Australian government's gathering of data from Netherlands), in her view it reflects a profoundly important shift in the political, philosophical, linguistic and cultural understanding of citizenship itself.

Andrew Buck and Charlotte Frew follow, examining the broader colonial context of the introduction of language tests across the British Empire. They note similarities with other settler societies, such as Canada and South Africa and insist on the historical background to modern debates about citizenship testing. They suggest that citizenship as a legal category in Australia is exclusive rather than inclusive. Buck and Frew argue that the development of Australian ideas and legislation on immigration and citizenship must be understood in the context of its colonial origins. Not only were the Australian settlements themselves colonies, they also shared features with the colonial settler societies of Canada and South Africa. Through a detailed examination of those colonial origins, Buck and Frew's Chapter 2 sheds new light on the legal and jurisprudential dimensions of the current debate over citizenship and language tests.

The implications of the developing historical context of citizenship testing in Australia throughout late nineteenth and twentieth centuries are at the core of Alison Holland's Chapter 3. She argues that citizenship testing has been an underlying assumption of citizenship policy from 1901, with an explicit function of vetting prospective citizens as suitable for a cohesive nation underpinned by shared values. Assimilationist policies of the 1950s and 60s, while aiming at inclusion, continued to be based on forms of testing. The White Australia Policy, designed to exclude non-Europeans, was predicated on an understanding of what a cohesive nation state would look like. Holland explains that even when the policy was no longer in place, the idea of testing immigrants remained to re-emerge as global population movements, asylum seekers and refugees became politicised.

Ian Tregenza, in Chapter 4, places the Australian case in the broader context of nineteenth-century philosophical debate, and identifies the particular flavour of Australian Idealist thought about citizenship. According to Tregenza, the period immediately before and after Australian federation was one in which there was extensive debate about the philosophical understanding of citizenship. Tregenza focuses on the 'new liberalism' inspired by the late-nineteenth-century British Idealists such as T.H. Green, D.G. Ritchie and Edward Caird. Tregenza identifies a positive conception of freedom, emphasising duties and responsibilities rather than rights, in new idealism. Among its strong features was an emphasis on community and a critical attitude to the free-market liberalism of the time. Paradoxically, Tregenza claims, it was the institutional success of a post-war expanded welfare state that, in part, led to the decline of this conception of citizenship. Debate about citizenship focused on rights and entitlements in reaction to which the new right has recently reminded us of the importance of the duties of citizenship. For Tregenza then there has been a shift from 'horizontal' obligations that members of a political community had, to values such as 'self-reliance'. While the new liberals wished to create linkages between the state and its members, the new right has returned to a model in which the two are described in opposition.

More recent debates surrounding the introduction of citizenship tests, and their appeal to a notion of 'Australian values' are the focus of Lloyd Cox's Chapter 5. He begins by outlining the recent controversy about Australian values and identity in reaction to the citizenship tests. He notes that both the Government and Opposition are committed to a discourse in which values are a key part of the foundation of Australian citizenship and national identity. Citizenship testing then becomes part of the role of the state. Cox takes issue with the substance of this argument and with its practical effects. He problematises the very notion of 'Australian values', while also providing a political and sociological explanation of its recent renaissance. With Alison Holland, he explores the resonances between historically disjoint but philosophically related forms of culturally prescriptive, exclusionary Australian nationalism.

Part II: Cross-National Perspectives on Citizenship: A convergence of testing regimes?

In this part, we consider various citizenship testing regimes against the socio-political background of their implementation. Particular emphasis is given to values and linguistic skills that are tested under those regimes.

Marian Hargreaves starts off this part with Chapter 6, identifying new directions taken in the Anglophone countries. As in Australia, so in Canada and the United States, tests or criteria for those wishing to take up citizenship have existed for more than a century. In these classical countries of immigration new citizens were the norm. In the post-colonial period, flows of migration have been far more complex. In the case of the United Kingdom, there is the vexed issue of citizenship in the colonial mother state for former subjects and legal moves to limit such immigration. Hargreave's Chapter 6 looks at citizenship testing in the United Kingdom, Canada and the United States. It provides an overview of the backgrounds in each country, the changing emphases and priorities for testing and the methods these countries now employ to assess potential citizens. The chapter considers the validity, reliability and practicality of current citizenship tests and highlights both their strengths and their weaknesses.

Western Europe has taken a different route to the regulation of citizenship. In both the Netherlands since the turn of the century (Chapter 7) and in Germany in 2008 (Chapter 8), there has been a reaction to the tensions of immigrant groups (many of whom came to the nations of Western Europe as guest workers) in the form of an introduction of formal testing for citizenship. Whereas the Netherlands had followed a liberal multicultural approach to immigration in the late twentieth century, Germany, up until 2000, had a very restrictive citizenship legislation regime.

Chapter 7 offers an examination of the context, values and linguistic skills in the Dutch immigration testing regime. When Theo van Gogh was shot in Amsterdam by a fundamentalist Dutch Muslim youth in 2004, the image of Dutch society as supremely rational and tolerant was exploded. In fact, the Netherlands tradition of acceptance of refugees and workers from North Africa had been under pressure since 2000 when a conservative government had imposed stricter tests on asylum seekers. The Dutch immigration regime is at the forefront of the wave of language testing in Europe, evaluating values and language skills of prospective migrants even before they arrive in the Netherlands.

Martina Möllering begins Chapter 8 by criticising the discrepancy between the *de facto* status of Germany as an immigration country since the late 1950s and the political stance of denying the reality of this status until the introduction of the new Nationality Act in 2000. The reform of German citizenship law in 2000 is described to be of crucial importance: the principle of *ius soli*, a territorial principle which allows for the acquisition of German citizenship by the fact of being born in Germany, is added to Germany's historic principle of *ius sanguinis*, a descent-based principle of national belonging. Comprehensive immigration legislation, with a new Immigration Act taking effect in 2005, has spurred heated debates on the merits of introducing formal citizenship tests.

Möllering analyses the debate surrounding the introduction of citizenship testing in Germany by linking it to the political debate of 'core' cultural values *(Leitkulturdebatte)*. She emphasises the value attributed to the German language in the current discussion of the integration of migrants in Germany and examines the role of language competency in the citizenship testing regime introduced in September 2008.

In Chapter 9, Emily Farrell examines citizenship tests as introduced in Australia in 2007 detailing both the specifics of the tests and the reactions of those subjected to its processes. Her chapter explores debates and reactions to the 2007 Australian citizenship test at the national level. The introduction of the test was both widely debated and, at the same time, shrouded in secrecy. Farrell explores the voices that contributed to the debate and how they were incorporated or ignored in the final document. She draws on a range of data that are directly or indirectly related to the 2007 Australian citizenship test. These include a corpus of solicited submissions to the Department of Immigration and the published summary of those submissions; submissions to a Senate inquiry and the Senate's subsequent Report; the resources published to help applicants prepare for the test, including earlier published drafts of those resources; media reports surrounding the introduction of the test; and blogs that engaged with the question of citizenship testing and interviews with migrants who reflect on their understandings of citizenship.

Part III: Citizenship Testing under Review: Philosophical and Popular Implications

Catriona Mackenzie's Chapter 10 interrogating the philosophical issues at the heart of the debate relating to citizenship testing opens the final part. Mackenzie explores how citizenship testing raises fundamental questions about the meaning of citizenship and conceptions of national identity in liberal multicultural societies. She draws on the work of Kymlicka *(passim)* in raising questions about the role of shared language and culture in developing national identity and a sense of belonging, the role of a shared group of core values among citizens. Mackenzie situates current debates about citizenship testing in the context of these broader philosophical debates, contrasting the models of assimilation and multiculturalism and examining the obligations of the state towards immigrants. Finally, she turns her focus to the question whether, in principle, citizenship testing is an appropriate model for developing a liberal multicultural society. She notes two areas for further debate: the limits of toleration towards those who preach intolerance, for example on religious grounds, and the limits of toleration towards religious and cultural practices that enshrine injustice towards women.

In Chapter 11, Murray Goot and Ian Watson report on their fine-grained analysis of social science data to chart how Australians actually think about new citizens. They identify strands in what they call 'nativism': the belief that to be Australian one needs to be born in Australia, lived most of one's life there or be of Australian heritage, and correlate those attitudes with education levels and broad political orientation. Not surprisingly, higher levels of education among Australian born non-migrants correlate with non-nativist views. On the other hand, among overseas born migrants, higher levels of education correlate with nativism. A further set of correlations show that opposition to immigration is related to education levels and probability of voting for parties of the right, but not to economic hardship. In their chapter, Murray and Watson explore: the extent to which nativism explains attitudes to immigrants and multiculturalism; how various fears – about job insecurity and economic decline, about law and order and about threats to the nation of other kinds – fuel nativist beliefs; and how being a nativist shapes one's vote, especially votes for One Nation. Their work provides an empirical basis for an understanding of attitudes to citizenship.

In the final Chapter 11 of this part, Martina Möllering and Linda Silaghi discuss the Woolcott Review of the Australian test of 2008, and the political context of developments in citizenship testing. The review itself highlights the narrow conception of cultural knowledge and the 'intimidating [...] and discriminatory' nature of the original Australian citizenship test of 2007. It also seeks an alternative focus for *what* is tested (namely, an understanding of the importance of the pledge of allegiance and hence of becoming an Australian citizen) and of *how* it is tested (by introducing pathways for those whose English skills are insufficient). Broadly speaking, the Rudd government has accepted the first point, altering the test and introducing citizenship education, but insists on competence in English in prospective citizens. Möllering and Silaghi suggest that while the focus of the test has moved from 'earning the privilege' to 'understanding the responsibilities' of citizenship, the insistence on language skills takes us back to a narrower understanding of the identity of citizens.

From the essays in this volume, it is clear that there are two opposed tendencies reflected in regimes of citizenship in the countries of immigration in the twenty-first century. On the one hand, processes of globalisation have undermined those national controls and national identities which had flourished over the previous two centuries in the developed world. The pressure of refugees, population movements and economic pressures have, on the other hand, led to a restatement of national cultural stereotypes which citizenship tests too often reinforce. It is our hope that the fine-grained analysis of the Australian case of debate about citizenship testing and of the international comparisons in the chapters that follow will add to our understanding of these new forms of testing which have such a significant impact on so many.

Notes on Contributors

Professor Andrew Buck

A.R. Buck is Associate Dean, Research, in the Faculty of Arts at Macquarie University and a Professor of Legal History in the Macquarie Law School. He is the author and editor of a number of books on law and history, including, most recently, *The Grand Experiment: Law and Legal Culture in British Settler Societies* (2008) and *The Making of Australian Property Law* (2006). He has been Visiting Professor of Law at the University of Western Ontario and the University of Florida, and the recipient of Research Fellowships at the Huntington Library, Los Angeles and the John Carter Brown Library, Providence, Rhode Island.

Dr Lloyd Cox

Lloyd Cox graduated with a BA and MA (Hons) from the University of Auckland and a PhD in political sociology from La Trobe University. He teaches units on Australian politics, nationalism and U.S. foreign policy at Macquarie University's Department of Politics and International Relations. His main research is in Australian and comparative politics, globalisation and nationalism. He is particularly interested in the intersection between accelerated globalisation and questions around national identity and citizenship, about which he is presently writing.

Dr Emily Farrell

Emily received her PhD in Linguistics from Macquarie University in April 2009. Her research came out of an ARC Discovery Grant project (awarded to Ingrid Piller) focused on highly proficient adult second language users of English in Sydney. Her interests lie at the intersection of sociolinguistics, discourse analysis and migration and transnationalism research. Emily has taught in the Linguistics departments at the University of Sydney and UNE and is currently involved in a DIAC-funded ethnographic project examining the relationship between language learning and settlement success at the AMEP RC. Her next research project will focus on migration and transnationalism in the art communities of Berlin, funded by the DAAD.

Charlotte Frew

Charlotte Frew is completing a PhD in the Macquarie Law School, Macquarie University. Her thesis examines the law that prohibited marriage to a deceased wife's sister in the nineteenth century; a topic that animated Victorian society in the United Kingdom and its colonies.

Professor Murray Goot

Murray Goot is an Australian Research Council Australian Professorial Fellow in the Department of Modern History, Politics and International Relations at Macquarie University. A Fellow of the Academy of the Social Sciences in Australia and a past President of the Australasian Political Studies Association, he held a Personal Chair in the Department of Politics at Macquarie University from 1997 to 2009. He has written widely on public opinion, political parties and the media; has been an election columnist for the *Australian Financial Review* and the *Sydney Morning Herald*; and has served as a consultant on public opinion to several government enquiries, including the FitzGerald Committee to Advise on Australia's Immigration Policy (1987–88). Murray is currently working on: a study of electioneering from the nineteenth century to the twenty-first; studies of the polls, the press and Australian politics since the 1940s; and a study of public opinion, political rhetoric and public policy in relation to Australia's involvement in the war in Iraq. His most recent book (with Tim Rowse) is *Divided Nation? Indigenous Affairs and the Imagined Public* (Melbourne University Press, 2007).

Marian Hargreaves

Marian's research interests include reading difficulty, rater reliability, assessment task development and curriculum development. She also has extensive practical experience in English language testing and assessment. Marian has an MA in History and recently completed her MA in Applied Linguistics, at Macquarie University, with a dissertation on language testing for Citizenship.

Dr Alison Holland

Alison Holland is a Lecturer in Australian History/Studies in the Department of Modern History. Included in her teaching portfolio is a Masters unit on Australian citizenship. Her current research interest is the historicisation of citizenship and human rights in Australia, with a particular interest in Indigenous citizenship.

Professor Catriona Mackenzie

Catriona Mackenzie is Professor in Philosophy at Macquarie University, Sydney. She received her PhD from the Australian National University and has taught at Monash University and, as guest professor, at Utrecht University, Netherlands. Her main research interests are in ethics, applied ethics, moral psychology, feminist philosophy and political philosophy. She is co-editor of *Practical Identity and Narrative Agency* (Routledge 2008) and of *Relational Autonomy: Feminist Perspectives on Autonomy, Agency and the Social Self* (Oxford University Press 2000). Her articles have appeared in numerous edited collections and journals, including *Australasian Journal of Philosophy, Hypatia, Journal of Applied Philosophy, Journal of Social Philosophy* and *Philosophical Explorations*. She was awarded the 2007 Australian Museum Eureka Prize for Research in Ethics.

Professor Martina Möllering

Martina Möllering is Professor in European Languages and Head of the Department of International Studies at Macquarie University in Sydney. She undertook her undergraduate tertiary education in Migration Studies and Language Teaching in Germany, followed by an MA and PhD in Linguistics completed in Australia. She has been a guest lecturer at the University of Essen, Germany, and has contributed to postgraduate programs of the Hellenic Open University in Patras, Greece.

Martina's language acquisition research has included computer-assisted language learning, with a particular interest in intercultural learning in computer-mediated communication. Martina's most current research, concerned with the theorisation of language, migration and identity construction in globalised contexts, is focused on the role of language competency in citizenship tests in Europe and Australia.

Professor Christina Slade

Christina Slade is at present Dean of Arts and Social Sciences at City University London, and holds an appointment as Professor at the University of Utrecht in the Netherlands. From 2003–8 she was Dean of Humanities at Macquarie University in Sydney.

She was educated at the Australian National University, Somerville College, Oxford and at the University of New England. She has lived in Canberra, Beirut, Nairobi, Islamabad, Brussels, New York and Mexico City, and has taught at the University of Canberra, at New York

University, at La Universidad Ibero Americana and the ITESM in Mexico City, Université de Québec à Montréal, the Univeristé Libre de Bruxelles and the Université de L'Etat in Mons, Belgium.

At present, she is working on issues at the intersection of questions of media and national identity. Her books include *The Real Thing: Doing Philosophy with Media*, (Peter Lang, 2002) and *Critical Communication* (Prentice Hall, 2000). Her recent articles have dealt with questions of media and national identity.

Dr Ian Tregenza

Ian Tregenza lectures in the Department of Modern History, Politics and International Relations at Macquarie University and is the author of *Michael Oakeshott on Hobbes: A Study in the Renewal of Philosophical Ideas* (Exeter: Imprint Academic, 2003). He is currently engaged in an Australian Research Council-funded project examining the history of philosophical Idealism in Australia, 1850–1950. A central component of this project concerns nineteenth and twentieth century debates on citizenship and Australian civilisation.

Dr Ian Watson

Ian Watson is a visiting Senior Research Fellow in the Department of Modern History, Politics and International Relations at Macquarie University. He has been an applied researcher for the last two decades, concentrating on the quantitative analysis of economic and social issues. His background is in the areas of labour market analysis, sociology and history. Prior to becoming a freelance researcher, Ian worked for 13 years as a Senior Research Fellow at the Australian Centre for Industrial Relations Research and Training at Sydney University. Ian has recently published in the areas of wage inequality, casualisation in the labour market, voting behaviour and social attitudes.

Professor Sue Wright

Sue Wright's research interest is language practice at the macro level and through time. How did communities of communication constitute themselves in the past? What caused language convergence and divergence? How have political structures and language practices influenced each other? Such study of the interaction of language, polity and people permits an understanding of how language both shapes and is shaped by the political, social and cultural context in which it develops. It illustrates how difficult it is to affect the process and is useful in showing the limits of language policy and planning.

In 2006, Sue Wright completed a project on language in the institutions of the European Union (EU). As they develop a new form of supranational political organisation, key EU actors appear to subscribe to several contradictory and competing language ideologies. On one level, member states continue to follow the nineteenth century European nation state system, link language and citizenship and strive for national communities of communication. On another level, the EU appears a laboratory where a post-national concept is being trialed: power is relocated at both supra- and sub-national level and there are new linguistic practices evolving in tandem with both processes.

Sue Wright is also editing a collection of essays on language and citizenship in Europe for a special issue of UNESCO's *International Journal on Multilingual Societies*.

Part I

Citizenship in Australia: From Empire to Multicultural State and Back

1
Shifting Landscapes of Citizenship

Christina Slade

Introduction

What it is to be a citizen is not a simple matter. For an individual to be a citizen is for that person to belong in a particular way to a community, be it a 'city' (as in the origins of the term), a nation state or some other broad grouping such as the European Union (EU). That an individual *is* a citizen of a community is a matter of law. However, the relationship also carries cultural connotations. Being a citizen implies that an individual shares certain beliefs with, and behaves as a member of, the community. The beginning of the twenty-first century has seen a number of nation states impose – or refine – tests to ensure that citizens to whom they grant the formal legal status have appropriate cultural attributes. Not only have the classical countries of immigration, such as Australia, Canada and the United States, strengthened or reintroduced stringent tests for migrants to become citizens, but the countries of Western Europe have, for the first time, also turned to testing regimes. Since the beginning of the century, the Netherlands and Germany have imposed tests of cultural knowledge for new citizens; the Netherlands has developed a civic integration regime which prospective migrants take before arrival; and the United Kingdom has revised its requirements of cultural knowledge and toughened its stance on visas and migration (Chapter 6). In a time of globalisation, it is remarkable that so many nations are insisting on nationally based cultural attributes for would-be citizens.

This chapter outlines the issues which underpin discussions of migration and citizenship in the early twenty-first century. Part I deals briefly with the historical and philosophical origins of the concept. Part II focuses on aspects of citizenship, ranging from the legal and political

3

understanding of the relationship at one extreme, to notions of cultural belonging on the other. Part III discusses the impact of new media on citizenship, followed by a case study contrasting assimilationist and multicultural approaches to those seeking citizenship. The penultimate part argues that models of citizenship testing are flawed. The conclusion deals with the pressing need to bring the varied discourses of citizenship together in discussions of citizenship-testing.

Globalisation has altered our understanding of citizenship. The power of the nation has been undermined by the rise of transnational entities such as the EU, of trading blocs such as the North American Free Trade Association, and by the increasing pace of globalisation of trade and information, especially with the Internet.[1] Yet legal citizenship remains a national affair. The fact that citizenship-testing regimes have been introduced in Western European nations since the beginning of this century shows how strongly states and their citizens still fear the loss of national identity. Sue Wright asks in her introduction to a recent volume of the *International Journal of Multicultural Studies*:

> Why at this precise point in time are so many states requiring would-be citizens to pass entrance tests? (2008, 1)

Wright considers two explanations for the rise of citizenship tests in Europe: fears for security and what she calls the issue of 'critical mass'. In the wake of 9/11 and the moral panic and fear of Islam following the attack on New York, security has dominated national agendas. This has certainly been a factor in the rise of citizenship testing. Debate has been framed in terms of what Huntington (1996) called a 'clash of civilizations'.[2] However, as is pointed out in the chapter dealing with the Netherlands (Chapter 7) in this book, the introduction of more rigorous tests for migrants predated 9/11 and, while certainly fuelled by fear, had deeper roots in the fear of loss of national identity. The nation state (with its concomitant national identity) is a relatively recent construct even in Western Europe, where the 1648 Treaty of Westphalia is often cited as the crucial starting point (cf. e.g. Held, 2003). In the New World, national identities were self-conscious creations of the last two centuries. While all national identities are to some extent social constructions, the recent scale of migration has led to concerns that new waves of migrants will undermine the practices and values of the West. There is a fear that a massive intake of migrants, or *newer* migrants in the case of Australia and the New World, will dilute traditional or hard-won identities, which will no longer have the critical mass necessary to maintain their culture. Citizenship-testing regimes are a response to those concerns.

This book focuses on the debate around the introduction of a test for citizenship in Australia, putting it into its international context. The Australian test was introduced by the Howard Government, following little more than a year of consultation, in October 2007. It was seen as a potential vote winner in the elections due that year. It was widely criticised at the time, in particular for its focus on a traditional construction of Australian culture (Chapter 9). It included questions about figures such as Donald Bradman, a cricketer now long dead. The new Rudd Government appointed Richard Woolcott to review the test in April 2008. His report, handed to the Government in August, was made public on 22 November 2008. The report, entitled *Moving Forward...Improving Pathways to Citizenship*, is broad ranging, considered and, with minor exceptions, has been accepted by the Government. The major change is that the test will no longer concentrate on questions of cultural knowledge such as the identity of cricketers, but will concentrate on an understanding of the Pledge of Allegiance.[3] The Pledge is key to the review committee's recommendations about the requirements for Australian citizenship. As the Minister for Immigration and Culture, Chris Evans, said in presenting the report to Parliament on 24 November:

> If there is any clear definition of what it means to be an Australian citizen then surely it lies in the very nature and content of this contract. [...] The establishment of the Pledge at the core of citizenship will give the test process a coherence and rationale it currently lacks. It is the missing link. (2008, 3)

It is in this spirit that the report called for greater clarity about the levels of English both used in the test and required for citizens, suggesting that the level of language skills should be that sufficient for understanding of the Pledge (Chapter 12).

The fact that some version of Australian test will be maintained, even after a critical review, is an example of the ubiquity of forms of testing. In the Australian, North American and European cases apparently disparate local debates led to broad similar approaches. While this *may* be a consequence of direct modelling, it reflects a profoundly important shift in the political, philosophical, linguistic and cultural understanding of citizenship itself.

Ideals and contexts of citizenship

Citizenship-testing regimes are not new; nor are they uniquely tied
to nation states. Indeed, language barriers were used in the British
Empire as exclusionary devices for British colonies from the beginning
of the twentieth century (Chapter 2). Citizenship as a political relation between the public and the private, the state and the individual,
has been constantly reconstituted as the shifting and philosophically
charged conceptions of public, private, state and individual alter; and
with those changes, the requirements to be a citizen have altered. While
there is a strong continuity in the philosophical understandings of citizenship, contemporary globalisation and media have created a new
context for regimes of citizenship, and of citizenship testing.

Normative and descriptive theories of citizenship draw on models
from widely different social and political contexts. The Athenian citizen, as described by Aristotle, was required to be engaged in the activities
and practices of the state. The ideal of the active citizen and of the public
sphere continue to be influential in modern theory particularly in the
twentieth-century Habermasian form. Yet the Athenian citizen was very
different from the modern counterpart, even in principle. For Aristotle,
even Plato's ideal state of just 5000 citizens was too large. As Heater
puts it:

> Aristotle was quite dogmatic that in order to discharge their func-
> tions effectively citizens must inhabit a city-state that is exceedingly
> compact and close-knit. (1990, 3)

Aristotelian citizenship was highly exclusive – there was even doubt as
to whether working men should be included. Modern forms of republicanism, drawing on the Athenian model, while differing markedly in
scale, insist on the participatory ('active') aspects of citizenship. Maynor
(2003, ch. 1) includes such thinkers as Hannah Arendt, Rawls and Sandel
as inheritors of the Athenian view of citizenship.

In this volume (Chapter 4), Ian Tregenza traces the transformations of
ideals of active citizenship in Australia. Tregenza draws on what Judith
Brett calls a 'virtue' model of citizenship as the underlying form of the
understanding of citizenship in the creation of the Australian state, and
contrasts it strongly with the 'value' conception characteristic of recent
approaches to citizenship. For Tregenza, the shift from active to passive forms of citizenship reflects the rise of a liberal tradition focusing
on rights. He distinguishes forms of liberalism of the mid-twentieth

century, in which 'rights were understood as deriving from duties which stemmed from membership of a political community', from neo-liberal conceptions of rights. For Tregenza, neo-liberal conceptions of citizenship emphasise the individual citizen as consumer. They then fail to incorporate the insights of political commitment to the group that earlier liberal conceptions were founded on. Tregenza makes a subdued call for the revival of active citizenship. This concern with the model of an individual citizen-consumer arises again in the next section, in the context of our understanding of cosmopolitan citizens. An active citizen proves citizenship through activities of participation in a political community.

In a quite different sense, the Athenian model of active citizenship has been taken up in Habermas' *The Structural Transformation of the Ideal Public Sphere* (1993). Habermas traces the transformations of the modern world and incorporates them into a model in which the *ideal* of reasoned debate among the citizenry maintains the function of legitimating democratic leadership. Writing in the aftermath of the Second World War, he was concerned to ensure that nation states maintained spaces of strong reflective debate about national actions. In the 40 years since he first published his work in German, the European and global context has been transformed again, into a genuinely transnational space.

The Roman Republic has likewise served as a model for accounts of citizenship from Machiavelli to theorists in recent years (Pettit, 1997, 2001; Skinner and Strath, 2003). In the current context, the transnational flavour of Roman citizenship is striking. While based on a city state, Roman citizenship evolved with the empire, culminating with the formal extension of Roman citizenship to all those in the empire, under the *Constitutio Antoniniana* in AD 212. Mathison (2006, 1015) argues that, in spite of some scepticism amongst scholars, citizenship in the later Roman Empire was genuinely transnational. As he says:

> during the later Roman Empire, the Roman government [...] created a functional equivalent of universal citizenship. This was done largely for purposes of administrative streamlining, but even the streamlining could not have happened if there had not been a pervasive belief in the world of Roman officialdom that people living under Roman authority ought to have access to Roman law. (2006, 1040)

Mathison contrasts this model with that based on the nation state and specifically questions whether the Roman model might not be appropriate to the modern globalised world. The question is one which has exercised many scholars (e.g. Habermas, 2001; Peters, 2005). There is no doubt that globalisation has undermined the ability of the nation state to manage independently of other nations. While normative accounts of the ideal global citizen exist in the literature (e.g. Held, 2003), philosophical debates surrounding notions of citizenship overwhelmingly continue to be framed in terms of the state.

Between passport and belonging

Citizenship-testing regimes exist under the control of individual nation states, and are essentially mechanisms of exclusion. They are generally imposed by nations where conditions of life are preferable to those in other countries (or perceived to be so), and aim to limit migrant influx into the preferred destinations, ostensibly to preserve those conditions that make the country desirable to live in. Citizenship tests also have an internal political role: to reassure voters that governments are keeping watch. (The political message may of course be cosmetic. Lloyd Cox in Chapter 5 points out that in the Australian case, a government rhetoric of exclusion during the Howard years was accompanied by increasing levels of immigration.) The mechanisms for citizenship testing are framed in international legislation and are hedged about with domestic and international structures. Only citizens can access consular protection, for instance, and the level of protection varies widely depending on the financial strength of the nation to which a citizen belongs. Australians, along with US and European citizens, have well-funded consulates to assist them if working or travelling in other countries; others, such as Pakistani and Indian workers in the Gulf, receive less assistance.

Possession of a passport is the minimal 'barest' form of citizenship, but there are other forms which are equally powerful. In his book *Cultural Citizenship*, Toby Miller distinguishes political, economic and cultural aspects of citizenship: the political, consisting of the politico-legal rights of citizenship; the economic, of rights 'to work and prosper'; and the cultural, which he defines as 'the right to know and speak' (2007, 35). He charts a web of political, sociological, philosophical, historical and legal arguments based on notions of cultural citizenship. The formal political and legal aspects of citizenship which define the rights of 'bare' citizenship lie at the far end of the spectrum from those forms of belonging which derive from economic and cultural activity. The conceptual space of citizenship debates could be modelled as a topological space. At one extreme of such space lies bare citizenship – the formal or political rights entailed by having a passport. At the other extreme lie cultural practices by which citizens define their identity and sense of belonging to a community, ranging from use of language, food, clothing and work habits, to sport and intellectual style. Between bare and cultural citizenship there lies an interconnecting web of concepts. The nature of these interconnections is much debated. This discussion draws on a range of sources, from Isin and Turner's (2007) exploration of the complex and shifting practices of citizenship, to traditional philosophical debate, focused on the normative underpinnings of our concepts of *good citizenship*.

The relation between the state, its citizens and their cultural identity is highly contested. Liberal conceptions of the state, for instance, see the role of the state as the guarantor of individual's choice as to their cultural practices. Somewhat paradoxically, versions of this liberal conception have led to a normative requirement of cultural uniformity among *would-be* citizens, in terms of citizenship testing.[4] To take a second example, much of the debate about diversity has been framed in terms of cultural citizenship as if cultural citizenship only exists where there is cultural diversity. Thus, when Pakulski writes:

> claims for cultural citizenship involve not only tolerance of diverse identities but also – and increasingly – claims to dignified representation, normative accommodation, and active cultivation of these identities and their symbolic correlates (1997, 77),

he is assuming that claims for cultural citizenship arise only when one is *not* associated with the dominant culture. Citizenship tests prove otherwise. In such tests, the dominant culture lays out its claims for cultural citizenship.

The complexities in conceptual discussions of citizenship derive from implicit assumptions about the connections between different aspects of the network of political, cultural and economic citizenship. The widespread assumption that citizenship constitutes a one-to-one relationship between a state and an individual often slides to a stronger claim that a citizen should have a unique *cultural* relationship to the nation state. The stronger claim is then read as the view that citizens owe allegiance and loyalty to the state to which they belong and to that state alone. Pledges of Allegiance, willingness to go to war and identification with national sports teams have strong emotional overtones which draw on this stronger view. Behind much of the rhetoric of national identity is the view that citizens should belong to and fight for the nation to which they belong, and also identify with the relevant national icons and symbols. A sense of national identity is assumed to be manifest in pride in sporting achievements or cultural achievement. Yet, the sense national identity is no longer so simple, if it ever was. To use the much-quoted phrase of Anderson (1983), 'imagined identities' are no longer bounded by the physical borders of the nation state. The one-to-one connection between nation and cultural identity is mythical, however potent that myth may be.

The view that each person should have one and only one national citizenship is best read as a *normative* claim about the relation between cultural and bare citizenship. It is striking that it was only really in the second part of the twentieth century that the idea of a unique (one-to-one) relationship between the state and its members really took purchase. In Australia, as pointed out by Alison Holland in Chapter 3, while there were strong legal conditions restricting entry to the country, Australian citizenship *per se* did not come into existence until after the Second World War. Until that time all Australians were British subjects. Nor did Australia have independent diplomatic relations until after that war and, even after the introduction of specifically Australian forms of citizenship, British citizens were permitted to vote and work permanently in the Australian Public Service. This did not at all prevent the self-conscious development of an Australian identity, begun well before Federation in 1901.

As immigration from Europe and the Middle East to Australia accelerated in the post-war years, the popular sentiment was that new Australians should take up citizenship and, with it, loyalty to Australia. Putting aside for the moment the assimilation/multicultural debate, at the level of bare citizenship the assumption was that migrants, the British excluded, in taking up Australian citizenship, should renounce former loyalties. Some countries of immigration, such as Italy, Lebanon and Iran, did not accept that their citizenship *could* be revoked; but in all other cases, Australian law was clear – choosing dual nationality was unacceptable. Those who took up alternative citizenships automatically lost their Australian citizenship (Rubinstein, 2008).

Australian law on dual citizenship changed in 2002, as it had earlier in the United States and in many European countries such as the Netherlands.[5] (Italy is so broad-minded on such issues that its parliament elects members representing the diaspora – an Australian citizen from Melbourne represents Australia and the Pacific in Rome.) In the case of Australia, as in the United States, acceptance of dual citizenship was driven by the need to attract economically successful citizens. In a globalised world, many live and work in places other than their nations of birth, and in doing so, contribute to the economic and social life of their new countries. However, as soon as dual citizenship is allowed, citizens can no longer be uniquely loyal to their country of citizenship. Dual citizens presumably have at least dual loyalties. The case is even more complex with the EU. By virtue of citizenship in any EU country, citizens automatically acquire transnational citizenship in the Union and thereby what is tantamount to multiple citizenships, increasing in number as membership expands. EU citizenship has been hedged about with constraints, for instance on the rights of citizens of more recent accession states to work in the states of 'Old Europe'; nevertheless such rights exist. Attempts to develop a notion of cultural citizenship for EU members (Weiner, 1998) have not been successful; but the notion that there *should* be such cultural citizenship remains a driving element in EU policy. The ideal EU citizen should exhibit multiple loyalties.

The developed nations of the West have come to a position which is, apparently, inconsistent: that some *must* and others *need not* develop cultural knowledge in order to be granted citizenship. Dual or multiple citizenship is offered to those who enter with economic benefit to the country without any test of cultural knowledge. A wealthy investor, a scientist or skilled tradesperson can take up citizenship without abandoning pre-existing cultural affiliations. British, Dutch, Australian, US and Canadian entrepreneurs, academics, knowledge workers, teachers and tradespersons have little difficulty with cultural hurdles: they are permitted to maintain the mother culture. By way of contrast, many immigrants, in particular those who come for family reunion, are subjected to rigorous and culturally specific testing and are expected to assimilate on their arrival. This is particularly evident in the Netherlands, where the pre-entry testing in Dutch does not apply to such 'Westerners' as Australians and New Zealanders (Chapter 7). To put it in controversial terms, those who are suitably cosmopolitan or transnational in their outlook are permitted diverse cultural attitudes, while those most in need are forced into cultural straightjackets.

Of course, governments have a right to vet prospective migrants in order to maintain economic well-being and the civil society of their nations. Governments argue (perhaps with good reason) that suitably cosmopolitan employees add to economic well-being and share a commitment to the core practices of a modern state. Less-educated migrants, in particular those from Islamic countries, may not share those values and could undermine the fabric of society. The consequence is that the new landscape of citizenship divides the world into those who are citizenship-rich, and those who are citizenship-poor. Those who are citizenship-rich possess passports or the right to live and work in at least one prosperous country (and potentially more). Others are citizenship-poor: refugees or those whose country of birth does not give great opportunity. Possession of a suitable passport is essential to a prosperous life. In the conceptual space that ranges from bare formal citizenship to cultural citizenship, bare citizenship is presupposed by all other forms of cultural engagement. And passports remain (except in highly unusual circumstances) in the gift of the nation state.

New media: New citizenship

In the twenty-first century, new technologies have put further pressure on the nation state. Global media networks and, to an even greater extent, Internet access have fractured national public spheres, introducing not just global information, but new types of allegiance and forms of political action – in effect new citizenships. In the last Part, I argued that notwithstanding globalisation, the nation state has emphatically reimposed control over bare, formal citizenship. Cultural citizenship is at the same time unprecedently globalised.

The immediacy of global news has altered the notions of time and geographical place (Giddens, 1990; Price, 2002). As media consumers we are part of a global space, in which distant events play out in real time via satellite feed. First CNN and now a range of satellite transnational media outlets, and critically the Arabic transnational media, have altered the state-based and local control of news creating mediated spaces independent of the nation (Chalaby, 2005; Miladi, 2003; Miles, 2005; Sakr, 2002). Technologies such as the Internet and the mobile telephone have altered patterns of social and political relations from a linear hierarchical model to a networked and associative style (Castells, 2001). The traditional model of public broadcasting as setting the agenda, at least in Europe and the former British Empire, is completely outdated. The public sphere of debate has become a *mélange* of transnational public spaces, fostered by proliferating transnational media access, and what Gitlin (1998) called 'public sphericules', sub-national spaces in which debate on public affairs occurs in groups.

In the case of Europe, the media environment has been utterly transformed from its past as separate nations dominated by separate state run public media. These days the media are no longer only available in national languages. What has emerged is not the hoped-for pan-European public sphere, but rather a multi-channeled, multi-lingual free-for-all; a fragmented set of sub- and super-national public spheres (Volkmer, 2007). Even where there is an assumption of shared political and social *mores*, national and sectarian differences emerge in the media space. The case is acute with diasporic groups. Diasporic media include the long-standing forms of newspaper, magazines, radio and television, all of which in principle were governed by state regulations. Newer technologies, in particular satellite television, cannot be so regulated. Indeed in Europe, regulation of satellite is possible only in the country of upload. This means that what is broadcast in France is not regulated, even in principle, by the French government.

The loss of control of media by the state has undermined the ability of the nation state to set the agenda of news and the civil society. For instance, Arabic language media have opened a pan-Arabic transnational space of debate. Thousands of Arabic language television channels are available on satellite. They include not just channels aimed at a transnational audience, such as *Al Jazeera* or *Al Manar*, but also the domestic Egyptian, Moroccan, Tunisian, Iraqi, Yemeni, Saudi and Syrian stations. In Europe, nine different satellites offer a selection of several hundred Arabic language channels. In Australia, apart from a short period when the major provider TARBS TV went into receivership, the landscape is equally densely inhabited. The newer space of Arabic language and Islamic media has fundamentally recast the world of the Arabic-speaking diaspora. Where once diasporic communities gathered and shared news of the birth country in *cafés* or read local diasporic media, they now can share the mediated public sphere of the birth country as well as other transnational media worlds in their mother tongue. The Arabic language media world cuts across the other linguistic and political boundaries of nation states, creating a new cross-national diasporic public.

The 'ideal public sphere' of Habermasian theory describes a nation state within which democratic processes are theorised as questioned and legitimated by a process of deliberation among citizens. Some argue that new forms of media give rise to a *transnational* public sphere (Bredt, 2006). Is the new landscape defined by mediated citizenship an *ideal* transnational public sphere? Nancy Fraser (2007) reminds us that what characterised the ideal public sphere was normative legitimacy and political effectiveness. Both are lacking in the new mediated transnational public sphere, which is neither democratically appointed, nor able to legislate. The issuing of passports is a clear case in point: however important global media may be for cultural citizenship, the nation decides formal citizenship. This is so even in the EU which *is* a genuine transnational public sphere, with legislative power and political legitimacy. Passports in the EU are awarded by the member nation, not by the Union. In any case, the EU is distinctly exclusionary, as the proposed EU common immigration policy shows (Chapter 7).

Transnational forms of political allegiance are not new. It is the mediated landscape of citizenship that has changed, divorcing control of the cultural agenda from the seat of political power. If citizenship testing shows the strength of the nation state in terms of bare citizenship, the new mediated environment shows its powerlessness when it comes to cultural citizenship.

Acquiring cultural citizenship: Multicultural or assimilationist?

Cultural citizenship for those who are already citizens is a complex matter. For migrants or would-be migrants, it is even more complex. Two models of incoming cultural citizenship dominated debate in the late twentieth century: assimilation, as in the French model, and multiculturalism, a version of which became the proud achievement of Australia, along with other nations of immigration, such as Canada. The literature on multiculturalism is extensive; and the issues are philosophically and politically challenging. Yet 'multiculturalism' as a label and as a strategy has fallen into disfavour. A brief case study of France and Australia illuminate the contrasts drawn in the book between regimes in the EU and those in classical countries of immigration.

The scale of Australia's post-war immigration is of a different order of magnitude from anything in Europe: almost one in four of Australia's 2000 population was a post-war migrant. Even in the period in which Europeans became exercised about the inflow of migrants, the net intake of immigrants as a percentage of population in Australia from 1950 to 2000 was 23.1 per cent; whereas in France the figure was only 7.9 per cent (Tiffen and Gittens, 2004, 10–11). Australia gave citizenship to 610 migrants per 100,000 population in the 1990s, while France to 173. There are other differences. Unlike in France, employment rates among recent Australian immigrants (with a few exceptions such as in the Lebanese Muslim Lakemba area of Sydney), equal those of longer-term residents of the country. The difference between Australia's multiculturalism and the French assimilationist attitude to immigrants is profound.

In France, since the Revolution, the model of citizenship that has underpinned migration has been assimilationist. As a member of the EU, France has now adopted the layer of transnational citizenship of the EU. But the myths and metaphors of an essentially eighteenth-century revolutionary *patrie* continue to underpin the understanding of what it is to be a citizen. This is true of Islamic French citizens as well. As Olivier Roy puts it, while British multiculturalism

> traditionally celebrated distinct ethnic or religious groups, French Islamists "brandished the tricolour". (2004, 245)

As with many in the new transnational entity of the European Union, the primary focus of loyalty is still to the nation state and its traditions.

The Australian model became self-consciously multicultural after the Second World War. Alison Holland explains in Chapter 3 how Australia moved beyond the White Australia Policy to disallow race as the basis of migration policy in the late 1960s and early 1970s. For instance, until the 1970s, while Lebanese Christians had been judged 'white' and hence eligible for immigration under the White Australia Policy, it was only after the Civil War that 'non-white' Lebanese Muslims were able to come to Australia in numbers. For the last 30 years, the policy of multiculturalism has allowed for different ethnicities, different languages and different social and cultural models to be accepted within the overarching community. Public policy and practice were synchronised over a long period, and even when the rhetoric of multiculturalism became unfashionable, attitudes towards those born outside Australia continued to be broadly positive.

Both assimilationist and multicultural models are increasingly under pressure. Habermas, in his discussion of the question of a European constitution (2001), distinguishes between citizens held together by ethnic identity and nations held together in the juristically neutral sense of 'state-constituting peoples' – what is here called 'bare' citizenship. He argues that modern democracy requires a more abstract neutral form of political participation and suggests that

> the multicultural self-understanding of the nations of citizens formed in classical countries of immigration [...] is more instructive [...] than that derived from the culturally assimilationist French model. (2001, 159–60)

At the same time, multiculturalism is under attack. In the Australian case, the rhetoric became heated in the wake of conflict on the beach of Cronulla in the Sutherland Shire of Sydney in December 2005. The fighting was between what were called 'Lebs', denoting the Muslims accused of inappropriate behaviour (in particular towards women on the beaches), and those who identified themselves as true ('native') Australians. The conflict was embodied in an image, which has since become iconic, of a young man who had painted on his chest:

We grew here! You flew here!

The underlying fear of those not born in Australia, discussed in Chapter 11 as 'nativism', is a potent force in Australian political life. By February 2006, both the then Prime Minister of Australia and Treasurer began to talk of the need for migrants to Australia to accept Australian laws and *mores*. Mr Howard, the then Prime Minister, marked his 10th year in power with a speech reported in the *Sydney Morning Herald* (25–26/2/06) in which he said: 'When you come to Australia you become Australian'. In the same article, Mr Costello, the then Treasurer, is quoted saying even more forcefully: 'Before becoming an Australian, you will be asked to subscribe to certain values. If you have strong objections to those values, don't come to Australia'. Similar remarks can be found readily in the British and Dutch press. The right wing Australian historian Keith Windshuttle argued even more trenchantly:

Multiculturalism is a reversion to tribalism that is anachronistic in a modern liberal urban society [. . .]. [It] has bred ethnic ghettos characterized by high levels of unemployment, welfare dependency, welfare abuse, crime and violence. (2005)

The new Rudd Government, while committed to reviewing citizenship testing, has been wary of returning to multiculturalism. Howard had removed the word 'multicultural' from the title of the federal government department concerned with immigration; the Rudd Government accepted the new name. Likewise the citizenship test signals a turn back in the direction of assimilationist models of citizenship, however carefully phrased. By testing language skills and shared values the test asks would-be citizens to conform.

Testing would-be citizens

What is it that would-be citizens should acquire? Is it a set of skills, such as speaking a language, or is it knowledge of cultural practices? Is it the disposition to obey the law? Is it a quality, or set of qualities, those who are already citizens should have? Or is it rather, as Minister Evans put it in the Australian case, an understanding of the Pledge of Allegiance? These are vexed questions which arise whenever citizenship tests are devised. The intense national and philosophical debates on these issues are the subject matter of Chapters 6–10 and Chapter 12.

There are two critical assumptions in the adoption of citizenship-testing regimes. The first assumption is that the dispositions which characterise a good citizen can be defined in a way which uniquely describes the desirable would-be citizen. But, as we have argued, there is no unproblematic form of citizenship to which aliens or immigrants can either assimilate or offer multicultural alternatives. From the time of the Roman Empire, the complexities of joint and multiple loyalties have been part and parcel of the notion of citizenship itself. To use the language of recent scholarship, tests must admit the existence of hybrid identities (Kraidy, 2005). Tests require of would-be citizens a special relationship to a nation, yet the sense of belonging to many communities is commonplace in the globalised world. As Beck argues, globalisation heralds a move from a 'monologic' nationalistic perspectives to a newer 'dialogic imagination' which involves 'the coexistence of rival ways of life in the individual experience' (Beck, 2002, 18). While governments seek to encourage their own citizens to learn languages and become cosmopolitans, the multiple loyalties, languages and 'rival ways of life' of would-be citizens are perceived as a problem. Of course, there *are* genuine concerns about multiple loyalties and belief systems. In Chapter 10, Catriona Mackenzie examines in some depth the philosophical basis of a liberal multicultural state and offers her reflections on the limits of toleration in such a state. Her concern is whether citizenship tests, even in principle, could serve the ends of such an ideal state.

The second assumption is that the dispositions which distinguish the good from the bad would-be citizen can be tested by the sorts of individual tests the regimes impose. Surely the test should focus on behaviour in groups, rather than individual knowledge? The issue parallels a question raised by Tregenza, as to whether modern neo-liberal accounts of citizenship, by focussing on an individual citizen-consumer, detach the individual from the activities and practices that define the community. In the Australian case, the Woolcott Report calls for citizens to understand the Pledge of Allegiance. Whether citizens do understand the Pledge can only be seen in their behaviour. Yet the test assumes that, by asking whether prospective citizens understand and know the Pledge, we can predict whether they will behave appropriately. The test resembles a consumer attitude survey, with the dispositions of each citizen-consumer measured by market research techniques and attitude surveys. But appropriate behaviour – and indeed cultural citizenship more generally – consists in practices, not attitudes reflected in surveys or tests.

Citizenship tests assume, as do most surveys, that each individual tells the truth about their beliefs and acts on those beliefs in predictable ways. Yet in answering questions on a test, any reasonable candidate will be able to predict the desired answer. Even those who sincerely ascribe to beliefs do not always act in accordance with those beliefs. To take an example: a person may believe that it is wrong to drive fast and when asked in a test would agree that they intend to obey the law. In a country where excessive speed is penalised they stay within the limits. When there is no penalty, they tend to speed, whatever the legal limit. It is the social and communal context – and in particular the penalties – that best predict drivers' speeding behaviour.

It is the *practices* of immigrant groups, as much as their beliefs, which cause concern and have led to civic integration and citizenship tests. Those tests are based on linguistic and cultural knowledge. However, linguistic or cultural knowledge does not stop undesirable behaviour. There is no good reason to associate undesirable behaviour with lack of cultural knowledge. Take the case of Mohammed Bouyeri (Chapter 7), who murdered Theo van Gogh in 2004 for his anti-Islamic views. He had been educated in the Netherlands and was fully acculturated. He was aware of cultural norms in Dutch society, and could have answered questions about those norms, yet his behaviour was precisely what the tests intended to screen out. Mohammed Bouyeri would have passed the strongest assimilationist test of cultural knowledge.

The revised Australian citizenship test was designed to be more sensitive to a multicultural model of citizenship than the earlier test. It takes the Pledge of Allegiance to be the 'missing link', knowledge of which should be at the core of the test. It is certainly a better test than one asking questions about obscure cultural icons. Moreover understanding and (sincerely) making the Pledge of Allegiance may be desirable among new citizens. But such pledges in no way guarantee that those who pass the test will behave as good citizens.

Conclusion

The discourses of citizenship themselves often seem to be incommensurable, untranslatable across theoretical and disciplinary divides. The discussion here touches on just of few of the extended and sophisticated debates relating to citizenship. The landscape of citizenship is difficult to map. Even where the topics are shared, the conceptual territory is so differently described as to be mutually incomprehensible. The rise of citizenship-testing regimes has made it acutely important to piece together the fragmented discourses relating to citizenship.

This chapter has focused on the fundamental tension between the impact of globalisation in a much-heralded post-national era, and the resurgence of discourses of nationalism evident in citizenship tests. Traditional accounts of citizenship are under pressure from new political circumstances, and the rise of the new media. The long-standing debate between proponents of multicultural and assimilationist models of citizenship plays out in the globalised domain in new languages of hybridity, cosmopolitanism and mobility. Soysal (1994) talks of new forms of post-national belonging emerging in Europe, based on culture not territory. Optimistic utopian visions tell of modern hybrid citizens who negotiate their identities between countries of residence, of passport and of ethnic and religious links. This chapter argues that while this may be true for the citizenship-rich, there is a dark dystopian world of those who cannot access passports. Those citizenship-poor are caught up in the world of national immigration regimes.

The image of a culturally unified nation state is implicit in the rhetoric which informs legislation and immigration policy on citizenship testing. The complex relationships between cultural and national identity, charted in Part II, underlie much debate. Fears have been reignited in the beginning of this century among wealthy populations following 9/11. Xenophobia is only likely to increase as the economic crisis bites. National identities are on the rise. Identity, emotion and territory are, as Berezin (2003) reminds us, closely interwoven. As she says:

> Territory is congealed identity that embeds relations of social, political cultural and political power in physical space. [...] Citizenship is more than simply a juridical relationship. It also signals an emotional bond that arouses feelings of national loyalty and belonging in a politically bounded geographical space. (2003, 10, 13)

There is no doubt that there is a powerful emotional component in the populist discourses that dominate citizenship debates in Europe, as there is in Australia. Nations and their peoples have a right to seek to ensure that society is secure and that the practices of citizens fit within the rule of law. Yet in adopting citizenship-testing regimes, nations fail to recognise the complexities of a post-national mediated world. The nation state is unlikely to relinquish its power to grant citizenship. Nor, in the present circumstances, should we expect that more complex notions of cultural belonging to inform debate. However it *is* worth asking whether present models of citizenship testing work. Testing prospective new citizens by enquiring of their values and language skills is not an effective way to ensure security or appropriate behaviour. The assumption is that by filtering migrants for citizenship the state can achieve a secure and law-abiding populace. That assumption remains in doubt.

Notes

1. For just some of the utopian and dystopian accounts of the transformations of citizenship, see Barbrook and Cameron, 1995; Barlow, 1998; Boeder, 2005; Boyle, 1997; Castells, 2001; Couldry, 2004; Gillespie, 1995; Gray, 2001; Grove, 2007; Miller, 1993; Poster, 1995; Vandenberg, 2000. For debate on the end of the nation state, see Castells, 2001; Giddens, 1990; Held, 2003; Miller, 2007; Price, 2002.
2. The phrase 'clash of civilizations' was first in fact used by the Princeton-based British political theorist Bernard Lewis at a meeting in Washington in 1957 where it was recorded in the transcript.
3. The Pledge of Allegiance runs as follows:

> From this time forward, under God*
> I pledge my loyalty to Australia and its people
> Whose democratic beliefs I share,
> Whose rights and liberties I respect, and
> Whose laws I will uphold and obey.

* A person may choose whether or not to use the words 'under God'.
4. cf. Kukathas (2008: 35) who charts a variety of liberal responses to the dual issues of integration and membership in the state
5. Although in recent years dual citizenship has again become a matter of debate in the Netherlands.

References

Anderson, Benedict (1983) *Imagined Communities: Reflections on the Origin and Spread of Nationalism* (London: Verso).
Aristotle (trans. Kenyon 1891) 'The Athenian Constitution', in F. Kenyon (ed.), *Aristotle on the Athenian Constitution* (London: G. Bell and Sons).
Beck, Ulrick (2002) 'The Cosmopolitan Society and Its Enemies', *Theory, Culture and Society* 19 (1–2): 17–44.
Berezin, M. (2003) 'Territory, Emotion and Identity: Spatial Recalibration in a New Europe', in M. Berezin and M. Schain (eds), *Europe Without Borders:*

Remapping Territory, Citizenship and Identity in a Post National Age (Baltimore, MD: Johns Hopkins University Press): 1–29.

Bredt, Stephan (2006) 'The European Social Contract and the European Public Sphere', *European Law Journal* 12 (1): 61–77.

Castells, Manuel (2001) *The Internet Galaxy: Reflections on the Internet, Business and Society* (Oxford: Oxford University Press).

Chalaby, Jean (ed.) (2005) *Transnational Television Worldwide: Towards a New Media Order* (London and New York: I.B. Taurus).

Couldry, Nick (2004) 'The Productive "Consumer" and the Dispersed "Citizen" ', *International Journal of Cultural Studies* 7 (1): 21–32.

Fraser, Nancy (2007) 'Transnationalising the Public Sphere: On the Legitimacy and Efficacy of Public Opinion in a Post-Westphalian World', *Theory, Culture and Society* 24 (4): 7–39.

Giddens, Anthony (1990) *The Consequences of Modernity* (Cambridge: Polity).

Gillespie, Marie (1995) *Television, Ethnicity and Cultural Change* (London: Routledge).

Gitlin, Todd (1998) 'Public Sphere or Public Sphericules?', in T. Liebes and J. Curran (eds), *Media, Ritual, Identity* (London: Routledge): 168–75.

Gray, C. H. (2001) 'Citizenship in the Age of Electronic Reproduction', in C. H. Gray (ed.), *Cyborg Citizen: Politics in the Posthuman Age* (New York: Routledge): 21–39.

Habermas, Jürgen (1993) *The Structural Transformation of the Public Sphere* (Cambridge, MA: MIT Press).

Habermas, Jürgen (2001) *The Postnational Constellation* (Cambridge: Polity).

Heater, D. (1990) *Citizenship: The Civic Ideal in World History, Politics and Education* (London: Longman).

Held, David (ed.) (2003) *Prospects for Democracy* (Cambridge: Polity).

Huntington, Samuel P. (1996) *The Clash of Civilizations and the Remaking of the New World Order* (New York: Touchstone).

Isin, E. F. and B. S. Turner (2007) 'Investigating Citizenship: An Agenda for Citizenship Studies', *Citizenship Studies* 11 (1): 5–17.

Kraidy, Marwan M. (2005) *Hybridity, or the Cultural Logic of Globalization* (Philadelphia, PA: Temple University Press).

Kukathas, Chandran (2008) 'Anarcho-Multiculturalism: The Pure Theory of Liberalism', in G. B. Levey (ed.), *Political Theory and Australian Multiculturalism* (New York: Berghan): 29–43.

Mathison, Ralph (2006) 'Peregrini, Barbari and Cives Romani: Concepts and Citizenship and Legal Identity of Barbarians in the later Roman Empire', *American Historical Review* 111 (4): 1011–40.

Maynor, J. (2003) *Republicanism in the Modern World* (Cambridge: Polity).

Miladi, N. (2003) 'Mapping the Al Jazeera Phenomonon', in D. K. Thussu and D. Freedman (eds), *War and the Media Reporting Conflict 24/7* (London: Sage): 149–60.

Miller, Toby (1993) *The Well-Tempered Self: Citizenship, Culture, and the Postmodern Subject* (Baltimore, MD: Johns Hopkins University Press).

Miller, Toby (2007) *Cultural Citizenship: Consumerism, and Television in a Neoliberal Age* (Philadelphia, PA: Temple University Press).

Miles, H. (2005) *Al-Jazeera: How Arab TV News Challenged the World* (London: Abacus).

Pakulski, Jan (1997) 'Cultural Citizenship', *Citizenship Studies* 18 (3): 360–79.

Peters, M. A. (2005) 'Between Empires: Rethinking Identity and Citizenship in the Context of Globalization', in P. Hayden and C. el-Ojeili (eds), *Confronting Globalization: Humanity, Justice and the Renewal of Politics* (Basingstoke: Palgrave Macmillan).

Pettit, Philip (1997) *Republicanism: A Theory of Freedom and Government* (Oxford: Clarendon Press).

Pettit, Philip (2001) *A Theory of Freedom: From the Psychology to the Politics of Agency* (Cambridge/New York: Polity/Oxford University Press).

Price, Monroe (2002) *Media and Sovereignty: The Global Information Revolution and its Challenge to State Power* (Cambridge, MA: MIT Press).

Roy, Olivier (2004) *Globalised Islam: The Search for the New Ummah* (London: Hurst and Co).

Rubinstein, Kim (2008) 'Loyalty and Membership: Globalization and its Impact on Citizenship, Multiculturalism, and the Australian Community', in G. B. Levey (ed.), *Political Theory and Australian Multiculturalism* (New York: Berghan): 171–87.

Sakr, Naomi (2002) *Satellite Realms: Transnational Television, Globalization and the Middle East* (London: IB Tauris).

Skinner, Q. and B. Strath (2003) *States and Citizens* (Cambridge: Cambridge University Press).

Soysal, J. (1994) *Limits of Citizenship: Migrants and Postnational Membership in Europe* (Chicago, IL: University of Chicago Press).

Tiffen, R. and R. Gittens (2004) *How Australia Compares* (Cambridge: Cambridge University Press).

Vandenberg, A. (2000) 'Cybercitizenship and Digital Democracy', in A. Vandenberg (ed.), *Citizenship and Democracy in a Global Era* (Basingstoke: Macmillan): 289–306.

Volkmer, Ingrid (2007) 'Governing the Spatial "Reach"? Spheres of Influence and Challenges to Global Media Policy', *International Journal of Communication* 1: 56–73.

Wiener, Antje (1998) *'European' Citizenship Practice – Building Institutions of a Non-State* (Boulder, CO: Westview Press).

Windshuttle, K. (2005) 'Ghetto Youth a Multicultural Legacy', *The Australian* 16 December 2005.

Wright, Sue (2008) 'Citizenship Tests in Europe: Editorial Introduction', *International Journal of Multicultural Studies* 10 (1): 1–9.

Online sources

Barbrook, R. and A. Cameron (1995) 'The Californian Ideology', *Mute* 3, http://www.alamut.com/subj/ideologies/pessimism/califIdeo_I.html

Barlow, John Perry (1998) 'A Declaration of Independence of Cyberspace'. February, http://www.eff.org/~ barlow/Declaration-Final.html

Boeder, P. (2005) 'Habermas' Heritage: The Future of the Public Sphere in the Network Society', *First Monday* 10 (9), http://www.firstmonday.org/issues/issue10_9/boeder/

Grove, Steve (2007) 'A Second Life in Politics' ABC News, 19 January 2007, http://abcnews.go.com/print?id=2809023

Poster, Mark (1995) 'Cyberdemocracy: Internet and the Public Sphere'. http://www.humanities.uci.edu/mposter/writings/democ.html

Woolcott, Richard (2008) 'Moving Forward... Improving Pathways to Citizenship: A Report by the Citizenship Test Review Committee, August 2008' Australian Department of Immigration and Citizenship. Accessed 22 November 2008, http://www.citizenshiptestreview.gov.au/_pdf/moving-forward-report.pdf

2
Citizenship and Language Tests in Australia: Issues of Law and History

A.R. Buck and Charlotte Frew

Introduction

Any discussion of citizenship and citizenship tests in twenty-first century Australia needs to take account of the origins of the existing legal and jurisprudential structures. The first point to be noted is that the Australian Constitution makes no mention and gives no definition of an 'Australian citizen'. In the context of the Australian Constitution, there are only 'subjects' and 'aliens'. Citizenship in Australia is a product of statute law, not constitutional law. And, as such, it is very recent, having been introduced with the passage of the Citizenship and Nationality Act (later renamed the Australian Citizenship Act) in 1948. This legal, historical and jurisprudential reality establishes the framework within which future reform may take place. In order to understand the current law, we must understand why the current law exists and what implications it holds for the future. In this chapter, two questions are posed. First, in the continuing debate over citizenship and language tests, to what extent can it be argued that Australia is a 'prisoner of its past'? Secondly, what insights might be revealed if we examine the Australian experience comparatively with reference to other jurisdictions of the former British Empire? Through a detailed examination of the colonial origins of the laws and values informing contemporary Australian citizenship this chapter will shed new light on the legal, historical and jurisprudential dimensions of the current debate over citizenship and language tests.

Both immigration and citizenship law and policy are discussed in this chapter. They are interrelated in the sense that an immigration test that contributes to narrowing immigration to specific cultural groups also defines which persons are able to apply for citizenship. In addition, language testing has been utilised both to exclude immigrants and to exclude potential citizens. In Australia, the fact that the Department of Immigration was responsible for citizenship matters highlights how much immigration was related to nationality issues. It was through control of immigration that the borders were prevented from being permeable. Thus, the rules about immigration are prior to and contain those about the acquisition of nationality once admitted (Davidson, 1997, 87).

There has been very little change in the discourse of immigration, subjecthood and citizenship in Australia since federation. Citizenship continues to be characterised by exclusivity and language tests which are intended to demonstrate who should and who should not be a member of our nation. The similarities between historical and modern citizenship discourse illustrate the circularity of Australian citizenship policy. Ideas of citizenship, particularly the notion of who 'deserves' to be part of the nation, and indeed the question of what the 'nation' actually means, have been reflected (and repeated) in Australian political rhetoric over the last 100 years. The rhetorical tone was set by the Australian Prime Minister, Alfred Deakin, in 1901:

> The unity of Australia is nothing if that does not imply a united race. A united race implies not only that its members can intermix, intermarry and associate without degradation on either side, but implies one inspired by the same ideas, an aspiration towards the same ideals, of a people processing the same general cast of character, tone of thought – the same constitutional training and traditions – a people qualified to live under the Constitution.
>
> (Macintyre, 1999)

Deakin's was the most influential speech of the Immigration Restriction Bill debate which would result in the implementation of the White Australia Policy and it can be seen that, though not explicit in the legislation, the politicians had no intention of hiding the real agenda behind the Bill. But how much has changed since 1901? Though the language of 'race' may have been replaced by that of 'common values' or 'culture' one would not be alone in supposing it was more recent Prime Ministers, John Howard or even Kevin Rudd, who made this speech at a much more recent time. In fact, the following extract from John Howard's speech on the eve of Australia Day in 2006 illustrates how citizenship discourse has remained stationary for over a century:

> our celebration of diversity must not be at the expense of the common values that bind us together as one people – respect for the

freedom and dignity of the individual, a commitment to the rule of law, the equality of men and women and a spirit of egalitarianism that embraces tolerance, fair play and compassion for those in need. Nor should it be at the expense of ongoing pride in what are commonly regarded as the values, traditions and accomplishments of the old Australia. A sense of shared values is our social cement.

(Howard, 2006)

As this chapter will demonstrate, the rhetorical continuity so displayed is crucial to understanding the distinctive nature of citizenship in Australia. An analysis of the origins of Australian citizenship law reveals that it has developed very little since its inception.

The idea of citizenship has developed concurrently throughout the settler societies of the former British Empire. What insights might be gained by examining the development of Australian citizenship from a comparative perspective? The reason for looking at the development of citizenship in Australia, Canada and South Africa, in particular, lies in their commonalities and the insights that can be gained from a comparative approach. All three countries were settler societies; all received, in varying degrees, English common law and English political institutions; and the legal and political development in each occurred mainly in the nineteenth century and is therefore relatively contemporaneous. In addition, the idea of 'national characteristics' in these countries is recent and fluid, and the rhetoric of the 'crimson thread of kinship' very powerful. Jeremy Martens (2006, 324) has pointed out that the 'importance of geographies of connection between white settler colonies should not be underestimated'. Legislative, political, economic and social relations in these jurisdictions were all heavily influenced by the colonial context. Australian ideas and legislation respecting immigration and citizenship were also 'colonial' in two important respects. First, in the sense of the relationship between the colonies and Great Britain and second, in the sense that patterns of development in the Australian colonies bear marked similarities with the development of the colonial settler societies in other parts of the empire.

The origins of citizenship in Australia: Why is it exclusive?

A comparative analysis of the political and jurisprudential history of Australia provides insight into how citizenship developed as a mechanism of exclusion and language testing came to be an enduring component of the acquisition of citizenship. The defensive project of the white man's country bound together white settler colonies around the world for a 'spatial politics of exclusion and segregation was common to them all' (Lake, 2003, 122). The exclusionary mechanism of language testing was first incorporated within immigration legislation because of pressure from the Colonial Office to mask the racial motivation for excluding particular groups of immigrants. The fact that language and knowledge testing remains a part of immigration and citizenship law demonstrates the continuity of citizenship as an exclusive legal category.

One of the most important historical moments in the history of Australian immigration law was on 24 June 1897 when the premiers of Canada, New South Wales, Victoria, New Zealand, Queensland, Cape Colony, South Australia, Newfoundland, Tasmania, Western Australia and Natal assembled at the Colonial Office in Downing Street to discuss 'certain Imperial questions' with Joseph Chamberlain, Secretary of State for the Colonies (Martens, 2006, 336). Prior to the meeting, New South Wales had submitted the Coloured Races Restriction and Regulation Bill (1896) for approval but it had not received royal assent. The Colonial Office was determined to keep the peace with the colony of New South Wales whilst preventing the passing of racist laws that might provoke nationalist anger in other parts of the Empire, particularly British India. Chamberlain made it clear that the Colonial Office was in full support of the colonies' rights to maintain a white society and protect labour. Chamberlain hoped that it might be possible for colonial governments to 'arrange a form of words which will avoid hurting the feelings of any of Her Majesty's subjects' and at the same time 'amply protect Australian Colonies against any invasion of the class to which they would justly object' (Martens, 2006, 337).

The Colonial Office encouraged the colonial representatives present to draft their exclusionary immigration legislation with reference to undesirable characteristics other than race and to model such legislation on Natal's new Immigration Restriction Act. The Act incorporated an educational test which could be given in any European language chosen by an immigration officer and had the affect of restricting Indian immigration without excluding Indians as a racial category. Western Australia was the first to adopt legislation modelled on the Natal test in 1897, New South Wales and Tasmania followed in 1898 and New Zealand in 1899. The Commonwealth of Australia incorporated a version of the Natal test in the Immigration Restriction Act (1901), stating under Section 3:

> The immigration into the Commonwealth of the persons described in any of the following paragraphs of this section [...] is prohibited, namely: –
>
> a) Any person who when asked to do so by an officer fails to write out at dictation and sign in the presence of the officer a passage of fifty words in length in a European language dictated by the officer.

The Section was a means of meeting the British halfway, as it was again based on arbitrary language testing rather than race. The Act virtually ruled out any coloured immigration for the better part of seven decades (Boyer et al., 2004, 13–4). Originally immigrants could be tested within their first year in Australia but in the 1930s this was changed to the first 5 years of residence. Between 1902 and 1905, 50 people passed the 'dictation test' but in 1906 the Customs Officers received a four-page pamphlet informing them that '[i]t is intended that the dictation test be an absolute bar to admission'. As a result, between 1906 and 1909, only two people passed the test and none of them were successful after 1909. The language test was administered in languages not understood by applicants and was simply a mechanism for exclusion. Such testing went on for many more decades. A customs officer writing about his experience administering the test in the 1950s said he would often choose the Sydney Morning Herald Editorial for immigrants to translate or he would make up his own test such as 'the harassed pedlar met the embarrassed cobbler in the cemetery gauging the symmetry of a lady's ankle in unparalleled ecstasy'. If a German came in, he recorded, he would test him in Ethiopian (Dutton, 2002, 35).[1] This illustrates the absurdity of such testing and its unfailing exclusionary role.

The meeting on 24 June 1897 and its outcomes was of great significance to the British Colonies represented because all were in the process of 'creating' national values in the late nineteenth and early twentieth centuries and this led to a strong public sentiment that those who did not hold British values should be excluded. Protection from the unknown was treated as essential in the British colonies because of the nervous task of creating new and successful societies and the wider popularity of eugenics and scientific understandings of racial difference. The Australian population was eagerly 'creating' a distinctive national identity but continued to rely on the values, political institutions and legal precedents of Britain. The nervousness of the young nation reinforced the exclusivity of immigration legislation and the concern was reflected in media reports referencing the language test. This is revealed clearly in the following extract from *The Bulletin* in 1901, the highly influential Australian journal of commentary and polemic, in its discussion of the new language test:

> Of course, it [the test] is not intended to apply indiscriminately [...]. The apparent idea is that the authorities will ask the man they want to keep out, and the man they want to let in won't be asked. [...] It appears to be a law which will work well so long as the people keep an anti-nigger Government in power, with a strong anti-nigger majority behind it, and keep a sleepless eye on both of them.

The issue of Australian citizenship requires an understanding of the influence of colonialism on the historical development of immigration and citizenship categories. It was distinctive colonial concerns that led to the development of immigration laws which excluded on the basis of language testing and later led to similar exclusionary restrictions with regards to citizenship.

In addition to the colonial relationship with Britain, the political institutions inherited from Britain influenced the development of citizenship law. Citizenship as an exclusive privilege rather than an inclusive right reflects the political context in which Australia developed in the late nineteenth and early twentieth century. Australians viewed government and the state positively, as a powerful collective means to improve their economic and social well-being (Buck, 2008, 238–46). Australians were proud heirs of the nineteenth-century British tradition and for half a century after federation continued to identify as British subjects. The lack of attention to citizenship in the Australian Constitution was unproblematic for Australians. Leaving the issue of citizenship to future parliaments reflected Australia's positive view of democracy and government (Chesterman and Galligan, 1999, 11). The principal reason why no citizenship clause was inserted in the Constitution was because the representatives of the colonies/states wished to retain power over citizenship issues including the power to discriminate against certain groups of people (24). It was within this liberal political context that citizenship was defined (or left undefined). On a few occasions, even prior to the easing of requirements in the late twentieth century, there were challenges to the privilege model of Australian citizenship. In 1953–56, Sir Tasman Heyes, Secretary of the Department of Immigration, introduced a rights-based charter but it was swiftly rejected and in 1958, Billy Snedden, a member of the House of Representatives at the time and later elected as the Minister for Immigration, made similar proposals provoking the same response. The attitude that an immigrant must demonstrate that he wanted to belong to the Anglo-Celtic family was firmly entrenched.

Contemporary citizenship: A prisoner of its past

A look at the development of Australian citizenship law reveals that it remains a prisoner of its past as it remains an exclusive legal category defined by values inherited from Britain. Australian citizenship is a relatively new phenomenon, however it is tightly linked with the idea of British subjecthood which existed before it. Australian citizenship has only existed since 1948, Canadian citizenship since 1947 and South African citizenship since 1949. As noted previously, the Australian Constitution makes no mention and gives no definition of the words 'Australian citizen'. The concept is statutory and prior to the Nationality and Citizenship Act (1948) most Australians (if not all) were British subjects. The subject/alien distinction made in the Constitution refers to those who are perceived to be members of the community and those who are not perceived to be members of the community. Before Federation, under British law, any person born in Britain or in any other British colony was a British subject by birth and each colony determined its own principles on the rights of aliens to become naturalised as British subjects (Goldlust, 1996, 11). Being a British subject in the nineteenth century gave the bearer entitlement to an imaginary international fellowship. It even suggested a type of superior character or 'breed' of manhood. The idea of the British subject was 'an abstraction compounded in equal parts of patriotism, physical toughness, skill at team games, a sense of fair play (sometimes called sportsmanship), self-discipline, selflessness, bravery and daring' (Boyer et al., 2004, 10). The popular response to the break out of war in 1914 is illustrative of the internalisation of these values by Australians. There was almost complete public consensus about the indivisibility of Australian and British interests. Almost 20,000 men rushed to enlist in the first few weeks of war and overwhelming Imperial loyalty was expressed in the press (Beaumont, 2007, 173). It is hardly surprising that the exclusivity of the British subject/alien distinction and the values encompassed within

British subjecthood came to define Australian citizenship and continue to characterise it today.

When the Nationality and Citizenship Act was introduced into the House of Representatives on 30 September 1948, the Immigration Minister Arthur Calwell stated, 'The Bill is not designed to make an Australian any less a British subject, but to help him to express his pride in citizenship of this great country' (Chesterman and Galligan, 1999, 30). The rights of British subjects without Australian citizenship were continually reinforced. This illustrates the powerful relationship between Britain and Australia and the colonial origins of citizenship in Australia. The 1948 legislation established citizenship but it contained no description of the rights of Australian citizens. In the parliamentary debates Mr Lang argued, unsuccessfully, that the provisions were skeletal and the government had wasted an 'opportunity to provide the structure of Australian citizenship with the life blood of freedom that should have been accepted by a democratic government' (Chesterman and Galligan, 1999, 31). This reveals the development of Australian citizenship as an arbitrarily defined, flexible mechanism of exclusion and protection rather than a fixed statement of Australian values or a commitment to the rights of members of the Australian nation. Even after the establishment of a legal category of Australian citizenship, it remained undefined and Britain continued to exert a strong influence on Australia's national self-perception.

Case law in the late twentieth century demonstrates the continuing role of citizenship as a mechanism of exclusion. In *Kio v West* (1985) it was argued that a child of parents who were temporary entrants and subjects to a deportation order was an Australian citizen and, therefore, entitled to natural justice.[2] The Court did not adopt this view and the case prompted a change in the legislation to prevent the abuse of citizenship to obtain an immigration advantage (Rubinstein, 2002, 12). The previous nationality by birthplace rule was changed in August 1986 and the new rule limited citizenship to those born in Australia to a parent who was an Australian citizen or permanent resident (11). Increasingly the statute was being moulded to allow for exclusion rather than general inclusion. This application of citizenship law mirrors the ideal of the British subject which encompassed exclusivity and the philosophical rather than practical value of membership.

Despite the fact that citizenship was incorporated into statute in 1948, it remained an elusive category barely defined. This illusiveness was necessary to allow for flexibility with regards to changing 'desirable characteristics' of new members of the nation. As Karen Slawner reminds us 'the legal definitions of citizenship always incorporate what is considered to be desirable activity' (Slawner, 1998, 83). The requirements for grant of citizenship were set out in Section 13 Australian Citizenship Act (1948) and include the following:

- The applicant must be a permanent resident;
- The applicant is over 18 years;
- Understand the nature of the application;
- Must have lived in Australia for 2 years in the 5 years preceding the application and 12 months in the 2 years before the application;
- Must be of good character;
- Must have a basic knowledge of English;
- Must have adequate knowledge of the responsibilities and privileges of Australian citizenship;
- Must be likely to reside or continue to reside in Australia.

Each of these represents both the desirable and undesirable characteristics of persons to be considered members of the nation. These specific requirements illustrate the nervousness of Australian society and the use of citizenship as a mechanism of migration control. On passing the required tests, a person would swear the following allegiance: 'I swear that I will be faithful and bear true allegiance to Her Majesty Queen Elizabeth the Second, her heirs and successors according to law, and that I will faithfully observe the laws of Australia and fulfil my duties as an Australian citizen.' As Davidson points out, the emphasis of the Act was on proving and affirming that you belonged, and then on acquiring not *active* rights as equal citizens but *passive* rights to consume benefits and privileges (Davidson, 1997, 91). The struggle to define one's identity is often accompanied by the formation of exclusive subcultures which reject the 'other' in order to create themselves. The Australian nation has undergone this process on a larger scale, perhaps more significantly than other nations, due to its colonial beginnings and struggle to create a national identity. A nation's understanding of its self is revealed by the categories of persons it regards as foreign, alien and 'other'. From 1948 to 1987, Australia's citizenship legislation defined an alien as a person who does not have the status of British subject and is not an Irish citizen or a protected person. Therefore citizenship was defined by reference to Anglo-Celtic inclusion and alien exclusion from the beginning. The concept of 'race' may well have been replaced by 'culture', however the more recent language and knowledge requirements for Australian citizenship remain heavily endowed with culturally specific questions designed to weed out the 'culturally' undesirable.

In *Re Frunz and Minister for Immigration and Multicultural Affairs* (2000), the Administrative Appeals Tribunal considered Section 13 (9)(a) of the Australian Citizenship Act which gave the Minister the discretion to grant citizenship to a person under the age of 18 years. The Department refused Mrs Frunz's application for citizenship for her 2-year-old daughter. Mrs Frunz was no longer an Australian citizen because she had become a Swiss citizen in 1997 and under Section 17 of the Australian Act she could not retain Australian citizenship concurrently. The Tribunal found that the discretion should not be exercised in favour of the applicant unless strict criteria are met and stated:

> while [the applicant's daughter] is only two years old and has not given the Immigration Department any cause to refuse her entry to, and stay in Australia, **the grant of Australian Citizenship is a privilege.**
>
> [emphasis added] (552)

The case law illustrates the continuing exclusivity of the legal category of citizenship and its formulation as a privilege granted at the discretion of the government according to flexible 'desirable characteristics'. This leads us to ask how such desirable attributes have been defined since the inception of citizenship in Australia. It has been argued that a number of overarching values are central to a distinctively Australian social and political ethos. These include Australia's democratic tradition, commitment to freedom of the individual, economic pluralism and the centrality of the English language as the basis of public administration and discourse (Goldlust, 1996, 20). All of these apparently 'distinctive' Australian values which have come to define Australian citizenship are clearly British legacies. John Howard made a direct reference to the British values and political traditions which are enshrined within the legal category of modern citizenship in his 2006 Australia Day speech:

> Most nations experience some level of cultural diversity while also having a dominant cultural pattern running through them. In Australia's case, that dominant pattern comprises Judeo-Christian ethics, the progressive spirit of the Enlightenment and the institutions and values of British political culture. Its democratic and egalitarian temper also bears the imprint of distinct Irish and nonconformist traditions.

The inheritance of citizenship values from Britain is further illuminated by a comparison with Canada where similar inherited ideals constitute citizenship. In *Re Gialedakis and Court of Canadian Citizenship* (1976), the Court concluded that the applicant did not meet the requirements for citizenship after examining him on geographical, historical and political–legal matters. The 24-year-old applicant had been in the country for 10 years but did not know where the western-most province of Canada was, how the French came to be in Canada or what was the basic duty of the representatives of the people in the Canadian political system (Pryles, 1981, 80–1). In another case, a woman was found to have met the requirements on the basis that she was a devout Christian and the doctrines of the Christian religion are the most comparable with the ideals of democratic government (82).

In 1975, in the Canadian case *Re Giancaterino* (1975), the Canadian Citizenship Appeal Court explored the meaning of 'adequate knowledge of the English language' (one of the requirements for citizenship in place at the time) and enunciated an objective test which referred to the basic ability to communicate with other members of the community (DLR (3d), 380). In 1984, the Australian test was changed from 'adequate knowledge of the English language' to 'basic knowledge' interpreted as the ability to speak and understand sufficiently to be able to work, obtain the necessities of life and understand the responsibilities of citizenship (Goldlust, 1996, 21–2).[3] The change to a lower standard of English accompanied the removal of the definition of British subject status, a reduction in the residency requirement to 10 years, and the elimination of the renunciation of 'any other allegiance' from the oath and affirmation of allegiance.[4] Despite the relative easing of requirements to gain citizenship, strict requirements remained. The similarities between Canadian and Australian requirements for gaining citizenship and its exclusive nature in both nations illustrate that values inherited from their British colonial beginnings and their shared history with regards to the events of 1897 are central to their notions of citizenship. This is further reinforced by the fact that it took almost a century for Australian colonial anxieties to settle and for the definition of British subject status to be removed from the Australian legislation.

Citizenship and the pathology of testing

In addition to being a mechanism for racial and cultural exclusion, the dictation test as an exclusive immigration policy was a mechanism of political control. Just as the Colonial Office had utilised restrictive immigration policy for political purposes, Australia in later decades would continue to do so. The cases of *Walsh and Johnson* and *Egon Kisch* made clear that a prior commitment to a very limited band of Anglo-Celtic values and political traditions was a precondition for rights to act politically in Australia (Davidson, 1997, 64–5). The former action was brought under Section 8AA (2) of the Immigration Act which allowed the Minister to deport from Australia anyone 'not born in Australia' if he was satisfied that that person had been hindering or obstructing to the prejudice of the public, the transport of goods or trade with other countries and that the presence of that person was injurious to the peace, order and good governance of Australia. In *Walsh and Johnson* attempts to deport seamen's union officials (who were communist) under this section failed because it could not be proven that they were immigrants. However, as Davidson points out, the notion that a person could be denied rights because his or her views were un-British was the leitmotif of some judgements. Egon Kisch's story is an even clearer example of the use of restrictive immigration laws to exclude persons with non-British political values.

Kisch was a Czechoslovakian communist invited to address the Congress of the Society Against War and Fascism in Melbourne in 1934. The Australian Government determined that he was 'undesirable as an inhabitant of, or visitor to, the Commonwealth' and subjected him to a dictation test in Scottish Gaelic, a language only spoken by one person in every 600 in Scotland at the time. Kisch, of course, failed the test. Ultimately, the High Court of Australia ruled that Scottish Gaelic was not a European language, highlighting the absurdity of the test (Cochrane). The case, discussed in detail by Holland in Chapter 3, illustrates the lengths to which the Australian Government was prepared to go in order to exclude undesirable persons; whether deemed so politically, mentally, racially or culturally.

The absurdity of the Kisch case was perhaps more easily overlooked at this time in history because of the broader context with regards to reliance on intelligence testing and eugenics. In examining the nature of the dictation test, it is necessary to explore the growing movement of eugenics in the late nineteenth and early twentieth century and the blind reliance on 'testing' of this kind throughout the world. Following the First World War, for example, the United States subjected 1 million men in the army to intelligence tests, the results of which showing that nearly half were not much more than morons (Nourse, 2008, 25). Instead of challenging the test itself, the response was one of panic. The public had enormous respect for such 'scientific' testing and the feeblemindedness of the Army men was viewed as fixed, permanent, inherited and illustrative of the intellectual decline of the nation's population. In Canada, the Sexual Sterilization Act of Alberta was enacted in 1928. Under the Act, individuals were assessed using IQ tests like the Stanford–Binet in order for the Alberta Eugenics Board to locate and sterilise the mentally deficient (McWhirter and Weijer, 1969, 424–31). Many new immigrants in Canada were sterilised under the act because their scores illustrated impaired intellectual functioning, mainly as a result of limited knowledge of the English language. These are just a couple of international examples which demonstrate the wider intellectual context in relation to language and intelligence testing.

What the Kisch case and the early twentieth century obsession with eugenics highlight are both the nervousness of modernising societies and the faith in 'scientific' testing, whether they be language tests or intelligence tests, as mechanisms that could identify and weed out 'undesirables'. It is sobering to reflect that we are still linking admission to citizenship to tests based on language and culturally specific knowledge, given the original intent of such tests.

As we have seen the language test, contained in Natal's Immigration Restriction Act was heralded by Joseph Chamberlain at the Colonial Office on 24 July 1897 as a model for other colonial governments. It should also not be forgotten that the Natal legislation, with its language test, also borrowed from the US Immigration Act of 1891 which was designed to exclude, among others, 'All idiots, insane persons, paupers, or persons likely to become a public charge, Persons suffering from a loathsome or contagious disease, Persons who have been convicted of a felony or other infamous crime or misdemeanour involving moral turpitude' (Martens, 2006, 333) . In other words, there was a close connection drawn in the late-nineteenth and early-twentieth century between racial exclusivity and a belief in eugenics. These were the motivations underlying the commitment to 'scientific' testing. And yet we still link access to citizenship to tests based on language or on knowledge of culturally specific values and data.

Conclusion

It is clear that an examination of the historical colonial origins of Australian citizenship reveals that Australia is a prisoner of its past. The legal category of citizenship remains exclusive, defined by British values and based on a model determined by privilege rather than rights. The limited coverage of the experience of other colonial nations in this chapter demonstrates the value of a comparative approach to this topic and the possibilities for further comparative research in this area. The collective experience at the Colonial Office meeting of 24 June 1897, the influence of Imperial political concerns and the creation of immigration legislation based on the Natal Bill resulted in similarly framed citizenship laws and similar outcomes in the courts. The public perception of what is 'Australian' and 'un-Australian' and who should be 'included' and 'excluded' as members of the nation has developed largely as a result of colonial beginnings. The fact that citizenship remains an exclusive legal category in contemporary Australia is what is most interesting about this analysis, particularly when the means to maintaining such exclusivity is linked historically with the social philosophy of eugenics. There cannot be any movement forward without an appreciation of how the current focus on testing language and national knowledge developed a century ago. If we continue to debate the question of citizenship, citizenship testing and language tests without a due appreciation of the historical background to both contemporary Australian law and contemporary Australian rhetoric, we may be condemned to simply re-invent the wheel.

Notes

1. See also Wall Moore, ex-Newcastle Customs Officer 'Administering the Dictation Test 1950s' at http://museumvictoria.com.au/customshouse/stories/dictation_test.asp accessed 3 March 2009.
2. *Kio v West* (1985) 159 CLR 550 at 559 (Gibbs CJ); at 588 (Mason J); at 603 (Wilson J); at 629 (Brennan J); at 634 (Dean J).
3. See also Section 14 (1)(g) *Australian Citizenship Act* 1948 for original language requirement.
4. See Nationality and Citizenship Amendment Act 1984.

Bibliography

Beaumont, J. (2007) 'Australian Citizenship and the Two World Wars', *Australian Journal of Politics and History* 53 (2): 173.

Boyer, P., Cardinal, L. and Headon, D. (2004) *From Subjects to Citizens: A Hundred Years of Citizenship in Australia and Canada* (Ottawa, ON: University of Ottawa Press).

Buck, A. R. (2008) 'The Age of State Socialism: Government, Economy and Society in the Early Twentieth Century', in D. Gare and D. Ritter (eds), *Making Australian History: Perspectives on the Past Since 1788* (Melbourne: Nelson Australia Ltd).

Chesterman, John and Galligan, Brian (eds) (1999) *Defining Australian Citizenship Selected Documents* (Melbourne: Melbourne University Press).

Cochrane, P. (2008) 'The Big Jump: Egon Kisch in Australia', The National Centre for History Education. Accessed 7 February 2009 http://hyperhistory.org/index.php?option=displaypage&Itemid=730&op=page

Davidson, A. (1997) *From Subject to Citizen: 1901–1996* (Cambridge: Cambridge University Press).

Dutton, D. (2002) *One of Us? A Century of Australian Citizenship* (Sydney: UNSW Press).

Goldlust, John (1996) *Understanding Citizenship in Australia* (Canberra: Australian Publication Service).

Howard, John (2006) 'Australia Day Address to the National Press Club', Parliament House Canberra. Accessed 5 February 2009 http://www.australian politics.com/news/2006/01/06–01–25_howard.shtml.

Lake, M. (2003) 'White Man's Country: The Transnational History of a National Project', *Australian Historical Studies* 34 (122): 346–63.

Martens, Jeremy (2006) 'A Transnational History of Immigration Restriction: Natal and New South Wales, 1896–97', *The Journal of Imperial and Commonwealth History* 34 (3): 323–44.

McWhirter, K.G. and Weijer, J. (1969) 'The Alberta Sterilization Act: A Genetic Critique', *The University of Toronto Law Journal* 19 (3): 424–31.

Macintyre, Stuart (1999) *A Concise History of Australia* (Cambridge: Cambridge University Press).

Nourse, V.F. (2008) *In Reckless Hands: Skinner v Oklahoma and the Near Triumph of American Eugenics* (London and New York: W.W Norton & Co).

Pryles, M. (1981) *Australian Citizenship Law* (Sydney: Law Book Co).

Rubinstein, Kim (2002) *Australian Citizenship Law in Context* (Sydney: Law Book Co).

Walter, James and MacLeod, Margaret (2002) *The Citizen's Bargain: A Documentary History of Australian Views Since 1890* (Sydney: UNSW Press).

Slawner, Karen and Denham, Mark (eds) (1998) *Citizenship after Liberalism* (New York: P Lang).

Case History and Legislation

Australian Citizenship Act 1948
Gialedakis and Court of Canadian Citizenship (1976)
Kio v West (1985) 159 CLR 550
Re Frunz and Minister for Immigration and Multicultural Affairs (2000) 31 AAR 550
Re Giancaterino (1975) 60 D.L.R (3d) 380

3
Australian Citizenship in the Twenty-First Century: Historical Perspectives

Alison Holland

When Australia's Federal Liberal Government introduced the idea of a citizenship test in September 2007, it was promoted, along with changes to citizenship legislation, as a modernising project. The 2005 Citizenship Bill would replace the old Nationality and Citizenship Act (1948: hereafter, NCA) bringing it 'into line with the reality of modern Australia'. Their discussion paper on citizenship testing, *Australian Citizenship: Much More Than A Ceremony*, pushed this line still further suggesting that a test represented 'new thinking' and a 'fresh approach to settlement and citizenship'. Yet, during the parliamentary debates which ensued several opposition politicians saw in the new apparitions of the old, including attitudes associated with the White Australia Policy. Such difference of view reflects what Judith Brett reminds us is the partisan nature of debate about citizenship in Australia (Brett, 2001). This had remained relatively contained over the preceding two decades. There had been broad bipartisan agreement about the need to reinvigorate the language of citizenship. However, the contemporary changes were radical. The reintroduction of a formal test, some 50 years after the abolition of the last, signalled the new use to which citizenship was being put. The Federal Government wanted to use citizenship to drive unity, insisting on it being the common bond at the heart of the nation. As David Dutton argues while this had been a long-standing and relatively stable theme of policy there had been changes in the ways the citizenry was imagined and the policies by which governments tried to fulfil their respective visions across the twentieth century (Dutton, 2002, 161). The twenty-first century vision was ultimately more backward looking than the then Commonwealth Government would concede.

The citizenship test must not be seen in isolation but as part of a *particular* focus on citizenship under the decade-long Howard regime. Howard made it clear that citizenship would be a focus of his government, declaring his 1996 election slogan as 'For All Of Us', thus drawing an imaginary line around a community of 'us' and, by inference, a community of 'them'. His government's discussion paper on testing suggested that the test would be a mechanism to ensure readiness for participation in the Australian community. Importantly, it would target only those wishing to apply for citizenship by conferral. As some commentators pointed out at the time, this was discriminatory, privileging Australian-born citizens. But such discriminatory treatment of would-be citizens was a deeply ingrained historic practice. It spoke to a tradition of anxiety about outsiders and newcomers that earmarked citizenship policy from its inception. Its insistence on English literacy and knowledge of Australian values spoke of an old, even foundational, view of Australia as an organic community of 'natural-born' people, sharing a common culture and displaying fixed characteristics and values. In utilising it Howard was using a remarkably entrenched and resilient ideal of what constitutes Australianness.

For most of the twentieth century this organic community was defined by racial exclusivity. Race, in this context, meant British. As members of a self-governing Dominion within the British Empire, Australians were 'natural-born' or naturalised British subjects whose primary allegiance was to the Crown (Chesterman, 2005). But, as Lake and Reynolds (2008) remind us, they were also white and, in the late nineteenth century, whiteness was thought to be threatened globally by the so-called rise of the 'coloured' man. In the thinking of the day non-white races were regarded as inferior stock, incompatible with Europeans with whom they should not mix. To ensure the purity of the race, to fortify whiteness, was to exclude undesirables – non-white and non-European – from entering and contaminating the body politic.[1]

It is no coincidence that in an effort to ensure racial purity and develop a mechanism for exclusion policy makers in Australia looked to language. During the course of the nineteenth century, language came to be understood as a marker of national character. This in turn contributed to the seismic shift in nineteenth-century racial science to polygenism, which held that mankind was divided into races whose characteristics were biologically fixed, not subject to historical or environmental change. The progress of British colonisation had done much to encourage this view and Australia had provided what was regarded as the perfect exemplar of the theory in the Aborigines. Considered too primitive to advance, Aborigines were consigned to oblivion. Although declared British subjects, they were internally excluded from the body politic; physically via removal to reserves, legislatively via exclusion from the rights of their fellow citizens and constitutionally via non-inclusion in the census. Being consigned to State rather than Federal control, they would not come within the newly created Commonwealth Government's determinations on citizenship policy.

The question for the Federal Government remained how to exclude all other undesirables, to ensure the unity of a common race and culture. As the previous chapter shows, language was the key. Exclusion was enshrined in the Immigration Restriction Act (IRA), the first substantive legislation passed by the newly formed Federal Parliament in 1901. Under the terms of the Act, customs officials were empowered to administer a dictation test, described as an education test, to test prospective immigrants on their competency in English. This involved an official reading out a passage of 50 words which the immigrant was required to transcribe. While it was a discretional test and applied only to non-Europeans, debate developed over the desirability of testing in English. Some politicians believed that this would enable educated non-Europeans' entry. This led to a change to testing in any European language. In 1906, the test was defined as an absolute bar to admission. Whereas some 50 or so immigrants passed the test till 1909, none did afterwards. Tests were given in German, Dutch, Spanish and many other languages, most notoriously Gaelic in the famous case of Czech communist Egon Kisch. For more than 50 years the test was the Commonwealth's chief tool for preventing the entry and deportation of non-Europeans from Australia.

The legislative framing of unity, where non-British, non-Europeans were excluded in the first instance, meant that understandings and practices of citizenship or subjecthood could be more fluid and, in many ways, more wide-ranging than later in the twentieth century when the White Australia Policy no longer pertained. For instance, there was a conception of citizenship as dual (if not three-tiered). As subjects of Empire and Commonwealth, Australians were citizens of city, state and dominion, according to the Premier of New South Wales (1927–30), Sir Thomas Bavin (Walter and Macleod, 2002, 25). At the same time, leading feminists of the period frequently referred to their dual status as citizens of nation and empire. As several commentators have noted, citizenship was as much a behavioural ideal as a political identity, denoting a certain type of person or community. Citizenship was about civilisation and character, implying morality, independence and respectability. Even so it remained highly selective. While the Chinese-born businessman and philanthropist, Quong Tart, could be celebrated in the 1890s as a model citizen because he approximated the British–Australian way of life, Aborigines who were thrifty, industrious, hard-working and Christian could not (Fitzgerald, 2007, 29). There were definite limits, then, as to how far unity could stretch.

The preoccupation with unity has remained central to citizenship policy. It was most evident immediately after the Second World War when, for demographic and economic reasons, the Commonwealth Government was forced to look beyond natural increase and British migration to modernise and fortify the nation. Although, in 1948, the NCA created the legal category of Australian citizen for the first time, Australian citizens remained British subjects simultaneously until 1984. But the Act was less concerned with natural-born Australian citizens than with the naturalisation of non-British migrants, mostly refugees from war-torn Europe (90 per cent of the population was of Anglo-Celtic descent in 1947 when the first government-assisted 'alien' immigrant arrived in Australia). It differentiated between British subjects (including Irish citizens and protected persons) and all others, who were defined aliens. It gave preferential treatment to the former and demanded assimilation of the latter.

As a doctrine of national unity, assimilation rested on assumptions of race and nationality which promoted homogeneity. Born in the post-war atmosphere of anti-racism, assimilation was the mid-century progressivist discourse promising inclusion and advancement to all. No less discriminatory in practice, race was replaced by culture and cultural conformity as the yardstick by which to measure assimilability. Migrants – New Australians – were discriminated against not only by being required to wait longer than British or Irish subjects before applying for naturalisation and to be competent in English, but also they were expected to leave their old cultures and allegiances behind and absorb the 'Australian way of life'. They were required to demonstrate renunciation of prior allegiance (family, social, economic and political) to qualify for naturalisation. This conflation of nationality and allegiance was evident in citizenship policy as early as 1917 when it was first introduced by the Commonwealth Government and as late as 1984 when it was finally abolished.[2]

One didn't need to look far to see to how unyielding government policies were under assimilationist doctrine. To maintain even the outward signs of one's culture was to show lack of commitment to the core or host society. It could lead to the revocation of citizenship. Nowhere was this clearer than in the case of Aboriginal Australia. Under assimilationist doctrine, citizenship for Aboriginal Australians was premised on conformity to non-Aboriginal culture. As Minister for Territories in the Menzies Liberal Government, Paul Hasluck defined assimilation in relation to Aboriginal policy as follows:

> that all Aborigines and part-Aborigines will attain the *same* manner of living as other Australians and live as members of a single Australian community enjoying the *same* rights and privileges, accepting the *same* responsibilities, observing the *same* customs and influences by the *same* beliefs, hopes and loyalties as other Australians [my emphasis].
>
> (Rowse, 1998, 110)

The impracticality of such a formulation was tragically played out in the case of Albert Namatjira, well-known painter from Central Australia who, in 1957, became the Northern Territory's first Indigenous citizen. Aboriginal people frequently equated citizenship with drinking rights. They sought access to what they identified as quintessential to the Australian way of life. However, it was an offence to sell or supply liquor to a ward (full-blood Aborigine, not a citizen). In sharing alcohol with his relatives in conformity with Arrernte traditions, Namatjira broke the conditions of his own citizenship. His citizenship revoked, he died not long after serving 3 months' detention at Papunya in Central Australia (Wells and Christie, 2000).

The promotion of the Australian way of life coincided with the abolition of the dictation test with the passing of the *Migration Act* (1958). Its abolition was a sign of the times, its racist undertones progressively out of touch with growing international and domestic opposition to racism following the Second World War. This clearly represented a break with the past. Dutton insists, however, that even as ideas about what constituted social cohesion – including conceptualisations of human difference – began to change, race remained an important, if increasingly elusive, element in the formulation of civic policies (Dutton, 2002, 66–8). The clearest example of this again appeared in relation to Aboriginal policy. When an Aboriginal person applied for and got an exemption certificate, called a 'Certificate of Citizenship in Western Australia', he or she was automatically declared non-Aboriginal. No longer a native or an Aborigine they could have all the rights, privileges and immunities of, and be subject to the same duties and liabilities as, all other natural-born or naturalised subjects.

Aboriginal policy also demonstrates how the idea of testing was not eradicated altogether either. Exemption certificates were promoted as the short-cut to citizenship for Aborigines. Once obtained, they freed individuals from the restrictions of the specific laws governing Aboriginal persons. However, to obtain an exemption certificate was an onerous task. One had to dissolve tribal associations 2 years prior to the application, adopt the manners and habits of civilised life, speak and understand the English language, be free from disease, have industrious habits and be of good behaviour and reputation, for which two recent written references from reputable citizens were required. As Namatjira's case illustrates once obtained citizenship could be suspended or cancelled for non-compliance. In varying degrees this situation applied until the various state-based legislative regimes earmarking Aboriginal people as different to all other Australian citizens were dissolved. Despite the widespread belief that Aboriginal people were given citizenship following the 1967 referendum, it was in fact never formally granted (Attwood and Markus, 2007). Chesterman has shown that Aborigines had been granted rights to voting and social services prior to the referendum (Chesterman, 2005) and the legislative regimes defining them as 'other' were slowly dismantled after it in the late 1960s, into the 1970s and as late as 1984 in Queensland.

The treatment of Aborigines demonstrates the shift in thinking about what constituted national unity, highlighting a conceptual shift away from anxiety over potential racial conflict to an interest in integrating outsiders into an homogenous population. In this sense, immigrants (and Aborigines) had to demonstrate capacity or readiness for integration and their 'test' was conformity to the Australian way of life. 'The Australian way of life' became the mantra for a whole range of attributes and values, racial and otherwise. Not a test, it was nonetheless an ideal, social and behavioural, not merely referring to a set of national attributes but to a lifestyle, a pattern of morality and mode of living that was hegemonic. One of the first amendments to policy in the 1950s was the possibility of the naturalisation of Asians who had residence in Australia for more than 15 years, compared to 5 for Europeans. But this was on the proviso that they were of good character, had adequate knowledge of English and had taken part in 'normal Australian life'.

It also became increasingly important for prospective immigrants to demonstrate an appreciation of the meaning and value attached to Australian citizenship. In promoting the NCA, the first post-war Immigration Minister, Arthur Calwell, suggested prospective immigrants should be able to demonstrate their appreciation of the value of

Australian citizenship. A grant of citizenship rested on a number of practical things such as years of residency, knowledge of English and good character. However, it was also important to demonstrate an understanding of the nature of the application for citizenship, including a conscious appreciation of the value of citizenship, along with knowledge of the responsibilities and privileges of citizenship. The length of residency for all non-Europeans was particularly important as was proof of commitment to Australia in processes such as involvement in community organisations. Citizenship ceremonies began officially in 1949 as part of an array of official functions intended to convey to the 'New Australian' the privileges of citizenship.

A line of continuity thus runs between the mid-century changes to policy and the Howard Government's definition of citizenship as 'more than a ceremony'. Howard wanted to make citizenship a value-added experience as much as it was value-laden. Like Calwell, he insisted on defining citizenship as a privilege not a right, consistent with its terms of definition over most of the twentieth century. Part of the justification for the citizenship test was to re-instil a certain gravitas to the attainment of citizenship which the Liberal Government felt had lapsed under Labour, in the words of one Liberal MP, to 'restore a pride in and a commitment to and understanding of what this Australian nation is about' (2006). But whereas in the preceding 50 years or so, changes to the original NCA demonstrated a gradual broadening of the terms of citizenship, including, under multiculturalism, social and cultural 'rights', Howard's linking of citizenship to privilege and responsibility spoke of a pre-multicultural vision where diversity was downplayed in the interests of homogeneity and unity.

Despite gradual liberalisations to policy during the 1960s, including assessment of non-Europeans on the basis of merit, social homogeneity remained the cornerstone of immigration policy. As the population slowly changed, debate ensued over whether different groups could coexist in socially harmonious communities. Some saw tension between the requirement for assimilability and the principle of merit. Into the 1970s, homogeneity was consistently emphasised. The terms used then to define homogeneity are almost identical to those used by Andrew Robb, Parliamentary Secretary to the Minister for Immigration and Multicultural Affairs in 2007. In his foreword to the Howard Government's discussion paper on the merits or otherwise of introducing a citizenship test, he referred to 'one family', 'one overriding culture', 'a common set of values'. Citizenship must assist social cohesion and successful integration. In addition to English skills and capacity to make a social and economic contribution to Australian society, according to Robb, it was critical that immigrants 'understand the Australian way of life and our shared values and demonstrate a commitment to contributing to that way of life and accepting those values'. A 1972 press-release from the McMahon Liberal Government lauds the notion of homogeneity:

> a society that does not have permanent minorities of people with extremely different backgrounds that will resist integration in the long-term. We want one Australian people, one Australian nation [...it is] a valid social objective of preventing the frictions and tensions which can come from enclaves and a divided nation.

The emphasis on one family and one culture in 2007 was not only a return to an older ideal of national unity but also a reaction to the direction of citizenship policy since the 1970s. When multiculturalism was promoted under the Whitlam Government in 1972 it was supposed to bury White Australia once and for all. In 1971, the Labour Party adopted a non-discriminatory policy, suggesting that the basis of immigration should be multicultural and include, 'avoidance of discrimination on any grounds of race, or colour, of skin or nationality' (Dutton, 2002, 79). As this suggests, multiculturalism was also about burying assimilation. In 1973, the Labour Government replaced a racially discriminatory and assimilationist conception of the national citizenry with a multi-racial, poly-ethnic and pluralist one (Dutton, 2002, 81). In 1973 and 1974, new selection procedures were introduced, eliminating race as a criterion for eligibility. At the same time, preference for British immigrants was finally abolished, identical conditions for the issue of visas for all migrants were established and race was removed as a criterion for assisted passage. The NCA, now rebadged the *Australian Citizenship Act* (1948–73), was amended so that all non-citizens were eligible for the grant of citizenship after 3 years residence. In 1984, the residence requirement was further reduced to 2 years.

This shift in policy was part and parcel of the worldwide discursive shift in conceptualising citizenship during the 1960s and 70s. It was also influenced by the failure of assimilation as policy. During this period, it became clear that assimilation did not work, either because migrants would or could not forsake their heritage and/or because racism barred their effective participation in Australian society (Davidson, 1997). Furthermore, the same era saw the notion of citizenship *rights* become a dominant concern. Where, in the inter-war and immediate post-war years, citizenship was widely perceived as a relatively passive status, the atmosphere of social protests in the 1960s and 70s fostered a revived understanding of the parameters of citizenship. While the language of duty and responsibility prevailed in previous years, the notion of citizenship rights (civil and social) dominated the 60s and 70s. The passing of the *Racial Discrimination Act* in 1975, under Whitlam, was the hallmark of this era.

During the early years of multiculturalism, emphasis shifted from attempts to facilitate substantive changes to citizenship in theory to the necessity of building infrastructure to meet migrant need. Nevertheless, multiculturalism was underwritten by a significant discursive shift in thinking about racial/ethnic difference, which was increasingly understood as cultural rather than biological. The issue of how to reconcile a growing diversity with the need to maintain national unity remained a core, bipartisan, concern. But so did the basic principle of non-discrimination in immigration policy. The momentum begun by Whitlam was carried forth under the Conservative Government of Malcolm Fraser (which admitted large numbers of Indo-Chinese refugees). It was then maintained in the 1980s and 90s by the Labour Governments of Bob Hawke (1983–91) and Paul Keating (1991–6).

To understand the Howard Government's particular focus on citizenship between 1996 and 2007, it is important to appreciate the changes made to policy and thinking about citizenship and immigration in the preceding two decades. In that period, ideas and practices of citizenship were not merely maintained but were developed and extended. Just as the migrant intake reflected a changing physical make-up of Australian society, particularly a growing increase in Asian migration, multiculturalism (or more precisely diversity) forced a rethink about what constituted national unity. As immigration policy it was premised on three key principles: social cohesion, cultural identity and equality of opportunity (Australian Ethnic Affairs, 1977). The Galbally Report, commissioned by Fraser in 1978, went so far as to identify maintenance of cultural and racial identity as a right, provided it 'is interwoven into the fabric of nationhood' (Walter and Macleod, 2002, 204). Fraser agreed that acceptance of ethnic difference within a framework of shared values provided the framework for social cohesion. But Labour had long since advanced the argument that multiculturalism was about migrants' needs and rights. Multiculturalism was seen as promoting socialcohesion via the avoidance of a migrant underclass. Hawke emphasised questions of access and equity, defining multiculturalism as a question of social justice. Importantly, the emphasis went from responsibility (of both migrant and host for commitment to and participation in society) under Fraser to rights – cultural and equalitarian – under Hawke.

Paul Keating's term as Prime Minister saw this approach developed still further. He saw multiculturalism as a progressive policy that provided a strong foundation for Australia's wider engagement in the Asia-Pacific region (Keating, 2000). Multiculturalism had made Australia a better place. But he saw it as a balance between rights and responsibilities. In his attempt to codify Australian citizenship, Keating not only talked of immigrants acquiring an understanding of and commitment to the Australian community and Australian values, but also identified a need to increase awareness and understanding of the rights and responsibilities of citizenship. This harked back to a criticism of multiculturalism under Hawke in the Fitzgerald Report of 1988. Fitzgerald identified a large part of Anglo-Australia who were resentful of the focus on migrant need and critical of multiculturalism as threatening national interests. It also continued that which Labour's *National Agenda For Multicultural Australia* had begun. In response to Fitzgerald, Labour emphasised the need for an overriding commitment by all Australians to Australia which should be based on acceptance of its democratic structure and values. But this should not be at the expense of a right to cultural identity. The *Native Title Act* (1993), which recognised land rights for Aboriginal Australians, was ultimately an expression of this view.

Labour's dominance in the 20 years of non-discriminatory immigration policy, from 1970 to 1990, demonstrated a movement away from the notion of a common people as the basis of policy to establishing some common ground rules (Walter and Macleod, 2002, 230). Walter and Macleod point out that this was more evident in the late 1980s and 1990s and reflected, in part, a worldwide trend precipitated by the impact of economic rationalism and globalisation and the consequent circulation (and migration) of peoples. Keating identified this time as a 'pivotal period of modern history', when the structures of the preceding 50 years were toppling and where globalisation and the technological revolution were gnawing at the foundations of the nation state itself (Keating, 2000). According to political theorists Kymlicka and Norman, the period is characterised by what they call 'citizenship worries' manifest in many Western Liberal democracies faced with the challenge of ethnocultural diversity and the potentially differentiated status which it implied (Kymlicka and Norman, 2000, 31). It was in this period that citizenship testing was introduced into some of these same democracies.

In the face of this community uncertainty and worry there was a concerted bipartisan commitment in Australia to invest citizenship with new meaning, to remind people of their community ties (Walter and Macleod, 2002, 229). Under Labour's stewardship, this took several forms which, in many ways, were mutually exclusive. While a commitment to multiculturalism and cultural rights provided a theoretical framework for citizenship, much emphasis lays on a more practical application, via education about citizenship's history and reigniting debate about civics education. One further strand, under Keating, was a critique of Australia's British inheritance. Keating saw in the 1990s an opportunity to reshape Australia for the future. Australia's independence was one strand of this, evident in his championing of republicanism and replacement of the Oath of Allegiance to the Queen of Australia with a Pledge of Commitment as a Citizen of the Country of Australia (ALP, 1993). It was also evident in his emphasis on the refashioning of Australian history to include Aboriginal Australia and acknowledge past injustice. His facilitation of native title was the ultimate expression of this because the Mabo decision, which underwrote it, overturned the basis of British sovereignty.

That the Australian people were not ready for Keating's future was evident in his loss of government to John Howard in 1996. Keating has since admitted that in the post-Cold War world it was still much easier to describe our lives in terms of what had passed rather than what was to come (Keating, 2000, 2). Howard's election slogan, 'For All Of Us', was appealing to what he defined as a mainstream disaffected by Labour's policies on multiculturalism and Indigenous Australians, among other things. In an election speech at the time, he said:

> There is a frustrated mainstream in Australia today that sees government decisions increasingly driven by the noisy, self-interested clamour of powerful vested interests with scant regard for the national interest [...] Increasingly, Australians have been exhorted to think of themselves as members of sub-groups. The focus so often has been on where we are different not what we have in common. In the process our sense of community has been severely damaged.
>
> (Markus, 2001, 96–7)

Howard's critique of multiculturalism occurred at a time of heightened anxiety over immigration generally and an increase in Asian and Middle-Eastern migration in particular. This was partly generated by the unprecedented global movement of asylum seekers and refugees which worried most developed democracies around the world from the 1990s. Mandatory detention for asylum seekers had been one response in Australia. From the late 1990s, the Howard Government whipped up national anxiety, describing the increased arrival of boat people as the 'greatest assault to our borders in history', thus evoking memory and a historical preoccupation with protecting borders from external threat (Wills, 2002, 79).

There had been an earlier rendition of this theme. It was during the 1980s, in the context of increased Asian migration, that expressions of disquiet were expressed in popular, academic and conservative circles about the changing complexion of Australian society and its alleged Asianisation. Memorable debate sparked by the historian, Geoffrey Blainey, centred on a threat to the traditional concept of the nation under multiculturalism. Conservatives saw in the policy a threat to Anglo-Australian identity. At the time, Howard suggested slowing down the rate of Asian migration in the interests of 'One Australia'. At the same time, he expressed his dissatisfaction with multiculturalism:

> The objection I have to multiculturalism is that multiculturalism is in effect saying that it is impossible to have an Australian ethos, that it is impossible to have a common Australian culture. So, we have to pretend that we are a federation of cultures and that we've got a bit from every part of the world. I think that is hopeless.
>
> (Curran, 2004, 253)

As already noted, the Fitzgerald Report tapped into this, describing widespread dissatisfaction with immigration. The Hawke Labour Government responded by talking up economic efficiency as a key justification of the policy and reiterating the need for all Australians to have 'an overriding and unifying commitment to Australia', including acceptance of its democratic structure and values. However, it simultaneously promoted multiculturalism as a good thing for Australia in its *National Agenda For Multicultural Australia* (1989), a trenchant defence of the policy.

Yet, if some of the leftist academic critics of multiculturalism are to be believed, the policy had always been about the promotion of an Australian ethos and a common culture (Davidson, 1997; Hage, 1998). Certainly, in much of the political literature, from Galbally's report in 1978 to Howard's *New Agenda for a Multicultural Australia* in 1999, the emphasis has been on a celebration of diversity within the context of an 'overriding commitment to Australia'. There has been broad bipartisan agreement on managing diversity in the interests of unity, of embedding multiculturalism in the basic structures and values of

Australian democracy. Yet, there is a difference of inflection between Labour's Agenda of 1989 and the Liberal New Agenda for Multicultural-ism a decade later. Whereas Labour defined multiculturalism as 'a policy for managing the consequences of cultural diversity in the interests of the individual and society as a whole', the Liberal New Agenda defines it as, 'the way Australians address the challenges and opportunities of cultural diversity'.

What dominates Labour's Agenda is the language of rights, social and cultural. This includes reciprocal rights and obligations: the right to one's culture and the responsibility to accept the rights of others. Under the Liberal Agenda, rights are embedded rather than empha-sised. It stipulates unity in diversity and describes 'moral values' such as respect for difference and a common commitment to freedom within the rubric of Australia's national interest. Importantly, it adds civic duty as a foundational principle of policy. This is defined as supporting the basic structures and principles of Australian society that guarantee free-dom and equality and enable diversity to flourish. Within the space of a decade, despite the veneer of bipartisanship, undercurrents of disagree-ment appear. The Howard Government's focus was more concerned to place unity before diversity.

That Howard was interested in refashioning citizenship and immi-gration is evident in his establishment of a new National Multicultural Advisory Council in 1997. It was to develop recommendations on pol-icy aimed at ensuring that cultural diversity was a unifying force for Australia. His New Agenda was the response. A year later, as the cente-nary of Federation drew near, he appointed an Australian Citizenship Council to advise the minister on contemporary issues in citizenship policy and law and how to promote increased community awareness of citizenship in the pursuit of national unity. The centrepiece of the Council's report was a non-partisan acceptance and promotion of a dec-laration, styled an 'Australian Compact'. Described as a statement of core civic values, it rested on the promotion of seven basic principles: respect and care for the land, maintenance of the rule of law and the ideal of equity, strengthening liberal democracy based on universal suf-frage and freedom of opinion, tolerance and fairness, recognition of Australia as an inclusive multicultural society which values diversity, is devoted to the well-being of its people and to value the unique status of Aboriginal and Torres Strait Islander people.

The Compact was the Council's answer as to how to promote citizen-ship as a unifying symbol. It argued that the promotion of a national 'civic' identity should replace the fixation with 'a' national identity, making the polity rather than the nation the focus of belonging. But it was to be more than the promotion of a civic identity all could share. The Council saw the Compact as sitting alongside and complementary to the principles of cultural diversity and racial tolerance, arguing that diversity, rather than uniformity, should be one of the bases of social harmony. It recommended a non-partisan parliamentary declaration on the significance and values contained in the Compact and the concurrent dissemination of the Joint Parliamentary Statement on Racial Tolerance unanimously passed by Parliament in October 1996 together with the principles of Australian multiculturalism enunciated by the multicultural advisory council. On the question of citizenship law, the Council argued for continuity rather than change, recommending some modernisation of the *Australian Citizenship Act*, including repeal of Section 17 to enable dual citizenship.

While the Government agreed with the latter, abolishing Section 17 by Act of Parliament in 2002, they rejected the idea of an Australian Compact. Rejected, too, was the close connection between the promotion of core civic values and the principles of multiculturalism with the suggestion that the two could proceed independently. However, the Government did accept the Council's recommendation that the inclusive and non-discriminatory approach to citizenship had worked well and should remain the basis of citizenship law and policy. This included retaining the provisions for the grant of citizenship such as 2 years residency, a basic knowledge of English (or 300 hours of English language tuition) and an adequate knowledge of the responsibilities and privileges of Australian citizenship. The Council recommended retaining the current testing for the latter at interview which the Government agreed to. The Government also took the Council's advice that the suggestion by some that a written examination, testing on the Australian constitution, government and civic duties, was extreme.

This was in May 2001, several months before 9/11 and the War on Terror were unleashed, a context in which we see a swathe of new legislative provisions around migration, border protection and anti-terrorism. This should not be surprising. As Dutton (2002) tells us war and concerns over national security have been important catalysts for developments in citizenship policy in Australia. He argues that this is because of the close connection between nationality and allegiance in citizenship's history. The retention of signs of foreign nationality meant the retention of political loyalty to another state. He cites the emergence of new criteria for eligibility in immigration and naturalisation around the First World War as demonstrating a concern with the entry of potentially threatening political values and beliefs. It was during that war, he argues, that foreigners were reconceptualised in close relation to subversion and disloyalty. Non-British Europeans were now thought of as potentially dangerous, as illustrated by the internment of enemy aliens and the dispersal and assimilation of alien communities throughout Australia during and after the war.

Dutton argues that the First World War set a precedent. Once established, actions, laws and policies could be, and were, replicated in times of national emergency or apparent threat. Nowhere is this pattern clearer than in the escalation of practices and policies in Australia over recent years in the context of the War on Terror. As Bashford and Strange have shown, the practice of alien internment, first enacted during the First World War, provided the framework for the mandatory detention of asylum seekers (Bashford and Strange, 2002, 518). The Anti-Terrorism Act (2004) amended the Crimes Act (1914) introduced during the First World War to handle, among other things, sabotage, treachery and related crimes. Further amendments to anti-terrorism legislation in 2005 upgraded the regime of surveillance with provisions for detaining suspects without charge and new powers of question, search and seize. These not only eroded civil liberties but also gave the Government considerable regulatory powers which were reminiscent of the War Precautions and National Security Acts of 1914 and 1939. Furthermore, many of the anti-terrorist measures are resonant with anti-communist measures from the 1930s to the 1950s which were, in themselves, built on notions of political loyalty and allegiance to come out of the war.

The terrorist bombings of London in 2005, and the heightened international concern over security which accompanied them, appear to have been a major catalyst for changes to citizenship law as well, including testing. This was not least because of advice from the Australian Security Intelligence Organisation (ASIO) concerning the need to rethink the conditions of admission into the citizenry. Like the anti-terror legislation, these changes looked back rather than forward. The Citizenship Bill introduced to Parliament in 2005 was targeted to those wishing to take up citizenship in Australia, that is, those applying for a grant of citizenship. The principle changes included an increase in the residency requirements from 2 to 3 years, security checks (a strategy which dates from the First World War) and an increase in the number and range of personal identifiers, including iris scans. The former effectively gave ASIO the power to veto a grant of citizenship, as the minister could not approve an application while an adverse or qualified ASIO assessment was in force. In other respects, the new legislative provisions gave unprecedented discretionary powers to the minister. As this and other aspects of the Bill were being debated in Parliament, the Government floated the idea of a citizenship test (see Chapter 5), including changes to language requirements. Then, in December 2006, Howard announced his government's intentions to introduce a formal test.

Looking back to 2001 and the Howard Government's response to the Australian Citizenship Council's report, it would seem that, within the space of a few years, it had significantly hardened its position on citizenship. Certainly, a lot had happened in that time but the introduction of a formal test put it, in the Council's terms, in the extreme category. Parliamentary debate on the changes being introduced in 2005 also suggests that they represented more than a response to the War on Terror. There was a clear sense of partisan disagreement over what citizenship meant or should mean. Some of this was demonstrated in debate over detail. When the Government tightened the residency requirements still further changing it from 3 to 4 years, effectively doubling it, Labour objected. Whereas Labour had agreed to 3 years as part of a whole-of-government response to the security intelligence, they saw the latter change as unjustified and born of political whim. There was also much criticism within Labour ranks of the English language provision of the test. Citing the Howard Government's cutting of funding to the Adult Migrant Education Program (AMEP) to the tune of 11 million dollars, they saw the measure as disingenuous at best.

More obvious was the Government's attempts to discredit Labour's approach to citizenship and immigration from the period of Labour's ascendency in the 1980s. A recurring sentiment from Liberal spokespersons was that under Labour citizenship had been reduced to its basic minimum. One Liberal MP even suggested that the Cronulla riots (a confrontation between local residents from the Sydney beach-side suburb of Cronulla, and their supporters, and groups of Middle-Eastern youths which resulted in racially motivated violence) had been caused by Labour destroying all substance of commitment to Australia. He was referring to amendments to the Oath of Allegiance in 1986 which removed the requirement to renounce all other allegiances. He argued that the renunciation clause was the legal link to cite to one who 'transgresses our understanding of what it is to be an Aussie'.

In many ways this demonstrates Dutton's thesis that race never entirely disappeared from citizenship policy, even if less frequently invoked (Dutton, 2002, 68). As Andrew Markus (2001) has shown, race had re-emerged with renewed vigour in Australia from the mid-1990s. And it was alive and well in 2006 when Andrew Robb summed up parliamentary debate on his government's new citizenship legislation. In justifying the increased residency requirement for citizenship by conferral he suggested that the sole motivation was to do with new patterns of migration to Australia. He cited the 200,000 new arrivals over the past decade who had come from Middle-Eastern and African countries whose cultures were 'far removed from the Australian culture'. He added, 'it is more difficult if you come not from Europe but from other cultures that are far removed from the Australian culture to get some understanding of what it is that makes Australian tick'. Furthermore, he suggested, language skills are necessary to grasp Australian values and the Australian way of life.

This notion of cultures closer or farther away from Australian culture invokes an understanding of racial hierarchy which dates back to the Enlightenment. Accordingly, Middle-Eastern and African peoples were ranked much lower on a sliding scale upwards to Europeans. They therefore had a more difficult task ahead and required more time adopting Australian values. But, as John Fitzgerald found in his study of Chinese Australians, so-called Australian values have long been the terrain over which inclusion and exclusion have traversed. As he argues, White Australia, with its supposed unique values, was articulated through an historical clash of cultures with Asian values (Fitzgerald, 2007, 21). Australian's commitment to egalitarianism, mateship, a fair go and liberal democracy were characterised as completely antithetical to Chinese values conceived as hierarchical, separatist and despotic. But if Australia was a community of values, under White Australia, it was also premised on an exact fit between race and value which no longer applies (Fitzgerald, 2007, 27).

In resuscitating this notion of a community of values the Howard Government was careful to identify what should be included and what should be excluded. Howard's changes to citizenship law and practice, including the test, were widely believed to have stemmed from the report of the Australian Citizenship Council in 2001. Yet, as we have seen, the Council discountenanced the idea of a test while talking up values in an Australian Compact which the Government rejected. As well, by labelling values as 'Australian', the Government diverged from the Council which had critiqued the use of values to construct *a* national identity. Yet, there are some overlaps between the values promoted by the Government and those promoted by the Council. There are also notable absences. The Government's list includes support for parliamentary democracy and the rule of law, equality under the law and tolerance, all of which appeared in the Council's Compact. However, missing from the Government's list is respect and care for the land, recognition and celebration of Australia as an inclusive multicultural society which values its diversity, the development of a society devoted to the well-being of its people and valuing the unique status of Aboriginal and Torres Strait Islander peoples. The Government's list included individual freedom, freedom of religion, freedom of association, equality of men and women, equality of opportunity and peacefulness. The Citizenship Council's freedom of opinion is replaced by freedom of speech in the Government's list. Importantly, such freedoms were not classified rights. Rather, new citizens had a responsibility to embrace them as (Australian) values.

Thus, in the contemporary context, values replace race as the exclusive boundary of Australian citizenship. As Andrew Robb suggested at the time, 'our values' are 'the glue that maintains and has sustained such a cohesive society'. But citizenship and values are one and the same. Under Howard's leadership, citizenship itself moved to centre stage. Where once it was race and then culture that provided the glue for national unity, now it was citizenship tied to values. As the Government argued in its response to the Australian Citizenship Council, Australian citizenship is the 'common bond at the heart of a unified and inclusive Australia'. But, as they made clear in their rejection of the Australian Compact and their attacks on multiculturalism, unity would not be found in valuing cultural diversity or Aboriginal and Torres Strait Islanders but in insisting on what 'we' hold in common. Or, as one Liberal MP put it, in accepting the privilege of 'becoming a member of a very significant club'.

In emphasising citizenship as a privilege rather than a right, the Howard Government was, in many ways, returning citizenship back to its foundations. As Dutton has argued, despite popular appreciation of human and citizenship rights, the primary purpose of Australian citizenship has been controlling the movement of people across borders and incorporating migrants (Dutton, 2002, 18). Howard was also emphasising the partisan nature of citizenship once so entrenched in Australian political culture. In critiquing Labour's policies as appealing to noisy minorities and sub-groups, Howard was invoking an old partisan use of citizenship. As Judith Brett has shown, an emphasis on duty and obligation (now responsibility) was central to non-Labour's claim to political virtue in contrast to the ALP's commitment to sectional claims regardless of national interest (Brett, 2001, 424–5). But as Dutton shows policy makers have emphasised privilege above rights for most of the twentieth century largely because citizenship rights are not enshrined constitutionally but understood as protected by the vigilance of governments. In the history of citizenship, then, Labour's emphasis on rights was aberrant.

Although reinstating a formal citizenship test, some 50 years after the abolition of the last, does not amount to the reinstatement of the White Australia Policy, the act must be situated within an historical framework in which that policy constitutes an important precedent. And there are similarities of context, particularly in terms of global geo-politics. Furthermore, just as some critics of the test today argue that it is prejudicial and if given to many Australian citizens they would not pass, so early commentators on the White Australia Policy argued the same about Englishmen undertaking the dictation test. Although separated by 100 years, voices were raised in both contexts about the excessive degree of ministerial discretion in the application of the tests. And values can be just as discriminatory as race once was. As the preliminary reports on the citizenship test revealed, it is the humanitarian and refugee entrants, with a higher citizenship uptake than any other migrant, whose failure rate is consistently higher than all others.

Notes

1. For further discussion of the legal constitution of Australian policy, see Buck and Frew in this volume.
2. Such ideas continued to find resonance in Australia's treatment of dual citizenship. Up until 2002, Australian citizens were prevented from holding dual citizenship, automatically forfeiting their citizen status upon naturalisation in another country, a remarkably backward approach compared to other Western democracies. By 2002, New Zealand and the United Kingdom, for example, had allowed for dual citizenship for over 50 years.

References

Government Reports

Australian Ethnic Affairs Council (1977) Australia as a Multicultural Society: Submission to the Australian Population and Immigration Council on the Green Paper, Immigration Policies and Australia's Population, Canberra.
National Agenda for Multicultural Australia (1989) Accessed 10 November 2007 (http://www.immi.gov.au/media/publications/multicultural/agenda/agenda89/toc.htm).
New Agenda for Multicultural Australia (1999) Accessed 10 November 2007 (http://www.immi.gov.au/media/publications/multicultural/agenda/index.htm).
Australian Citizenship for a New Century (2000) A Report by the Australian Citizenship Council.

Australian Citizenship ... A Common Bond (2001) Government Response to the Report of the Australian Citizenship Council.
Australian Citizenship: Much More Than a Ceremony (2006) Discussion Paper. Consideration of the Merits of Introducing a Formal Citizenship Test.
Australian Government (2007) Becoming an Australian Citizen.
Australian Citizenship Act (2007).
The Senate, Standing Committee on Legal and Constitutional Affairs. Australian Citizenship Amendment (Citizenship Testing) Bill 2007 [Provisions], July 2007.
Australian Citizenship Test. Snapshot Report (2008).

Other

Attwood, Bain and Andrew Markus (2007) *1967 Referendum: Race, Power and the Australian Constitution* (Canberra: Aboriginal Studies Press).
Bashford, Alison and Carolyn Strange (2002) 'Asylum Seekers and National Histories of Detention', *Australian Journal of Politics and History* 48 (4): 509–27.
Brett, Judith (2001) 'Retrieving the Partisan History of Australian Citizenship', *Australian Journal of Political Science* 36 (3): 423–37.
Chesterman, John (2005) *Civil Rights: How Indigenous Australians Won Formal Equality* (St Lucia: University of Queensland Press).
Chesterman, John (2005) 'Natural-Born Subjects? Race and British Subjecthood in Australia', *Australian Journal of Politics and History* 51 (1): 30–9.
Curran, James (2004) *The Power of Speech: Australian Prime Ministers Defining the National Image* (Melbourne: Melbourne University Press).
Davidson, Alastair (1997) *From Subject to Citizen. Australian Citizenship in the Twentieth Century* (Cambridge: Cambridge University Press).
Dutton, David (2002) *One of Us? A Century of Australian Citizenship* (Sydney: University of New South Wales Press).
Fitzgerald, John (2007) *Big White Lie. Chinese Australians in White Australia* (Sydney: University of New South Wales Press).
Hage, Ghassan (1998) *White Nation: Fantasies of White Supremacy in a Multicultural Society* (Sydney: Pluto Press).
Holland, Alison (2005) 'The Common Bond? Australian Citizenship', in Martyn Lyons and Penny Russell (eds), *Australia's History. Themes and Debates* (Sydney: University of New South Wales Press): 152–71.
Keating, Paul (2000) *Engagement: Australia Faces the Asia-Pacific* (Sydney: Pan Macmillan).
Kymlicka, Will and Wayne Norman (eds) (2000) *Citizenship in Diverse Societies* (Oxford: Oxford University Press).
Lake, Marilyn and Henry Reynolds (2008) *Drawing the Global Colour Line: White Men's Countries and the Question of Racial Equality* (Melbourne: Melbourne University Press).
Markus, Andrew (2001) *Race: John Howard and the Remaking of Australia* (Sydney: Allen and Unwin).
Rowse, Tim (1998) *White Flour White Power, From Rations to Citizenship in Central Australia* (Cambridge: Cambridge University Press).
Tavan, Gwenda (2005) *The Long, Slow Death of White Australia* (Melbourne: Scribe).

Walter, James and Margaret Macleod (2002) *The Citizens' Bargain. A Documentary History of Australian Views Since 1890* (Sydney: UNSW Press).

Wells, Julie and Michael Christie (2000) 'Namatjira and the Burden of Citizenship', *Australian Historical Studies* 31 (114): 110–30.

Wills, Sara (2002) 'Unstitching the Lips of a Migrant Nation', *Australian Historical Studies* 33 (118): 71–89.

4
From Virtues to Values: Conceptions of Australian Citizenship

Ian Tregenza

Introduction

In her study of the Australian Liberals, Judith Brett (2003) points to a deep conceptual shift that has taken place in the meaning of citizenship, and political culture more generally, over the past century. Where today citizenship is generally conceived in individualistic and passive terms and as connected with a series of rights and entitlements owed to us by the state, in the first half of the twentieth century the prevailing understanding of citizenship was active, communal and tied up with notions of service, obligation and duty. The earlier conception on which Australian Liberals drew was, according to Brett, 'as much moral as political [...] The good citizen was not just someone who fulfilled their political rights and obligations, the good citizen was also a good person and their fulfilment of their citizenship obligations was but an aspect of this goodness' (Brett, 2003, 58). Moreover, morality here should not be equated with adherence to a set of values, as is so much of the contemporary discourse on citizenship, but with virtue – the cultivation of certain qualities of character that enhance the life of the community. Whereas values, Brett suggests, '[imply] attitudes and opinions held by the self and detachable from it; "virtues" are constitutive of the self, part of its very character or very nature, and immune from the relativising morality inherent in the concept of value' (Brett, 2003, 9–10).

Though the idea of character was a leading motif of Victorian and Edwardian social and political thought,[1] this 'virtue' conception of citizenship owes a great deal to the tradition of New or Social Liberalism inspired by late nineteenth- and early twentieth-century British Idealists such as T.H. Green, Bernard Bosanquet, D.G. Ritchie and Henry

Jones.[2] These thinkers were not only widely read in Australia, a number of their disciples taught in Australian universities and influenced key public figures such as Alfred Deakin, H.B. Higgins, H.V. Evatt, Frederick Eggleston and Walter Murdoch.[3] The concept of citizenship was so central to Green's political theory that it has been suggested that he offered nothing short of a 'religion of citizenship' (Vincent, 1986), while Tim Rowse, in his pioneering study of Australian liberalism, claimed that, 'those in Australia influenced by T.H. Green's theory of the ethical state were for a time convinced that Australia was its purest example. They believed that a capacity for compassion and social responsibility in each Australian citizen was expressed in aggregate form in the reformist policies of leaders like Deakin, Fisher, and Higgins' (1978, 22).

The reasons for the rise of Idealism in late nineteenth-century Britain are complex, stemming as much from religious and metaphysical concerns as from social and political (den Otter, 1996). At the social and political levels, the Idealists responded to the moral philosophy of Utilitarianism as well as the classical or *laissez faire* Liberalism of figures such as Herbert Spencer, who famously set up a sharp dualism between the state and the individual. Drawing on disparate intellectual resources including evangelical Christianity, civic republicanism and Kantian and Hegelian metaphysics, the Idealists developed an alternative conception of the individual and of the relationship between the individual and the state. At the heart of this view was the positive theory of freedom, which stressed civic participation as a key component of self-realisation. The Idealists advocated a co-operative relationship between state and individual, and the primary purpose of state action was not to protect a series of negative rights, but to foster individual freedom understood in positive terms. This was to be promoted by (in the words of Bosanquet) 'hindering hindrances to the good life'. Many of the social welfare reforms of the period – old-age pensions, unemployment relief, social insurance and, in Australia, compulsory industrial arbitration – owe a good deal to the moral arguments of the Idealists. John Docker suggests that, '[f]rom 1880–1910 the philosophy of Green's school could be found penetrating and fertilising every part of the national life, and popular image has it that he was the philosophical inventor of the Welfare State' (1982, 62). Indeed, the inheritors of the New Liberal tradition – William Beveridge, J.M. Keynes, and T.H. Marshall in Britain, and in Australia, H.C. Coombes, who had been a student of Walter Murdoch in Perth before post-graduate study at the London School of Economics in the 1930s (Rowse, 2002) – were instrumental in establishing the welfare state in the middle decades of the twentieth century. But it was the institutional success of the New Liberal agenda that, in part, led to the decline of the 'virtue' conception of citizenship and its replacement with a passive or rights-based understanding (see Vincent, 2001).

While the language of responsibility and obligation has returned in recent debates on Australian citizenship, the wielders of this discourse have principally (and paradoxically) been the classical or neoliberal critics of the welfare state. This is a sign that while our moral language is heavily dependent on concepts drawn from the past, we have largely lost the social context within which many of these concepts – such as virtue – made sense. As Alasdair MacIntyre has suggested, 'In the conceptual *mélange* of moral thought and practice today fragments from the tradition – virtue concepts for the most part – are still found alongside characteristically modern and individualist concepts such as those of rights or utility' (MacIntyre, 1984, 252). Moreover, conceptions of citizen virtue sit uneasily within a public culture of individualism. Understanding the social and political contexts of this revival of duties talk is crucial as it reflects the loss of the kinds of civil bonds that earlier Liberals had seen as the focus of our citizen duties, and its replacement with a vertical state-centric understanding of citizenship. Despite its rhetoric of dismantling state welfare provisions in the name of individual responsibility, the neoliberal agenda is deeply influenced by the state-centred managerialism of the past 50 years. According to Brett, 'when talk of duties was revived it was in the changed context of coercive attempts by governments to wind back their services and withdraw entitlements from people, as in the context of mutual obligation which governments were using to renegotiate various welfare entitlements' (Brett, 2003, 134).

This chapter is in large part devoted to outlining this earlier conception of citizenship as well as tracing its decline. In doing so it will hopefully avoid two hazards that Will Kymlicka and Wayne Norman identify in attempts to theorise citizenship. The first of these is the potentially limitless scope any theory of citizenship entails stemming from the fact that most questions in political theory invariably come back to the relationship between the citizen and the state. The second danger, and perhaps the more important one in the Australian context, concerns the way in which two conceptions of citizenship – first as legal category and second 'as desirable activity' – are sometimes conflated (Kymlicka and Norman, 1994, 353). The dominant concern of Australian historians and theorists has focused principally on the first of these – citizenship as legal category – which undoubtedly stems from the widespread assumption that Australia has a weak citizenship culture dominated by legalism (Davidson, 1997) and to the extent that Australians think of citizenship at all it is largely in 'statist and passive terms' (Hudson and Kane, 2000, 2). In focusing on the moral conception of citizenship, or 'citizenship-as-desirable activity', this chapter offers a partial corrective to such assumptions and contributes to the ongoing recovery of the Social Liberal tradition in Australia.

Citizenship, character and the individual

As a body of theory, New Liberalism contained many diverse, sometimes conflicting, strands. Perhaps the most fundamental tension was between, on the one hand, the support of the fully developed human personality as expressed in the form of the active citizen and, on the other, the promotion of an expanded welfare state, potentially threatening individual initiative. As will be discussed further below, such tension ultimately led to the undermining of the New Liberal tradition in the middle decades of the twentieth century as a significant gap developed between public policy and individual character. James Walter and Todd Moore have made the case that in Australia New Liberalism – as represented by figures such as Elton Mayo, C.H. Northcott, Meredith Atkinson and Frederic Eggleston – was also characterised by a certain infatuation with expert knowledge that contained a strong authoritarian streak (Walter and Moore, 2002).

This concern with enlightened leadership was undoubtedly an important feature of Australian New Liberal thinking, but it coexisted, albeit at times uneasily, alongside the ideal of the active citizen (see Walter, 1998). Frederic Eggleston, for instance, was well aware of this tension pointing out that while the 'principle of responsibility in leadership is relatively well understood; it is not so surely realised that the responsibility of the citizen is just as definite; responsibility in the leader is useless without a reciprocal responsibility in the citizen'. Overemphasis on the role of leadership, Eggleston claimed, is closely connected to the mistaken idea that the state is to be understood as a *deus ex machina*, assuming responsibilities and solving social problems that should lie with individual citizens. Such a conception involves setting up a false dualism between the state and the citizen. 'The State', Eggleston suggests, 'is ourselves. State action has unique value in any political system; it may co-operate with active citizens to secure results of great importance, but if it comes to be regarded as a substitute for individual action, releasing the citizen from responsibility, the result must be bad' (Eggleston, 1932, 14–15).

Perhaps the most influential articulation of the civic ideal in early twentieth-century Australia came from the popular writings of Walter Murdoch. Judith Brett alludes to Murdoch's biographer, John La Nauze's observation that Murdoch would prove a useful figure for future social historians wanting to understand the thinking of educated Australians between the wars (Brett, 2003, 58–9).[4] Murdoch is an excellent Australian example of what Stefan Collini (1991) has termed a public moralist, and a very important disseminator of Idealist Liberalism, writing best-selling textbooks on citizenship and freedom (Murdoch, 1903, 1912), as well as regular newspaper columns in the quality press on literary and political themes. According to Marian Sawer, through his textbooks, Murdoch did 'his best to ensure that a generation of Australian children was inculcated with Green's views' (Sawer, 2003, 44).[5]

The guiding presupposition of Murdoch's account of citizenship, as it was for Green, was the Aristotelian dictum that man is by nature a political animal. 'You may', says Murdoch, 'determine not to be political, but it would be just as sensible to determine not to be an animal'. It follows that ' "Citizen" is simply the name we give to a human being when we think of the political side of him' (Murdoch, 1912, 18). Citizenship follows from our social nature, and it is not something granted to us by the state. A good deal hinges on this basic insight. Whereas in the classical Liberal view the purpose of state action was the protection of a series of pre-political and individualistically conceived rights, from Murdoch's New Liberal perspective rights follow from a pre-existing communal identity.

As Brett suggests, for Liberals in early twentieth century Australian 'citizenship was not primarily a status conferred by the state but a capacity of the individuals on which the polity depended' (Brett, 2003, 63). Likewise, Helen Irving has claimed that:

> This notion of citizenship entailed commitment, belonging, and contribution. It did not begin with a list of rights. Rather, from the idea of citizens as particular type of person, an argument for rights emerged. The claim was the reverse of what we commonly make today. We tend to see the acquisition of rights as a means of becoming a citizen. Last century, people identified themselves as citizens and thus claimed rights.
>
> (Irving, 2000, 12)

From this conception of the social or political nature of the human person followed a positive conception of freedom at odds with the negative conception of classical Liberalism.

For the Idealists, freedom did not consist in the absence of restraint or freedom *from* interference, but in the freedom *to* realise our higher ends which are invariably connected to the common good or the general will of the community. 'Self-realisation' could not be achieved in isolation, but only in relation to others, by full participation in the life of the community. For Green, freedom meant 'a positive power or capacity of doing or enjoying something worth doing or enjoying, and that, too, something that we do or enjoy in common with others' (Green, [1881] 1986, 199). In this respect Murdoch takes to task J.S. Mill who is sometimes seen as a transitional figure between classical and new Liberalism. According to Murdoch:

> [Mill] takes liberty as a negative thing, as the absence of restraint from doing as one likes; we have learned to see more in liberty than that. He sees the supreme end of life as self-realization, the development of one's self to the fullest possible extent; he does not seem to see that the self can only be fully developed as a member of a society. The individual is really an abstraction apart from society, just as society is an abstraction apart from the individuals composing it.
>
> (Murdoch, 1938, 32)

For Murdoch, Mill's antithesis between society and individual, along with Spencer's antagonistic understanding of the relationship between state and individual, belong to an outmoded brand of Liberalism that figures such as Green had put to rest. Indeed, according to Murdoch, 'Green has done more than any other modern thinker to show the falsehood of the old antithesis of Individual and State [...] [whereas] Spencer's *The Man versus the State* is the great, the classical expression of this reactionary individualism' (Murdoch, 1910, 65).[6]

The freedom of citizens and the role of the state

From the claim that the state and the individual are not separate and that 'a man can attain his supreme good only as the citizen of a state' (Murdoch, 1910, 65) follows an argument for state action that goes well beyond the protection of basic civil rights. The purpose of state action is to enable individuals to realise their potential by becoming full participants in the life of society. 'The work of the state is to remove from every person's path the obstacles which would prevent him from living his best life' (Murdoch, 1912, 14). And since freedom is intimately connected with willing the common good, it follows that the relationship between state and individual should not be seen in zero-sum terms.

An increase in state action does not necessarily entail (as in Spencer) a diminution of the freedom of individuals. Rather, state action which takes the form of removing obstacles to the good life expands the realm of human freedom. For the Idealists, freedom is what Charles Taylor has more recently referred to as 'an exercise-concept which involves "self-direction...the actual exercise of directing control over one's life"' (Taylor, 1985, 214). According to Murdoch, when freedom is understood in a positive sense:

> as freedom to do, to be, to enjoy, to understand [...] you will find that, in innumerable ways, government sets us free. The measure of a man's liberty is the measure of his opportunities; and a modern civilized man, living under a government which imposes numerous and elaborate rules upon him, has a thousandfold more opportunities than a primitive savage has or can have.
>
> (Murdoch, 1912, 209)[7]

The classic, late-nineteenth-century expression of this view of the role of the state in expanding human freedom was Green's lecture on 'Liberal Legislation and Freedom of Contract'. Green argued in this lecture that although the principle of freedom of contract had done much good work in the early nineteenth century by undermining class and corporate privileges, by the mid-Victorian period it had become a tool for justifying economic exploitation and its rigid application was a major barrier to the realisation of freedom. So while one of the central functions of government is, according to Green, 'to uphold the sanctity of contracts [...] it is no less its business to provide against contracts being made, which, [...] instead of being a security for freedom, become an instrument of disguised oppression' (Green, [1881] 1986, 209). In the name of a greater freedom government has the right to interfere with the classical liberal principle of freedom of contract:

> Our modern legislation [...] with reference to labour, and education, and health, involving as it does manifold interference with freedom of contract, is justified on the ground that it is the business of the state, not indeed directly to promote moral goodness, for that, from the very nature of moral goodness, it cannot do, but to maintain the conditions without which a free exercise of the human faculties is impossible.
>
> (Green, [1881] 1986, 201–2)

As Sawer has argued (2003, ch. 3), this critique of unfettered contractual freedom was institutionalised in Australia in the early work of the Court of Conciliation and Arbitration in the first decade of the twentieth century. Henry Bournes Higgins, the Court's first president and author of the landmark 'Harvester' judgement (1907), which established the principle of the 'fair and reasonable wage', justified this decision and the work of the court in terms strongly reminiscent of Green:

> As a rule, the economic position of the individual employee is too weak for him to hold his own in the unequal contest. He is unable to insist on the 'fair thing'. The power of the employer to withhold bread is a much more effective weapon than the power of the employee to refuse to labour. Freedom of contract, under such circumstances, is surely misnamed; it should rather be called despotism in contract; and this Court is empowered to fix a minimum wage as a check on the despotic power.
>
> (Higgins, cited in Sawer, 2003, 59)

Sawer plausibly argues that we have here a translation of one of Green's central teachings into the Australian idiom of the 'fair go'.

For New Liberal thinkers, economic equality was not the goal of state action. Rather, the goal was the relief of material insecurity to enable the full development of human personality. As mentioned earlier, the tension entailed in the promotion of state action for the purpose of encouraging individual responsibility was recognised by New Liberal thinkers.[8] Eggleston, for instance, suggested that, 'the scope of human action can be enlarged by social re-organisation and co-operation, provided that the machinery created does not smother individual initiative and diminish personal responsibility' (Eggleston, 1953, 6). Tim Rowse suggests that, in Australia, this kind of criticism was pressed against welfare state reforms, undermining New Liberal arguments: 'the doctrine of personality could just as easily be construed *against* New Liberal reforms, as in the argument that state welfare payments would undermine the growth of independent personality' (Rowse, 1978, 40).

From duties to rights and back again

The tension within New Liberalism was also reflected in broader debates about the meaning of citizenship over the past 100 years. Andrew Vincent (2001) has pointed to three distinct phases of British thinking about citizenship through the twentieth century, which was also echoed in Australian debates. The first is the phase we have thus far discussed (1880–1914) which centred on an ethical conception of citizenship, and an argument for ameliorative state action facilitating this goal. New Liberals in this period certainly discussed rights, but rights were understood as deriving from duties which stemmed from membership of a political community.

After the First World War, many of the New Liberal reforms of the earlier period were consolidated and the foundations of the Welfare state were established. This led to the second phase of theorising on citizenship during the period from 1945 to the late 1950s. The classic work on citizenship in this period was T.H. Marshall's *Citizenship and Social Class* (1950), which will be discussed further below. Marshall was an inheritor of New Liberalism, but his emphasis was on rights – civil, political and social – and the concept of duty drops away. This was also the heyday of Keynesianism and the rise of professional economics. Solving the 'social problem' was increasingly understood in technocratic and economic terms, and ideas such as self-realisation, character and the ethical state took on an increasingly antiquated hue. Here a much thinner conception of citizenship was developed. It was technocratic, managerial and concerned with balancing social solidarity through the welfare state, with the need for wealth creation through the market. Moreover, the mid-twentieth century saw the institutionalisation of certain originally individual virtues such as thrift, and according to Vincent, 'Duty became largely institutionalised into the willingness to pay marginally higher levels of direct taxation. The civic component, in this scenario, began to draw back subtly from its ethical resources' (Vincent, 2001, 210).

Brett has described a similar development in the Australian context with the rise of both Keynesianism and the expansion of affluence and credit following the Second World War. Keynesianism broke the nexus between personal financial management and the national economy – or private virtue and public benefit. Earlier political leaders such as Andrew Fisher and Joseph Lyons could successfully mobilise Australians' civic duty in the form of thrift campaigns in response to national crises. In the case of Fisher this involved the purchase of war bonds, while Lyons's case involved the repayment of national debt as a consequence of the Depression. Both cases involved questions of national honour, which citizens could defend by exercising certain economic virtues. Keynesianism introduced a counter logic to traditional economic management, which involved an increase in public spending in bad times. The relationship between private virtue and public benefit was less obvious than it once appeared. According to Brett, 'The gradual acceptance of Keynesianism which decoupled the logic of the household economy from that of the nation's also began to decouple the stability of the personality from the stability of the financial system' (Brett, 2003, 112). Likewise, the easy availability of credit through the spread of hire purchase after the Second World War profoundly changed people's spending habits. Market values ('organized selfishness' as Frederic Eggleston phrased it (cited in Brett, 2003, 139)) were superseding traditional economic virtues such as thrift. It is common today to hear the complaint that, in public life, citizens are increasingly treated as consumers or that economics has replaced politics. This is not a new criticism and is the result of the twin developments of Keynesian fiscal management and the vast spread of consumer markets in the middle decades of the past century. 'Like the logic of Keynesianism', Brett suggests, 'the logic of the market undermined the causal links between the virtues of individuals and their households and the strength and prosperity of nations on which Australian Liberals' ideas of citizenship had depended' (Brett, 2003, 139).

Vincent's final phase of citizenship – in the post-1980s period – needs to be understood as a reaction to the influence of Marshall's 'passive' conception. As mentioned above, the shift from duties to rights in the middle decades of the twentieth century was reflected in the widespread acceptance of Marshall's rights-based argument for citizenship. For Marshall, citizenship entails full participation in the life of a community which can only be attained through the exercise of rights – civil, political and social. These three distinct groups of rights roughly correspond to the last three centuries of British political experience: civil rights – such as freedom of speech, assembly, property, legal equality and freedom of contract – were won in the eighteenth century; political rights – the right to vote and to stand for public office – were developed in the nineteenth century; and social rights – the old age pension, education, health care, unemployment protection: those rights that enable a person 'to live the life of a civilised being according to the standards prevailing in society' – were the products of twentieth century developments. According to Marshall, the full range of these rights is best secured in a liberal–democratic political system with a strong welfare state. The capitalist market is needed to generate wealth to fund social welfare programmes. Nevertheless, there is a fundamental tension between social rights, which are designed to ensure social solidarity, and the inequalities generated by the market, which Marshall himself acknowledged. Social inequalities that are the direct result of the market are incompatible with the full realisation of citizenship. Hence, under the influence of Marshall, citizenship came to be associated with the 'rights' and 'entitlements' of the welfare state.

The new social movements of the 1960s and 70s, while advocating active political participation, nevertheless drew on the orthodoxy established by Marshall. The inequality and oppression experienced by minority groups were to be alleviated through state action, which, if anything, simply augmented the decline of the New Liberal conception of citizenship of the early twentieth century. According to Brett, the new social movements (like organised labour before them):

> Came to the state as claimants and their attention was directed not so much at what people might do for society as at what society had done to people and how that might be changed [...]. The direction of the imaginative link between citizens and the state was thus reversed from one in which the state was created from the actions, decisions and capacities of its citizens to one in which the citizen was mainly conceived as a bearer of rights and entitlements bestowed by the state.

> (Brett, 2003, 134)

This passive, welfare model of citizenship came under attack from neoliberal critics of the welfare state, who aimed to re-moralise citizenship in terms of independence, responsibility and self-reliance, along with a resuscitation of the earlier language of duty in the form of mutual obligation, which was largely limited to work for the dole schemes. But although the language of obligation returned, it did so in the context of a fundamental change in the way that the relationship between the state and the citizen is understood. The new public sector management which emphasised 'choice', 'freedom' and individual responsibility was arguably as state-centric as its Keynesian predecessor. 'For all its talk of the freedom of individuals', Brett suggests, 'the new contractualism is fundamentally statist, with the very top levels of government (where the steerers dwell) harbouring the only people empowered to act in the interests of the whole. They alone seem to be beyond self-interested behaviour as they impose disciplinary strictures on the rest of the citizenry whose claims to act in a public-minded way are dismissed as so many self-serving illusions' (Brett, 2003, 175). While it is an overstatement to suggest that neoliberal economics is little more than 'organized selfishness' (to borrow from Eggleston), nevertheless the model of the actor at the heart of the neoliberal (or economic rationalist) orthodoxy is a far cry from the other-directed conception of the citizen advanced by New Liberals from Green to Eggleston. Moreover, to the extent that new right thinkers (or public figures who borrow from them) consider citizenship as a theoretical category, they trade heavily on neoliberal economics. In this context, Capling, Considine and Crozier make a valid observation by suggesting that despite former Prime Minister John Howard's rhetorical allusions to family and community, his understanding of the independent, self-reliant individual, on which his government's industrial relations programme was based makes a 'virtue of the lack of any sustained or necessary social ties or reciprocal social obligations to one's fellow citizens' (Capling et al., 1998, 138).

Virtues, values and cultural diversity

Beyond this, one of the other major changes to the Australian polity that works against any simple rehabilitation of the social liberal conception of virtue is the experience of multiculturalism. As is often noted, much of the discourse of Australian citizenship through the twentieth century has been conducted in terms of the relationship between inclusion and exclusion, where the 'White Australia Policy' occupies a position of central significance (Dutton, 2002). Indeed, Murdoch's case for cultivating the ordinary virtues assumed a certain moral consensus, which was bound up with an understanding of the essential Britishness of the Australian nation. And in his 1912 textbook Murdoch could quite naturally slide from a discussion of the British character of the Australian community to the assertion of the importance of 'racial purity' in preserving its integrity (Murdoch, 1912, 148). This is not, he hastens to add, because 'Asiatics' are inferior – we should give up 'the foolish habit of speaking about "superior" and "inferior" races' – but because '[t]heir idea of civilization is not our idea, and will not fit in with our idea. It is so utterly different, that the two races could not live happily side by side; they would never form a true community' (Murdoch, 1912, 147).[9]

The White Australia Policy was the consequence of a racially based communitarian reading of the Australian nation. Race is, of course, just one possible criterion for determining the boundaries of any community, but fundamental to the communitarian model is the right of exclusion and admission on the grounds of perceived kinship or cultural affinity. According to Michael Walzer, for instance, without the rights of exclusion and admission, 'there could not be *communities of character*, historically stable, ongoing associations of men and women with some special commitment to one another and some special sense of their common life' (Walzer, 1983, 62).[10]

While New Liberalism should be seen as an attempt to broaden the Liberal tradition beyond the protection of a series of negatively defined rights, its case for positive freedom, as with much contemporary communitarian thinking, draws on a loosely Aristotelian understanding of the person, where the virtues are not the possession of the individual *qua* individual, but as a member of a moral community. The argument for citizen virtue as the expression of the true freedom of the individual largely depends on some such communal setting as Murdoch was appealing to. This is not to suggest that, during the first decades of twentieth century, the Australian political community was anything like the Athenian polis translated to Antipodean shores (for a start there is the small matter of geographical proportion that Aristotle thought so important in defining the polis). But Murdoch's argument for positive freedom and the citizen life as the best possible human life had far greater resonance in a society marked by much greater cultural, and indeed, ethnic homogeneity than we have grown accustomed to in recent years.[11]

If the virtues in any remotely Aristotelian sense exist today, they are more likely to be found within those very migrant communities that have transformed the Australian polity over the past half-century. Here I am echoing the point made by Alasdair MacIntyre in *After Virtue*, where he writes that the virtue tradition survives 'in certain communities whose historical ties with their past remain strong' (1984, 252). But as critics have often pointed out, the communities MacIntyre identifies as bearers of this tradition – some Irish Catholics, some Orthodox Greeks, Orthodox Jews and black and white Protestant communities from the US South (MacIntyre, 1984, 252) – are notable for their lack of critical dialogue with liberal modernity (Poole, 1991, 146–151). There are then some obvious dangers inherent in the endeavour to recover citizen virtue. It can all too easily become an exercise in nostalgia – a longing for the 'warmth of communal ties'[12] – if not a reactionary attempt to revive a tradition that is either threatened or lost.

The way in which the contemporary discussion of citizen virtue jostles with the discourse of values is further evidence of this perception of threat. Citizenship tests, in Australia and elsewhere, are generally centred on knowledge of a prescribed set of abstract values – 'mateship', 'the fair go', equality, tolerance, commitment to the rule of law and so forth. The energy spent in recent times in the endeavour to codify or package a list of abstract Australian (or indeed, British or American) values is a sign that such 'values' are less secure or self-evident than some would have us believe. While the intention of citizenship tests is, at least in part, the laudable one of providing migrants – those with no necessary experience of Australian life – with some *entrée* into Australian culture, and hopefully thereby generating a level of civic commitment, such exercises invariably have an artificial quality about them. As critics have suggested, the first version of the Australian citizenship test (2007) looked remarkably like a game of trivial pursuit offering little guidance or help to migrants in dealing with the kinds of challenges they are likely to face in establishing themselves in a new country. Not only is superficiality an inevitable consequence of the endeavour to test values, but also the language of values is itself loaded with the sort of arbitrariness and subjectivity that those who most assert them claim they want to overcome. The more political leaders (particularly those of a conservative stripe) feel the need to self-consciously assert Australian values, the more they seem to reinforce the subjectivity and contestability of such values. If values are things that individuals can freely choose, then equally they can be rejected. The cost of trading in abstractions like 'Australian values' is, if anything, a reinforcement of the moral relativism and fragmentation of Australian political life. It is a sign that certain forms of conservatism are in fact more deeply implicated in the post-modern condition than its proponents appreciate (cf. Boucher and Sharpe, 2008).

But likewise, for those who want to rescue citizenship from conceptions of the individual drawn from neoliberal economics run the risk, as Michael Ignatieff has suggested, of moral narcissism: when 'the rhetoric of citizenship is used, not to understand market society but simply to express moral distaste for the vulgarity of market values'. Here, the call to citizenship becomes 'a rhetoric of complacency whose result is to reassure those who cannot bear the moral complexity of a market society that they are sensitive and superior beings' (Ignatieff, 1991, 29). In other words, 'citizenship' or 'civic virtue' can easily become further ideological abstractions doing little more than providing therapeutic value to those who appeal to them. Criticism of the neoliberal understanding of citizenship in the name of an altruistic 'civic virtue' will fall flat unless the complex ways in which such conceptions have historically been translated into arguments for extending government power are understood.

Acknowledgement

I would like to thank Jim Walter, Kay Ferres and Gwenda Tavan for their valuable responses to this paper at the 'From Migrant to Citizen' conference at Macquarie University, 3–5 December, 2008.

Notes

1. See, for instance, Stefan Collini's work *Public Moralists: Political Thought and Intellectual Life in Britain, 1850–1930* (1991), esp. ch.3 'The Idea of Character: Private habits and Public Virtues'.
2. Though 'philosophical Idealism' was one of the dominant sources of 'new liberalism', the terms should not be thought of as synonyms. The American pragmatist John Dewey was also an important contributor to New Liberal thinking as were the prominent British critics of the Idealist theory of the state L.T. Hobhouse and J.A. Hobson.
3. For an overview, see Sawer, 2003, chs. 1–4.
4. On Murdoch's influence, see La Nauze, 1977, esp. ch.7.
5. Murdoch was also a close friend and biographer of Alfred Deakin and they shared a common intellectual and political outlook. Regarding Deakin, Stuart Macintyre has suggested that 'The moral purpose that animated him and that he sought to realise in national life is so far removed from our own values as to be unintelligible' (Macintyre, 2000, 40). One way of entering into Deakin's moral universe is through the political writings of Murdoch. For a sample of their correspondence on political and literary themes, see La Nauze and Nurser (1974).
6. This was a review of J.H. Muirhead's *The Service of the State*, a study of Green's political thought. After reading the review in the *Argus*, Deakin immediately sent a congratulatory note to Murdoch mentioning the similarity of Green and Henry Jones. The latter had visited Australia the year before giving a series of public lectures which were later published as *Idealism as a Practical Creed*. Murdoch and Deakin attended the Melbourne lecture and dined with Jones. For Henry Jones's lecture tour, see Boucher, 1990.
7. See also Bosanquet (1893) for a forthright exposition of this view. For Bosanquet, 'liberty, in the plainest and simplest sense of the word, does not depend on the absence of legislation, but on the comprehensiveness and reasonableness of life' (1893, 379).
8. On Bosanquet's concern that state action can potentially hinder the development of character, see Collini, 1976.
9. Despite Murdoch's invocation of the racial character of the Australian nation he was, along with many of his Idealist contemporaries, a liberal internationalist believing that the British Empire provided something of a model for a co-operative world order. Along with other Idealists, such as Francis Anderson (Professor of Philosophy at the University of Sydney, 1890–1922), Murdoch worked in the inter-war years for the League of Nations Union. For some discussion of the Australian Idealists' views on the international order, see Hughes-Warrington and Tregenza, 2008.
10. Walzer takes the phrase 'communities of character' from Otto Bauer.

11. This is even more obviously the case in late-Victorian Britain where Green's arguments for a kind of Christian citizenship had so much force.
12. The phrase comes from Michael Oakeshott, 'The Masses in Representative Democracy' (in Oakeshott, 1991).

References

Brett, J. (2003) *Australian Liberals and the Moral Middle Class: From Alfred Deakin to John Howard* (Melbourne: Cambridge University Press).

Bosanquet, B. (1893) 'Liberty and Legislation', in B. Bosanquet (ed.), *The Civilization of Christendom and Other Essays* (London: S. Sonnenschein & Co.).

Boucher, D. (1990) 'Practical Hegelianism: Henry Jones's lecture tour of Australia', *Journal of the History of Ideas* 51: 423–52.

Boucher, G. and M. Sharpe (2008) *The Times Will Suit Them: Postmodern Conservatism in Australia* (Sydney: Allen and Unwin).

Capling, A., M. Considine and M. Crozier (1998) *Australian Politics in the Global Era* (Melbourne: Addison Wesley Longman).

Collini, S. (1976) 'Hobhouse, Bosanquet and the State: Philosophical Idealism and Political Argument in England, 1880–1918', *Past and Present* 72: 86–111.

Collini, S. (1991) *Public Moralists: Political Thought and Intellectual Life in Britain, 1850–1930* (Oxford: Clarendon Press).

Davidson, A. (1997) *From Subject to Citizen: Australian Citizenship in the Twentieth Century* (Melbourne: Cambridge University Press).

den Otter, S. (1996) *British Idealism and Social Explanation: A Study in Late Victorian Thought* (Oxford: Oxford University Press).

Docker, J. (1982) 'Can the Centre Hold? Conceptions of the State 1890–1925', in Sydney Labour History Group, *What Rough Beast?: The State and Social Order in Australian History* (Sydney: Allen and Unwin).

Dutton, D. (2002) *One of Us? A Century of Australian Citizenship* (Sydney: UNSW Press).

Eggleston, F.W. (1932) *State Socialism in Victoria* (London: P.S. King & Son).

Eggleston, F.W. (1953) *Reflections of an Australian Liberal* (Melbourne: F.W. Cheshire).

Green, T.H. ([1881], 1986) 'Liberal Legislation and Freedom of Contract', reprinted in Harris and Morrow (eds), *T.H. Green: Lectures on the Principles of Political Obligation and Other Writings* (Cambridge: Cambridge University Press).

Hughes-Warrington, M. and I. Tregenza (2008) 'State and Civilization in Australian New Idealism, 1890–1950', *History of Political Thought* 29 (1) 89–108.

Hudson, W. and J. Kane (2000) 'Rethinking Australian Citizenship', in W. Hudson and J. Kane (eds), *Rethinking Australian Citizenship* (Cambridge: Cambridge University Press).

Ignatieff, M. (1991) 'Citizenship and Moral Narcissism', in G. Andrews (ed.), *Citizenship* (London: Lawrence & Wishart).

Irving, H. (2000) 'Citizenship before 1949', in K. Rubenstein (ed.), *Individual, Community Nation: Fifty Years of Australian Citizenship* (Melbourne: Australian Scholarly Publishing).

Kymlicka, W. and W. Norman (1994) 'The Return of the Citizen: A Survey of Recent Work on Citizenship Theory', *Ethics* 104: 352–81.

La Nauze, J.A. and Nurser, E. (eds) (1974) *Alfred Deakin and Walter Murdoch on Books and Men* (Melbourne: Melbourne University Press).

La Nauze, J. (1977) *Walter Murdoch: A Biographical Memoir* (Melbourne: Melbourne University Press).

MacIntyre, A. (1984) *After Virtue: A Study in Moral Theory* (London: Duckworth).

MacIntyre, S. (2000) 'Alfred Deakin', in M. Grattan (ed.), *Australian Prime Ministers* (Sydney: New Holland Publishers).

Marshall, T.H. (1950) *Citizenship and Social Class* (Cambridge: Cambridge University Press).

Murdoch, W. (1903) *The Struggle for Freedom* (Melbourne: Whitcombe & Tombs).

Murdoch, W. (1910) 'Social Service', in W. Murdoch (ed.), *Loose Leaves* (Melbourne: George Robertson & Co.).

Murdoch, W. (1912) *The Australian Citizen: An Elementary Account of Rights and Duties* (Melbourne: Whitcombe & Tombs).

Murdoch, W. (1938) *The Victorian Era, Its Strengths and Weaknesses* (Sydney: Angus and Robertson).

Oakeshott, M. (1991) *Rationalism in Politics and Other Essays. New and Expanded Edition*. T. Fuller (ed.), (Indianapolis, IN: Liberty Press).

Poole, R. (1991) *Morality and Modernity* (London and New York: Routledge).

Rowse, T. (1978) *Australian Liberalism and National Character* (Melbourne: Kibble Books).

Rowse, T. (2002) *Nugget Coombs: A Reforming Life* (Melbourne: Cambridge University Press).

Sawer, M. (2003) *The Ethical State? Social Liberalism in Australia* (Melbourne: Melbourne University Press).

Taylor, C. (1985) 'What's Wrong with Negative Liberty', in C. Taylor (ed.), *Philosophy and the Human Sciences: Philosophical Papers II* (Cambridge: Cambridge University Press).

Vincent, A. (1986) 'T.H. Green and the Religion of Citizenship', in A. Vincent (ed.), *The Philosophy of T.H. Green* (Aldershot: Gower Publishing).

Vincent, A (2001) 'The New Liberalism and Citizenship', in A. Simhony and D. Weinstein (eds), *The New Liberalism: Reconciling Liberty and Community* (Cambridge: Cambridge University Press).

Walter, J. (1998) 'Understanding Australian Citizenship: The Cultural Constraints (and Unmined Legacy) of a Civic Ideal', *Southern Review* 31 (1): 18–26.

Walter, J. and T. Moore (2002) 'The New Social Order? Australia's Contribution to "New Liberal" Thinking in the Interwar Period'. Paper presented to the Jubilee conference of the Australasian Political Studies Association, Australian National University, Canberra. Accessed 15 June 2006 http://auspsa.anu.edu.au/proceedings/2002/Walter+Moore.pdf

Walzer, M. (1983) *Spheres of Justice: A Defence of Pluralism and Equality* (Oxford: Basil Blackwell).

5
The Value of Values? Debating Identity, Citizenship and Multiculturalism in Contemporary Australia

Lloyd Cox

Introduction: Identity anxiety and citizenship testing

It is the lot of immigrant societies to experience periodic bouts of identity anxiety. This refers to collective apprehension by a named population about what distinguishes it from other named populations. Identity anxiety is manifested in a public discourse that is preoccupied with notions of authenticity (what constitutes the real 'us'?), signs of demarcation (what are the external signifiers that distinguish 'us' from 'them'?) and the dangers of border transgressions (what will be the negative consequences of our borders – understood in territorial and symbolic senses – being breached?). It is a condition that is both exploited and reproduced by politicians, impacting on policy formation and political positioning alike. In recent years, this condition has revealed itself locally in the controversy over Australian values and citizenship testing.

In a sense, the issue of Australian identity and values is never far from the surface of Australian public life (Howe, 2007). With the massive influx of migrants in the decades following the Second World War, and with the subsequent shift from white Australia to multiculturalism, the question of what are Australian values has been repeatedly asked (Galligan and Roberts, 2004, 72–5, 145–50). This has often been conflated with a similar but distinguishable question about what constitutes 'Australian-ness' or Australian identity, with answers to the latter frequently assumed to be premised on answers to the former. The implication is that to be authentically Australian and to manifest

Australian-ness is to be committed to Australian values. I will return to this conflation, and to the imputed content of Australian values, in due course. For now, it is worth emphasising that the issue of Australian values and identity has always been articulated in, and has derived a sense of urgency from, specific political contexts. In the 1970s and 1980s, it was the (relatively) bi-partisan shift to multiculturalism that provoked much soul-searching about Australian values (Lopez, 2000). The refugee crises of the early 1990s and early 2000s, whether real or imagined, prompted a similar preoccupation (Jupp, 2007). The recent issue of citizenship testing is but the latest instantiation of this fixation with Australian values and identity, the latest manifestation of the identity anxiety with which it is underpinned.

Australia has always had citizenship testing of sorts, in so far as the state has routinely applied various criteria to assess the suitability of prospective immigrants for Australian citizenship (Cronin, 1993; Hawkins, 1991; also see Holland's and Tragenza's chapters in this volume). Interviews with immigration officials aside, however, it has been rarer for individual immigrants to have to sit tests designed to assess their cultural knowledge and/or value commitments, the English dictation tests of the early twentieth century being the most infamous examples (see Dutton, 2002, 20–43). The distinctiveness of the most recent drive for citizenship testing is precisely that it is administered individually, ostensibly as a way of determining the social and cultural fitness of a prospective Australian citizen. The presumed nexus between such cultural fitness, on the one hand, and Australian-ness and Australian values, on the other, is born out in the pronouncements of politicians from both sides of parliament, as we will see. Whether one is of the political right or left, it seems, the nationalist ethos is not accepting of silence or indifference on the value of Australian values.

In this chapter, I discuss the political significance of the discourse on Australian values, as revealed in recent debates around citizenship testing. I do so not to provide yet another laboured contribution to debate about the substance of 'real' Australian values and identity, but as a critical contribution that rejects citizenship testing as fundamentally flawed and which problematises the very notion of Australian values. In the first section of the paper, I outline the evolution of the citizenship testing debate from 2005 to 2007, as revealed in the speeches and comments of Coalition and Labor politicians. I then identify the main thrust of their arguments in favour of citizenship testing and go on to critique them. I conclude by sketching the main elements of a politically grounded account of why the issue of citizenship testing and Australian values has been reanimated in recent years. Given limitations of space, I frame this more as a hypothesis requiring further research than a fully elaborated explanation.

Citizenship testing and Australian values, 2005–2007

While issues of border protection and the effective political management of immigration were important throughout much of the Coalition's time in office, it was not until the second half of 2005 that the specific issue of citizenship testing and its relationship to Australian values came into sharper focus (see Holland's chapter in this volume for further discussion on the historical contextualisation of citizenship testing). At first, testing was only hinted at, as various Coalition politicians prepared the political ground with comments about the link between citizenship and Australian values. For example, in a series of comments in August 2005, explicitly directed at Muslim Australians who had supposedly expressed divided loyalties, the Treasurer Peter Costello suggested that only those with a knowledge of and commitment to Australian values should be permitted citizenship: 'If you are thinking of coming to Australia, you ought to know what Australian values are,' Costello said. He continued:

> Essentially, the argument is Australia expects its citizens to abide by core beliefs – democracy, the rule of law, the independent judiciary, independent liberty. You see, Tony, when you come to Australia and you go to take out Australian citizenship you either swear on oath or make an affirmation that you respect Australia's democracy and its values. That's what we ask of people that come to Australia and if they don't, then it's very clear that this is not the country – if they can't live with them – whose values they can't share [*sic*]. Well, there might be another country where their values can be shared.
>
> (Costello, 2005)

This echoed comments made by the John Howard around the same time. On 7 August, in the aftermath of the home-grown terrorist attacks in London, the Prime Minister asserted that if you come to this country you 'have the responsibility to endorse and imbibe and embrace the values of our society.' In the same interview, he also raised the possibility of revoking citizenship for those who do not embrace Australian values: '[...] if somebody has come from another country and has failed to properly embrace the values of this society [...] then the idea of taking away their citizenship is one that ought to be looked at' (Howard, 2005).

Almost imperceptibly, values became linked with the issue of language proficiency. In an intimation of things to come, on 15 September 2005, Liberal Party backbencher Sharman Stone argued in a radio interview that there was a need for greater English language proficiency amongst new migrants, and that better testing of such proficiency was needed (Jolliff, 2005, 1). Her position was endorsed by Coalition colleagues at the time, and was later elaborated on in major speeches by Prime Minister John Howard and Treasurer Peter Costello.

In his 2006 Australia Day Address, given in the shadow of the Cronulla riots of the previous December, John Howard concluded that 'the divisive, phoney debate about national identity' was over, after having spent a good part of his speech emphasising his own understanding of Australian identity, and assuming that all alternatives had been dispatched by history: '[...] Australians are now better able to appreciate the enduring values of the national character that we proudly celebrate and preserve' (Howard, 2006). While immigrants of the past did not have to sit a citizenship test, Howard said, they did have to commit to democratic values and to master the common language of English (which, of course, is not true). Australians are right to celebrate diversity, he went on, but it 'must not be at the expense of the common values that bind us together. Nor should it be at the expense of ongoing pride in what are commonly regarded as the values, traditions and accomplishments of the old Australia.' For the first time, he explicitly raised the spectre of testing 'Australianness': 'The truth is that people come to this country because they want to be Australians. The irony is that no institutions or code lays down a test of Australianness' (Howard, 2006).

In a provocative speech to the Sydney Institute on 23 February 2006, Peter Costello reiterated some of these themes, and expanded on his comments from the previous August. He chastised what he referred to as 'mushy multiculturalism,' and suggested that people become Australian citizens because they are 'looking for Australian values, our values and want to embrace them.' If immigrants had strong objections to Australian values, Costello asserted, they should not come. Finally, and significantly, given what he and other Coalition colleagues would go on to argue in the following months, the Treasurer said that there would be more respect for Australian values 'if we made more of the demanding requirements of citizenship' (Costello, 2006). John Howard defended these remarks the following day, and reasserted that 'Australia's core set of values flowed from its Anglo-Saxon identity' (cited in Humphries, 2006).

The issue of citizenship testing was explicitly put on the national political agenda in late April. In a speech to the Sydney Institute, Parliamentary Secretary for Multicultural Affairs, Andrew Robb, emphasised the importance of the English language and Australian history for effectively integrating new citizens into this country:

> It is asserted that a citizenship test, which requires a functional grasp of English and a general understanding of Australian values, customs, systems, laws and history, will help people integrate more successfully into our community. It is in their interests and in the community interests. For this reason I am prepared to have a serious look over the next couple of months at the merits of introducing a compulsory citizenship test.
>
> (Robb in Iggulden, 2006)

Over those next couple of months, a veritable storm broke out over the anticipated citizenship test. Some, such as Keith Windshuttle, welcomed it, claiming that it would help break down 'the sort of tribalism that the multicultural policy that's dominated immigration affairs for the past 30 years' had allegedly instituted (cited in Cica, 2006). Businessman Hugh Morgan was also positive about the citizenship test, giving it a national security gloss. He suggested that 'a person who is a citizen of two countries has at least the beginning of a bipolar disorder' (cited in Murray and Berryman, 2006). This is supposedly a symptom of divided loyalties, and hence a threat to national security. *The Australian* columnist, Janet Albrechtsen (2006), went further, gushing that Robb's proposal was 'reclaiming pride in Western values.'

Others, however, greeted citizenship testing with derision, if not downright hostility. Islamic groups, refugee advocacy organisations, church leaders, many academics, members of the press and others rejected a citizenship test as divisive, discriminatory and unnecessary. Amongst other things, it was argued that the proposed test, and its timing, was a cynical political manoeuvre to gain electoral favour and wedge the Opposition; that similar tests in Europe had been tried and found wanting; that it was ill-suited to achieve its stated purposes; that those purposes – improved integration of immigrants and the testing of knowledge of and loyalty to Australian values – were vague, highly contested and hence not self-evident social goods to which the government should commit; and that the test was more about excluding certain categories of immigrants than it was about social inclusion or integration (see, for example, Barnes, 2006; Murray and Berryman, 2006; Summers, 2006).

The response from the Federal Opposition was at first relatively muted – limiting criticism to the proposed new 4 years residency requirement and the proposed English language test – clearly mindful of the possible electoral consequences of taking a firmer stand against citizenship testing. But state and territory Labor politicians were not so cautious. John Pandazopolous, Victorian Minister for Multicultural Affairs, argued that the test would be 'patronising' and 'insulting,' while Tony McRae, the West Australian Citizenship Minister, said that the test was a 'backward step.' John Hargreaves, the ACT Multicultural Affairs Minister, pointed out that, 'If this policy had been in place over 50 years ago, the Snowy hydro-electric scheme would not have been constructed, and the nation is in debt to those non-English speaking migrants' (cited in Topsfield, 2006). When the then federal Labor leader, Kim Beazley, did finally clarify his position, it was not greeted with universal enthusiasm amongst his own caucus. On the fifth anniversary of the 9/11 terrorist attacks, Beazley unveiled his own Australian values crusade. He called on Australians to stand up for 'mainstream Australian values' of mateship and fairness. Further, he suggested that if a values test was good enough for prospective Australian citizens it was also good enough for immigrants more generally:

> What needs to go on the visa form for somebody who is looking at permanent entrant position in this country is that they have an understanding and respect for Australian values – freedom, democracy, tolerance, our institutions, rule of law'.
>
> (Beazley, cited in Anon., 2006a)

The proposal was roundly derided from all quarters of the political spectrum, including from erstwhile supporters within his party (Coorey, 2006; Fraser, 2006; Shanahan, 2006). The proposal would not see out the coming weeks, and would be quietly forgotten as Beazley was replaced by Kevin Rudd as Labor's leader.

In the meantime, the Government pushed ahead with its plan, defending the need to increase from 2 to 4 years the residency time required to become a citizen, promoting the importance of citizens having a commitment to Australian values, and endorsing the benefits of a compulsory English language test for prospective Australian citizenship. As the federal Health Minister, Tony Abbott, memorably summed up, 'It is impossible to be a first class Australian if you can't speak the national language' (Abbott, cited in Anon., 2006b, 1). Ethnic and community groups greeted these comments with outrage, as did some in the press. The Australian Greens Senator, Bob Brown, condemned the proposal as a step backwards towards the White Australia Policies of yore: 'It simply means it's going to become harder to come to Australia if you don't have an Anglo background, and that's not what this country ought to be,' he said (Brown cited in Anon., 2006c). Veteran ANU immigration scholar James Jupp endorsed this view. He told *The Canberra Times* that the new citizenship test was a shift from multiculturalism back to the mono-culturalism of the 1950s: 'We're going backwards [...] The emphasis on English is going back to a preference for the British, which was, of course, very strong in the '50s and '60s' (cited in *The Canberra Times*, 2006, B02).

But John Howard and his government were not to be dissuaded. Andrew Robb released a major discussion paper on 17 September, which provided the most definitive statement to date on the government's plans for a citizenship test. In comments promoting the release of the new paper, Rob said that 'Australian citizenship is a privilege. It in a sense gives us our identity. It tells who we are, where we fit in the world. It is a unifying force in Australia and if we give it away like confetti, it is not valued.' Consequently, people had to be made to feel that 'they have earned the privilege of citizenship' (Robb cited in Anon., 2006d, 1). To earn this privilege, migrants seeking to become citizens would have to demonstrate that they understood Australian values, including the 'spirit of the fair go.' He went on to provide a compendium of additional Australian values that new citizens would be tested on. These included 'respect for the freedom and dignity of the individual, support for democracy, our commitment to the rule of law, the equality of men and women, the spirit of the fair go, of mutual respect and compassion for those in need' (Robb cited in McManus and Power, 2006, 3). In the wake of debate generated by the paper, the new Australian Citizenship Bill was debated in Parliament in early November, public submissions closed shortly after, and the Bill became law in 2007. Not wanting to repeat electoral mistakes of the past, the new Labor leader Kevin Rudd went along with the regime of testing, limiting any criticisms to the form and implementation rather than the substance of the new tests. Once elected, in November 2007, Labor would retain citizenship testing, albeit with modifications, a position that they still hold.

We can observe, then, a sequential unfolding of the citizenship test-ing issue between August 2005 and the early months of 2007. Initial comments made by the Prime Minister and his Treasurer in August in the wake of the London terrorist bombings link citizenship to Australian values. In the following months, this issue is incorporated into more specific proposals concerning English language testing and the integration of migrants. By April 2006, the possibility of citizenship testing was explicitly raised by the government. This was repeatedly reaffirmed over the coming months, and crystallised into a major statement by the government in September 2006. A new citizenship bill was debated in Parliament in November, and citizenship testing became a reality in 2007. So much for the chronological unfolding of the debate; what of its actual content? What were/are are the main arguments for citizenship testing, and are they plausible?

The arguments

While a variety of arguments were/are used in favour of citizenship testing, and while justifications were/are sometimes ad hoc and shifting, the main contours of the positive position on testing is clear enough. These can be summarised in a number of core propositions.

1. English is the dominant language in Australia, proficiency in its use promotes the smooth integration of new citizens, and therefore the government should test for this proficiency
2. Australian citizenship is valuable, and hence the *obligations* entailed by membership rights should be impressed on those who would become Australian citizens, and citizenship testing is one means to this end
3. There are a number of core Australian values that prospective citizens should know and to which they should commit, and such knowledge and commitment can be determined through a test

The first clause in proposition 1 is true but trivial. Everyone knows that English is the dominant language in Australia, and that being able to speak, read and write the language has considerable benefits for an individual. But what is at stake here is not whether proficiency in the English language has benefits for an individual living in Australia – it does – but whether compulsorily testing that proficiency helps people integrate and has an overall benefit for Australia. As we have seen, the Parliamentary Secretary for Multicultural Affairs, Andrew Robb, crystallised precisely this argument: 'It is asserted that a citizenship test, which requires a functional grasp of English and a general understanding of

Australian values, customs, systems, laws and history, will help people integrate more successfully into our community. It is in their interests and in the community interests' (cited in Iggulden, 2006). I deal with the Australian values part of this equation below. For now, let us concentrate on the issue of the English language, integration and testing.

The first point to make is that social integration and cohesion is a function of a variety of variables of which language proficiency is but one. You do not have to be a structural–functionalist sociologist of the Durkheimian variety to recognise that social networks, paid employment, religious and political affiliations, access to transport, health and education services and participation in clubs and organisations, all play a part in determining social integration and cohesion. One may speak the English language with all the refinement of the entire Oxford University debating team, but still be poorly integrated into society if one is without work, without transport and without social connections. It is the interplay between individuals and groups and what some social scientists refer to as 'social capital' that determines integration, rather than a narrowly conceived proficiency in this or that language (see Putnam, 2000). This is why, and this is my second point, particular individuals and distinguishable groups may be perfectly good English language users, but still be socially alienated and poorly integrated within the broader frame of Australian society. The unemployed Anglo youth who were the main participants in the Macquarie Fields riots in 2005, for instance, were, if press coverage is to be believed, mostly citizens and native English language speakers. Yet this did not ensure their integration.

The defender of citizenship and English language testing might accept these points but still insist that, all other things being equal, proficiency in English promotes social integration. Expressed differently, if we hold the other variables influencing integration constant, they will say, new citizens have a better chance of integrating into Australian society if they are proficient in English than if they are not. This claim requires empirical verification, which has not been forthcoming. But even if we do accept this claim, it hardly clinches the case for making passing an English language test a condition of Australian citizenship – my third point. Australian governments could promote English language proficiency amongst new immigrants and citizens in various ways, and therefore achieve the anticipated end of improved integration, without linking it to a testing regime. Earlier generations of immigrants did not have to sit such a test as a precondition of Australian citizenship, and yet went on to make meaningful and productive contributions to the political community into which they were accepted. There is no reason to think that this would not be the case with future generations of immigrants seeking Australian citizenship. *Testing* people's English does not help integrate them; it merely creates a self-selecting process that excludes people whose English is not up to an arbitrarily imposed standard at the time that they sit the test. We should also remember, as Labor's spokeswoman on Citizenship and Multicultural Affairs, Annette Hurley, reminds us, that at the same time that Andrew Robb was highlighting the importance of English 'the Howard government [had] slashed almost $11 million of funding to English language programs' (cited in Grigg, 2006). So it seems that the Coalition's position was inconsistent and hypocritical in equal measure.

The first clause in the second proposition is relatively unproblematic. Australian citizenship – which is to say recognised membership of the political community called 'Australia,' with all the rights and obligations that this entails – *is* valuable to its bearers. To be an Australian citizen is to have access to certain rights, privileges and material advantages unavailable to non-citizens. A citizen can reside indefinitely in Australia and leave and return freely. They can work and access state-subsidised welfare, health and education (some of which, at least, is not even available to permanent residents). They are able to participate in political and civic life, and are equal before the law. Granted, social and political access and legal equality does not entail actual equality or even equality of opportunity – for Australia remains a class-, gender- and ethnically-divided country – but it is nevertheless valuable. It is certainly recognised as valuable by stateless persons, refugees and even many citizens from poorer countries, even if current Australian citizens sometimes take their citizenship for granted.

But if we can agree that Australian citizenship is valuable, what of the additional claims that we should, therefore, impress upon prospective members the obligations of citizenship and, furthermore, that a test is one way of doing this. This seems to be what Peter Costello was suggesting when he commented that, 'No one is going to respect a citizenship that is so undemanding that it asks nothing.' He continued, 'People will not respect the citizenship that explains itself on the basis of the mushy multiculturalism I have described earlier. We are more likely to engender respect by emphasising the expectations and the obligations that the great privilege of citizenship brings' (Costello, 2006). That citizenship rights bring with them obligations no one disputes. Whether one has a 'thick' or a 'thin' conception of such obligations, most would agree that, at a minimum, being a citizen requires paying taxes, abiding by the law and voting. And yet in Australia, no citizen has a choice about any of these obligations, or at least their choice is circumscribed by the sanctions that they face if they do not comply. The educational effect of studying for and sitting a test that emphasises such obligations, therefore, seems rather dubious if not superfluous.

The defender of citizenship testing might reply that the minimal requirements set out above represent a rather impoverished conception of citizenship. They will argue that citizenship is about much more than just paying taxes and voting, and instead entails a more active commitment to and engagement with the Australian community and Australian values. Thus, arguments about this second proposition often resolve into arguments about the third, to which I now turn.

As we have seen, 'Australian values' have been repeatedly invoked as a key justification for citizenship testing. Given the political heat generated by the issue, it might appear that the content of Australian values – what they are, what they imply and how they are expressed – has been fiercely contested. This is not altogether true, or at least it is not true of politicians who have dominated the debate, from both the Coalition and the ALP. For here we find some well-worn, shared themes concerning Australian values, many of which were recycled from an earlier debate about the preamble to the Constitution. In Peter Costello's initial foray into the values debate, for example, he cited 'democracy, the rule of law, the independent judiciary, [and] independent liberty,' as being central Australian values (Costello, 2005). At the end of his speech to the Sydney Institute in February 2006, he added 'loyalty' and 'tolerance.' The leader of the opposition compiled a similar list, lauding 'freedom, democracy, tolerance, our institutions, rule of law' (Beazley, cited in Anon., 2006a), to which he also added 'mateship' and 'fairness.' These words could well have come out of John Howard's mouth, though he would add that they 'flowed from [Australia's] Anglo-Saxon identity' (cited in Humphries, 2006). As we have seen, Howard's Parliamentary Secretary for Multicultural Affairs, Andrew Robb, gave the most exacting list of supposedly Australian values in comments supporting his September 2006 discussion paper. These included, 'respect for the freedom and dignity of the individual, support for democracy, our commitment to the rule of law, the equality of men and women, the spirit of the fair go, of mutual respect and compassion for those in need' (Robb cited in McManus and Power, 2006, 1).

There are a number of general points to note about such lists. To begin with, there is a routine conceptual slippage between, and therefore a repeated conflation of, abstract political principles and institutions on the one hand, and generalised cultural dispositions on the other. Political principles such as the valuing of individual liberty and democracy, for example, become conjoined with supposed Australian cultural attributes such as 'mateship' and 'the spirit of the fair go' (Dyrenfurth, 2007, 211). In this way, the lexicon of the Australian suburban vernacular is married with the broader Western philosophical tradition of Liberalism, and presented as something distinctly Australian. Through a rhetorical sleight of hand, politics is infused and confused with culture, which makes it all the more effective as politics. Political values whose chief attribute is universality are enlisted in the frontline of a war to promote Australian particularity. Values that all Western liberal democracies (and perhaps even a good many other states) would recognise and proclaim as characterising their own political culture are appropriated as the essence of Australian values and central to Australian national identity. This might make for effective politics and be reassuring to those experiencing identity anxieties, but it is hardly a plausible basis for justifying a regime of Australian citizenship testing. Testing such values would clearly not be a test about anything uniquely Australian.

Apart from their universality, another striking attribute of the principles listed as Australian values is the abstractness with which they are expressed. Individual liberty, democracy, the rule of law and tolerance are all fine phrases, but they tell us little and commit us to less in the absence of specifying how they are to be understood. With individual liberty, for instance, do we have a negative or positive conception to follow the famous distinction made by Isaiah Berlin (Berlin, 1969)? That is, do we understand liberty simply as an absence of constraint on the individual (the negative conception), or do we understand it as a condition in which the individual is positively enabled to develop their multiple potentials as a human being (the positive conception)? If we hold the latter conception, how might institutions be arranged to realise such positive liberty? Similarly, by democracy, do we mean *formal* mechanisms of majority rule, or do we have a conception that encompasses more demanding *substantive* criteria like mass political participation and engagement, protection of minorities, equality of access to the political process and checks on the arbitrary exercise of state and corporate power? Further, is the 'rule of law' a principle to which we should abstractly commit ourselves in the absence of knowing what laws rule and for whom do they rule? Finally, does 'tolerance' denote a cultural and political relativism where anything goes, or does it imply a dominant cultural and political centre from which decisions are made about what and who will be tolerated (see Hage, 2000, 78–81)?

In the discussion on Australian values initiated by citizenship testing, questions like these are rarely asked let alone answered. They are certainly not asked or answered by those politicians who routinely raise the spectre of values. They instead have a preference for the abstract and largely empty sound-bite, packaged for the 24-hour news cycle. This is not surprising and nor is it a weakness for the promoters of citizenship testing. Indeed, the abstractness of 'Australian values' is a source of strength. It means that the content of this or that value can be filled differently as circumstances require. It means that both spruikers and consumers of Australian values can attach an individually tailored meaning to this or that value as they see fit. All things to all people, 'Australian values' serve as a shifting, all purpose rhetorical device around which the national 'us' can be mobilised. Given this protean character, it is difficult to see how one's knowledge of, much less one's commitment to, Australian values could be tested. This is why the most recent manifestations of the citizenship test have moved increasingly to asking more concrete historical and empirical questions, with values quietly falling off the testing agenda. This might be helpful for improving the aspiring citizen's general knowledge about Australia, but is it really necessary for citizenship, and does it tell us anything about their commitment to Australian values? The answer is surely self-evident.

The abstractness of values is closely related to the final point I want to make in respect of citizenship testing and values. This is the inadequacy of thinking about and discussing values in isolation from the institutional frames, and quotidian practices of social life, within which they may or may not be embedded. Martin Leet, of the Brisbane Institute, nicely encapsulates the point:

> Values have no meaning unless they are expressed in the routine operation of institutions and in everyday social and economic practices. The practical glue holding together any nation is to be found in such institutions and practices, not in values articulated merely as beliefs.
>
> (Leet, 2006, 2)

Leet goes on to show that the Howard Government was undertaking its values drive at the same time it was undermining the institutions that could give, and once gave, those values practical effect. The values of individual freedom and commitment to the rule of law, for example, have been hollowed out by anti-terrorism legislation that has expanded the state's capacity for the surveillance and monitoring of citizens (see Hamilton and Maddison, 2007). The dismantling of the industrial arbitration system and the atomisation of the workplace undermined the social solidarity upon which 'the spirit of the fair go' was once premised. The erosion of many welfare programmes, manifested in welfare to work legislation, could only in the most Orwellian of readings be understood as expressing Andrew Robb's 'mutual respect and compassion for those in need.' It seems that the more sharply reality departs from idealised values, the more shrill become calls for citizens to embrace those values.

Given all this, I would tend to agree with Liberal Party backbencher Petrou Georgio when he said that citizenship testing, and the testing of Australian values more specifically, is a solution in search of a problem (Georgio, 2006, 13). It creates a problem, or more accurately the appearance of a problem, where there is none. But if there was not a problem, and if the justifications for testing Australian values, and those values themselves, are highly suspect, why was the issue reanimated in 2005–07?

Symbolic politics and electoral advantage

As I intimated earlier in this chapter, the linking of Australian values and identity is not new. Indeed, over the course of his political career, John Howard progressively perfected the political art of discursively tethering identity to values, such that the two became mutually constitutive. This was forcefully expressed in his long-held and well-documented antipathy to multiculturalism, which goes back to the early 1980s, if not earlier (Jupp, 2005, 175). It was expressed in his repeated efforts to reassert a normative conception of Australian identity that emphasised the country's Anglo origins and dominant culture. This political art form, if I may call it that, reached its fullest flourishing during Howard's years as Prime Minister.

In an important essay, Carol Johnson provides incisive commentary on this linking of values and identity over the course of the Howard Decade (Johnson, 2007). She notes that in the months immediately before winning office, Howard decried what he viewed as Paul Keating's efforts to impose a stereotype on Australian identity. And yet before and after making this allegation, Howard himself attempted to impose his own stereotype, which was far more exacting and rigid than anything his immediate predecessor had articulated (Johnson, 2007, 195). This stereotype appropriated traditional left-wing motifs such as 'battler,' 'mateship' and the 'fair go,' and intertwined them with privileged white, Anglo-Celtic identity and values, which were presented as being the essence of what it is to be Australian (also see Dryenfurth, 2007, 216–25). Immigrants could only become truly Australian to the extent that they assimilated these values, though for obvious reasons Howard preferred to use the less contentious term 'integration.' Tellingly, integration is here assimilated to 'assimilation.' To integrate is, in Howard's conception, to conform to an idealised and stereotypical pattern of Australian identity and values, which is but another way of demanding assimilation to what he described as 'mainstream' Australia.

But this did not exhaust Howard's and the Coalition's rhetorical construction of Australian identity and values. Johnson goes on to show that Howard also privileged Judeo-Christian, conservative values on the one hand, and entrepreneurial culture on the other. The former manifested itself in the controversies around same-sex marriage – which Howard presented as incompatible with Australian values – and in Howard's comments about the unique difficulties of integrating Muslim migrants (Johnson, 2007, 199–201). The latter was routinely expressed in Howard's injunctions that Australia was or should become an 'enterprise culture,' and that its people are inherently 'aspirational' (Johnson, 2007, 202–3; Dyrenfurth, 2007, 222). Both were linked with the normative, Anglo-Celtic conception of Australian identity already described, to become key pillars in what we might call the Howard consensus on Australian values. It can usefully be termed a 'consensus' not because everyone in Australia agreed with it, far from it, but because sufficient numbers did that it became a potent electoral weapon for the Coalition, as I discuss below.

Clearly then, the linking of values and identity long pre-dates the controversy over citizenship testing. It was deployed by Howard in the 1980s, and had successive iterations during the Coalition's 11 years in office, reappearing in several guises and being used as a response to multiple issues. It was first harnessed to the cause of combating Keating's multiculturalism and tilt towards Asia, and was then brandished in the History Wars and debates on reconciliation in late 1990s. It provides a backdrop to controversies over asylum seekers in the early 2000s, before again being mobilised around the debate over citizenship and testing in the mid-2000s. To identify a recurring ideological disposition, however, does not account for why it is reanimated or intensifies at particular points in time. Howard's and his Coalition's long-standing readiness to deploy the language of identity and values does not explain why it appears in the guise of citizenship testing in the period from late 2005 to 2007. The social and political environment bequeathed to the Australian government after 9/11, many would argue, is an important part of the explanation.

One of the most significant developments impacting on the articulation of the Coalition's identity politics in the first half of the 2000s was the moral panic around Muslims. In the wake of 9/11, the Bali bombings, and the terrorist attacks on Madrid, London and Casablanca, respectable fears were aroused that such actions manifested some inherently militant strain within Islamic religion. This was grist to the mill of talk-back radio – Alan Jones infamously referred to 'Middle Eastern grubs' when railing against the bashing of three life-guards at Cronulla beach, which would be followed by rioting – and provided fertile ground for populist vilification of Muslim Australians. 'We grew here, you flew here' declared the body adornment of an Anglo-Australian youth on the day that 'men of middle eastern appearance' became an endangered species on the streets around Cronulla. This encapsulated the sentiment of a sub-set of the constituency to which the reinvigorated Australian values rhetoric was appealing.

It was in this general context of Islamophobia, or at least the problematising of the integration of Muslim-Australians, that the issue of Australian values and identity was reanimated in the second half of 2005. As I have already documented, Howard's and Costello's comments on Australian values and citizenship in August of that year were prompted by the atrocities in London, and explicitly mentioned the difficulties of integrating Muslims into 'mainstream' Australia. In his speech to the Sydney Institute on 23 February 2006, Costello crystallised the opposition between Muslim values and allegedly secular, Australian values: 'There are countries that apply religious sharia law, Saudi Arabia and Iran come to mind. If a person wants to live under sharia law these are countries where they might feel at ease. But not Australia.' The Australian citizenship pledge, he continued, 'should be a flashing warning to those who want to live under sharia law' (Costello, 2006, 3). The implication, presumably, is that there are sufficient numbers of Muslims in Australia who want to live under Sharia law that we should be concerned; concerned enough to reassert the value of Australian values. If the moral panic about Islam was a key contributor to *precipitating* the latest Australian values and citizenship debate, however, it too does not provide a sufficient *explanation*.

As with Howard's general ideological predisposition towards Anglo-Celtic culture and values, Islamophobia long pre-dates the citizenship testing debate, as even a cursory acquaintance with the past decade would confirm. If it is the explanation for the latter, then the question arises as to why citizenship testing did not become an issue much earlier? The reason, and indeed the explanation for the timing of the citizenship testing debate, lies in politics. More specifically, it lays in the electoral advantages to be gained from engaging in symbolic politics, at a time when the text and sub-text of Howard's Australian values had a strong resonance with a large part of the electorate, at a time when Labor was divided on the issue and at a time when other OECD countries had recently moved towards citizenship testing.

It is tempting to see citizenship testing in general, and English language testing in particular, as political strategies designed to exclude. Indeed, much of the negative response to testing has been premised on the assumption that one can draw a straight line from Tampa[1] and the Pacific Solution to citizenship testing; that the latter represents an essential continuity with the former, with both being part of the Coalition's general exclusionary agenda. In this view, both episodes represent attempts by the Coalition to exclude particular categories of people who would otherwise settle in Australia. This view confuses political strategy with tactics, and misidentifies the nature of the continuity between the Pacific Solution and citizenship testing.

The idea that the Coalition Government's *strategic* orientation to immigration and citizenship was, in its totality, exclusionary is unsustainable. The intake of permanent migrants into Australia progressively increased under the Coalition, so that by the time of their defeat more than 100,000 persons per year were settling in Australia (Jupp, 2007, 197–202). At a time of skills shortages, low unemployment and demographic changes that portended an older population increasingly dependent on a tax base that would shrink relative to the demands placed on it, the Australian corporate sector was, with few exceptions, demanding an increased migrant intake. The Howard Government obliged. But in a post-Hanson era, and in an era haunted by the spectre of terrorism, it did so while constantly peddling its border protection credentials. This it contrasted with the befuddled, ambiguous and supposedly 'soft' positions adopted by the ALP, which found itself constantly wedged on issues of border protection. The Government's response to Tampa, and the Pacific Solution that followed, must be viewed in this light. The language of 'queue jumpers,' 'illegals' and 'border protection' was motivated by *tactical*, electoral considerations. It gave the appearance of being tough on immigration per se, when in fact this toughness was applied very unevenly, with the harshest measures reserved for asylum seekers arriving by boat. But this was not, nor could it be, part of a general strategy to exclude immigrants and new citizens. Rather, it was central to a *symbolic politics* that appealed to and reinforced xenophobia – in a context of identity anxiety and widespread unease over border security – in pursuit of concrete electoral advantage. It was a symbolic politics that permanently wedged the ALP and the Labor movement more generally.

Similarly, the Coalition Government's hyping of citizenship testing and Australian values was part of a symbolic politics and electoral calculus designed to help win government for a fifth term. In circumstances where the difficulties of winning a fifth term were widely recognised, and in circumstances where from late 2006 Labor was resurgent, citizenship testing was part of the government's tactical arsenal to improve its electoral chances. Surveys conducted by *Newspoll* in late 2006 confirmed the possibilities of this electoral tactic. In September and December, the poll showed that 90 and 93 per cent of Coalition respondents, respectively, supported the government's plans. More importantly, the corresponding figures for Labor respondents were 70 and 79 per cent (see Goot and Watson's contribution to this collection). The electoral advantages of a testing regime were obvious, with few if any apparent disadvantages.

Given this, it seems clear that citizenship testing was not part of a political strategy to roll back immigration or exclude people from becoming Australian citizens. To the extent that it might have this effect, only if applied rigorously enough with sufficiently difficult tests, this would be an unintended consequence that flowed from the Coalition's tactical gamble. This conclusion is supported when we remember that the early testing of the test saw success rates of around 93 per cent, with those failing being able to re-sit the test. Coalition Ministers were quick to point to such successes, while constantly reaffirming the necessity of testing as a way of vetting the social and cultural fitness, which is to say the suitability, of prospective Australian citizens. The symbolism could hardly be clearer: here was a government that was still firmly committed to border protection and to upholding Australian values, which was reason enough to cast one's vote for the Coalition. Citizenship testing and its rhetorical linking with Australian values was thus more about symbolic politics for electoral advantage than it was about exclusion. Herein lays the real continuity between citizenship testing and the Pacific Solution.

I have shown above that the contemporary linking of Australian values and citizenship testing begins in the second half of 2005 and progressively unfolds over the following 18 months. When the content of arguments in favour of citizenship testing and Australian values is put to the test, I have argued, they are revealed as superficial and misleading. They masquerade under false pretences. They are more about electoral politics than they are about determining whether migrants know about or are committed to Australian values. Indeed, what are Australian values is the wrong question. Instead, we should ask what are human values to which Australians and Australian governments should commit themselves and, more importantly, what are the institutional arrangements that can best embody those values? Only then will values talk have some real value, rather than being the political instrument that has been its purpose in the counterfeit controversy over citizenship testing.

Note

1. In August 2001, the Norwegian ship *Tampa* rescued 438 Afghans from a distressed fishing vessel in international waters. The Afghans had hoped to come to Australia, but the Australian government, opposed to so-called 'boat people' reaching Australia and the protection of its courts, insisted on their disembarkment in Nauru where they could be processed as overseas refugees. Politically this strategy became known as the Pacific Solution.

References

Albrechtsen, J. (2006) 'Open Market on Democratic Ideals', *The Australian*, 3 May 2006: 12.

Anon. (2006a) 'Beazley Stands by Values Form', *AAP Bulletin Wire*, 15 September 2006: 1.

Anon. (2006b) 'Abbott Backs English Test Plan for Migrants', *AAP General News Wire*, 15 September 2006: 1.

Anon. (2006c) 'Greens Condemn Planned Citizenship Changes', *AAP News Wire*, 15 September 2006: 1.

Anon. (2006d) 'Citizenship must be Valued: Robb', *AAP Bulletin Wire*, 17 September 2006: 1.

Barnes, G. (2006) 'Much-vaunted Values Should be Enshrined in a Bill of Rights', *The Canberra Times*, 2 May 2006: 11.

Berlin, I. (1969) 'Two Concepts of Liberty', in I. Berlin *Four Essays on Liberty* (London: Oxford University Press).

Cica, N. (2006) 'For All the Furore, Citizenship, Like Charity, Must Begin at Home', *The Age*, 1 May 2006: 15.

Coorey, P. (2006) 'PM Scorns Values Pledge for Visitors', *Sydney Morning Herald*, 14 September 2006: 5.

Costello (2005) 'Respect Australian Values or Leave', Interview on ABC's *Lateline* with Tony Jones, broadcast 23 August 2005. Accessed 27 November 2008. http://www.abc.net.au/lateline/content/2005/s1444603.htm

Costello (2006) 'Worth Promoting, Worth Defending: Australian Citizenship, What it Means and How to Nurture it', Address to the Sydney Institute,

23 February 2006. Accessed 27 November 2008. http://www.treasurer.gov.au/DisplayDocs.aspx?pageID=&doc=speeches/2006/004.htm&min=phc

Cronin, K. (1993) 'A Culture of Control: An Overview of Immigration Policy-making', in J. Jupp and Kabbala (eds), *The Politics of Australian Immigration* (Canberra: Australian Government Publishing Services): 83–104.

Dutton, D. (2002) *One of Us? A Century of Australian Citizenship* (Sydney: UNSW Press).

Dyrenfurth, N. (2007) 'John Howard's Hegemony of Values: The Politics of "Mateship" in the Howard Decade', *Australian Journal of Political Science* 42 (2): 211–30.

Fraser, A. (2006) 'Beazley Values list "has to go" ', *The Canberra Times*, 14 September 2006: 1.

Galligan, B. and Roberts, W. (2004) *Australian Citizenship* (Melbourne: Melbourne University Press).

Georgio, P. (2006) 'Why the Focus on English?', *The Age*, 5 October 2006: 13.

Grattan (2006) 'Culture War Victory; Howard's Australia Day Call for History Lessons', *Taranaki Daily News*, 27 January 2006: 8.

Grigg, A. (2006) 'Citizenship Exam Proposed for Migrants', *Financial Review*, 18 September 2008: 5.

Hage, G. (2000) *White Nation: Fantasies of White Supremacy in a Multicultural Society* (New York: Routledge).

Hamilton, C. & Maddison, S. (2007) *Silencing Dissent: How the Australian Government is Controlling Public Opinion and Stifling Debate* (Sydney: Allen and Unwin).

Hawkins, F. (1991) *Critical Years in Immigration: Canada and Australia Compared* (Montreal, QC: McGill-Queens University Press).

Hodge, B. & O'Carroll, J. (2006) *Borderwork in Multicultural Australia* (Sydney: Allen & Unwin).

Howard, J. (2005) 'Interview with Barry Cassidy', 7 August. *Insiders* ABC TV. Accessed 14 December 2006. http://www.abc.net.au/insiders/content/2005/s1431937.htm

Howard, J. (2006) 'A Sence of Balance: The Australian Achievement in 2006', *Media Centre: Speeches of Hon John Howard*. Canberra: Department of Prime Minister and Cabinet. Accessed 14 December 2006. http://www.pm.gove.au/News/Speeches/speech1754.html

Howe, B. (2007) *Weighing up Australian Values: Balancing Transitions and Risks to Work and Family in Modern Australia* (Sydney: UNSW Press).

Humphries, D. (2006) 'Live Here, be Australian', *Sydney Morning Herald*, 25 February 2006: 1.

Iggulden (2006) 'Liberal MP Proposes Compulsory Citizenship Test' 27 April *Lateline*. Accessed 2 July 2007. http://www.abc.net.au/lateline/content/2006/s1625552.htm

Johnson, C. (2007) 'John Howard's "Values" and Australian Identity', *Australian Journal of Political Science* 42 (2): 195–209.

Jolliff, A. (2005) 'Libs Call for Tougher Citizenship Tests', Interview with Sharman Stone on *The World Today*, broadcast 15 September 2005. Accessed 2 July 2007. http://www.abc.net.au/worldtoday/content/2005/s1461172htm

Jupp, J. (2005) 'Immigration and Multiculturalism', in C. Aulich and R. Wettenhall (eds), *Howard's Second and Third Governments* (Sydney: UNSW Press).

Jupp, J. (2007) *From White Australia to Woomera: The Story of Australian Immigration*. 2nd edition (Cambridge: Cambridge University Press).

Leet, M. (2006) 'Australian values', Accessed 1 December 2008. http://www.brisinst.org.au/resources/leet_martin_values.html

Lopez, M. (2000) *The Origins of Multiculturalism in Australian Politics 1945–1975* (Melbourne: Melbourne University Press).

McManus, G. and E. Power (2006) ' "Fair go" test for Migrants, Aussie Culture Quiz for Aspiring Citizens', *Herald Sun*, 18 September 2006: 3.

Murray, P. and A. Berryman (2006) 'Heed Europe's Mistakes on Citizenship', *The Age*, 1 May 2006: 15.

Putnam, R. (2000) *Bowling Alone: the Collapse and Revival of American Community* (New York: Simon & Schuster).

Shanahan, D. (2006) 'Aussie Values Test for New Migrants', *The Australian*, 14 September 2006: 7.

Summers, A. (2006) 'New Language Barrier No Way to Build a Tolerant Society', *Sydney Morning Herald*, 2 May 2006: 11.

The Canberra Times (2006) 'Test to Be True Blue', *The Canberra Times*, 23 September 2006: B02.

Topsfield, J. (2006) 'States Attack Proposed English Test for Migrants', *The Age*, 19 July 2006: 7.

Part II

Cross-National Perspectives on Citizenship: A Convergence of Testing Regimes?

6
Citizenship Testing in the Anglophone Countries: The UK, Canada and the USA

Marian Hargreaves

Introduction

Language skills have played a significant role in the history of assessment of applicants for citizenship. The United Kingdom, Canada and the United States have a long history of political, cultural and social interaction and each country has, on occasion, looked to the others when considering possible solutions to issues such as immigration and citizenship. The link of a common language, despite the development of different standard varieties, has facilitated this interaction and all three countries now stipulate that citizens should be able to speak basic English. This chapter focuses on how these countries assess English language skills as part of the process for naturalising adult applicants. An overview is given of the backgrounds to testing in each country, the changing emphases and priorities for testing, and the methods now employed to assess potential citizens. The validity, reliability and practicality of the current citizenship regimes are considered and finally an analysis is made of the vocabulary employed in each of the tests.

Background, emphasis and priorities

The background to language testing and citizenship varies in each country, as the political policies, popular attitudes and educational provision are very different. Even the format and content of the tests vary significantly, despite the common concern with civic values.

The United Kingdom

The Nationality, Immigration and Asylum Act (2002) was the first British Act to stipulate that 'those who apply for naturalization as a British citizen have sufficient knowledge about life in the United Kingdom'. The Act also required that English language skills be defined and tested.

The legislation reflected a recent period of change. The question of immigration had been an issue for some time, particularly with the flow of immigrants from former British colonies in the 1960s and early 70s. Previous governments had begun restricting immigration with the Commonwealth Immigrants Act (1962) and redefining citizenship with the British Nationality Act (1981). By the end of 2001, the UK Government, under Tony Blair, felt that the issue of citizenship needed to be readdressed, both in schools and in assessing potential citizens (Somerville, 2007). Factors which affected this decision included the perceived increase in delinquency amongst young people, the decline in the number of young people voting in general elections in the United Kingdom, the impact of the 9/11 attacks on America and the 'War on Terror'. With respect to naturalisation it was felt that the requirements then in place were too loosely defined and largely unoperationalised. The Government wanted to appear tough, but also to ensure that immigrants learned enough to integrate successfully into British society. It saw education as playing a vital role as part of a reinvigorated policy towards citizenship and integration. An Advisory Group Report stressed 'the mutual responsibility and civic duty of both the new and the old to learn about each others' ways' (UK Home Office, 2003). The Active Learning for Active Citizenship Programme was set up in 2004 to 'build strong, empowered and active communities' (Blunkett, in Mayo and Rooke, 2006) and the Take Part Programme is now taught throughout the United Kingdom (Bedford et al., 2006).

The United Kingdom's first citizenship ceremony was held on 24 February 2004 (Alexander et al., 2007) and the citizenship test in the United Kingdom became a bar, defining requirements for citizenship while also providing a practical (and compulsory) educational tool to help immigrants become useful and 'active' citizens (Crick, 2007). It was a definitive example of the way in which the major Anglophone countries were re-thinking the effectiveness of multiculturalism as a policy platform. This was a move that was also reflected in other countries discussed in this volume.

Since that time the British Government has further addressed issues of immigrant knowledge and commitment to the United Kingdom, as well as national security by developing a new procedure for acquiring British citizenship. In February 2008, the Green Paper 'The Path to Citizenship' was published for public consultation, aiming to 'make the immigration system clearer, more streamlined and easier to understand, in the process reducing the possibilities for abuse of the system, maximising the benefits of migration and putting British values at the heart of the system' (UK Home Office, 2008). Most significant is the introduction of a new time-limited probationary citizenship period, between temporary residence and British citizenship or permanent residence. Following a consultation period, the Government now plans to create a new path to citizenship in which 'rights and benefits of citizenship are matched by responsibilities and contributions to Britain' (UK Border Agency, 2008). In their analysis of the consultation responses it was found that a significant majority of those polled agreed that, before becoming citizens, migrants should have good English literacy standards and pass a test about the British way of life. Testing for citizenship has therefore been strengthened and its exclusivity reaffirmed.

The United Kingdom increasingly views the granting of citizenship as the ultimate reward for the successful completion of a journey. The process of becoming a UK citizen has become both longer and more complicated. But while successful integration is a primary aim for migrants that seek to become citizens, active civic education and participation for all UK residents is an acknowledged goal of the current government. The form of the test itself remains problematic but educational courses and official study materials have been increased to assist applicants for citizenship (Kiwan, 2008).

Requirements for Citizenship through Naturalisation: Applicants for British citizenship must be over 18, of sound mind and good character. They should have resided legally in the United Kingdom for at least 5 years and have English language skills at ESOL Entry level three or above. They must have sufficient knowledge about life in the United Kingdom to pass the citizenship test, though some exemptions are granted to applicants over 65 years old and applicants suffering from a long-term illness or a disability that restricts their mobility and ability to attend language classes. Applicants with a mental impairment that impedes their ability to learn English are also exempt. Following a successful application, new citizens are required to take an Oath (or Affirmation) of Allegiance to the Queen, and a Pledge to the United Kingdom at a citizenship ceremony. The new Immigration and Citizenship Bill was programmed for discussion in 2009 to replace all existing immigration legislation. Following agreement by both Houses on the text of the Bill it received Royal Assent on 21 July 2009. The Bill is now an Act of Parliament.[1]

The United States

Naturalisation in the United States was first enacted in 1790, reflecting both the immigrant composition of the American population and the early break from United Kingdom (following the Boston Tea Party (1773) and Declaration of Independence (1776)). Immigration was strongly encouraged in the 1860s and 70s, but enthusiasm turned to fright and the restriction movement blossomed in the late 1880s and 90s (Higham, 1952). The first general immigration law was enacted in 1882 to establish federal supervision and exclude groups unable to support themselves. The American literacy test of 1887 was devised to further discourage illiterate southern and eastern European immigrants. The Naturalization Act (1906) required that applicants for citizenship, in addition to showing good moral character, attachment to the United States and the ability to demonstrate knowledge of United States history and government, must also show that they can speak and understand English. In 1950, this was extended to include the ability to both read and write English.

Later legislation reflected the pressure for Anglo-conformity and the intensely nationalistic feeling first expressed in the Americanisation movement of the early twentieth century. The work of Raymond Crist and Richard Campbell in developing a program for education reflected the 'nation-wide drive to rapidly assimilate new immigrants through programs of citizenship education and instruction in the "American way of life", part of the progressivism that grew out of a general sense of disorder and overwhelming change that enveloped the country at the turn of the century' (Gordon, 2007). Restrictions enacted in the Immigration Act (1917) reflected the assumed moral qualities of different national groups and suspected political subversives (Gordon, 2007).

The Immigration Reform and Control Act (1986) saw the development of a bank of 100 questions which formed the basis for the naturalisation exam. In 1997, the US Commission on Immigration Reform returned to consider what the United States expects of immigrants and how they will be received. This continuing re-examination was dramatically affected by the 9/11 terrorist attacks in 2001 and security continues to be a major concern with respect to immigration and naturalisation, demonstrated by the creation of the Office of Citizenship under the US Citizenship and Immigration Service (USCIS) and the Department of Homeland Security. However, the Naturalisation Test came under considerable criticism, not least for asking meaningless questions within an un-standardised framework. It was therefore revised to ensure that the civics test effectively assesses whether applicants have a meaningful understanding of US government and history through a more standardised and fair naturalisation process.

Although the methods are different, the aims of the American test are similar to the British: to encourage citizenship applicants to learn and identify with the basic values of the United States, and to exclude applicants who do not demonstrate those values. The redesigned test was publicly introduced on 27 September 2007. Naturalisation applicants began taking the revised test on 1 October 2008 (USCIS, 2008).

The United States also sees the granting of citizenship as a reward, but appears less keen to assist migrants on their journey. The procedure for application is far from simple. While some study guides are available, the provision of English language courses for migrants varies across the states and is very limited (McKay, 2007). The onus of achievement is on the migrant, and the host nation sets the bar. This is reflected in the policy towards the test itself. While it has been seen that considerable efforts have been made to make the questions in the test more fair and meaningful, the test is still conducted by interview, with all the associated hazards of bias that that method implies.

Requirements for Citizenship through Naturalisation: Applicants for US citizenship must be over 18 years old and demonstrate that he or she has been a person of good moral character for the mandatory 5-year period of permanent residency. Applicants must show that they have the ability to read, write, speak and understand words in ordinary usage in the English language, and must also demonstrate a knowledge and understanding of the fundamentals of the history, principles and form of government of the United States. Exemptions from the English test are offered to applicants over the age of 50 who have lived as permanent residents in the United States for at least 20 years, and applicants over the age of 55 who have 15 years permanent residency. However, all applicants must take the test in civics. Any person who provides medical evidence of a permanent physical and developmental disability or mental impairment so severe that it prevents acquiring or demonstrating the required knowledge of English, may be eligible for an exemption. Following a successful application, new US citizens must take an Oath of Allegiance at a citizenship ceremony.

Canada

Canada's would seem to occupy a middle ground between the United States and British situations. According to official policy, the nation welcomes migrants and offers them generous levels of education when compared to the provision of the United States (although levels vary according to state). Canada differs from the United Kingdom and the United States in having two official languages. However, the background to the current regime is not dissimilar to that of the United Kingdom.

The Citizenship Act (1947) reflected a growing interest in the issue, but it was not until Patriation in 1982, when the British Parliament ceased to be the final authority in matters pertaining to the Canadian Constitution and Canada adopted a Charter of Rights and Freedoms, that there was a renewed interest in immigrant citizenship. As part of a move to centralisation, the Departments of Citizenship and Immigration were merged in 1992 to form Citizenship and Immigration Canada (CIC). Standardised questions were written for an existing but revised (1995) booklet *A Look at Canada* to form a consistent, standardised test for citizenship assessment.

This desire for consistency reflected the fiscal conservatism predominant in the major political parties (Joshee and Derwing, 2005). Personal, flexible arrangements, whereby applicants first met with a citizenship officer and then a judge, were replaced by a standard test that made the assessment procedure more economical, efficient and consistent. There are now four basic steps to citizenship: determination of eligibility; application for citizenship; taking the test; and attending a citizenship ceremony. However, under new, streamlined processes that came into effect in 2009, citizenship may be granted to certain individuals who have lost it, and to others who will be recognised as citizens for the first time (CIC, 2010).

The language requirement for citizenship currently focuses on the communicative ability of the applicant. It is stipulated: 'You must know enough of one of the two languages to understand other people and for them to understand you. That is, you need to be able to speak English or French well enough to communicate with people' (CIC, 2008). However, the test has been criticised for trivialising citizenship, encouraging rote learning and not providing an opportunity for applicants to 'think more deeply about citizenship or discuss these thoughts with others during their citizenship acquisition process' (Joshee and Derwing, 2005, 70–3).

Requirements for Citizenship through Naturalisation: Applicants for citizenship must be over 18 and be permanent residents in Canada for at least 3 of the past 4 years before applying. A health check is required and a criminal record may prohibit citizenship. Applicants must demonstrate the ability to speak English or French well enough to communicate with people. They must also show knowledge of the rights and responsibilities of citizens, Canada's history and geography and its political system. Applicants over 55 are exempt from the citizenship test. At the Minister's discretion, adults who hold a medical certificate proving a condition that prevents them from sitting the test may also be exempt. Illiterate adults may have a hearing with a citizenship judge after taking, and failing the exam. Successful applicants take an oath, accepting the rights and responsibilities of Canadian citizenship (Table 6.1).

Table 6.1 Requirements for citizenship

	UK	Canada	USA
Residency	5 years	At least 3 years (1,095 days) in the past 4 years before applying.	5 years
Visa	The necessary permission, under the immigration laws, to be in the UK.	Permanent resident	Permanent resident
Age	18	18	18
Character and Criminal Record (Background checks)	Applicants must be of sound mind and good character. Character checks will include, but are not restricted to, enquiries of the police. Photo ID required.	A criminal record may prohibit citizenship. A health check is also required.	An applicant must show that he or she has been a person of good moral character for the statutory period. A health check may also be required.
Language	ESOL Entry Level 3	The ability to speak English or French well enough to communicate with people.	The ability to read, write, speak and understand words in ordinary usage in the English language.
Knowledge of the country	Have sufficient knowledge about life in the UK.	The rights and responsibilities of citizens, Canada's history and geography and its political system.	Demonstration of a knowledge and understanding of the fundamentals of the history and of the principles and form of government of the United States.
Expression of commitment	Oath (or Affirmation) of Allegiance, and Pledge, taken at a citizenship ceremony.	Oath of Citizenship, taken at a citizenship ceremony.	Oath of Allegiance, taken at a citizenship ceremony.
Dual citizenship allowed	Yes	Yes	Yes
Cost of application and test	£655 adult application for citizenship £34 (test) £9.99 (handbook)	$200 adult application for citizenship	$595 + $80 biometrics fee, where applicable

Table 6.1   (Continued)

	UK	Canada	USA
Exemptions from the citizenship test	Adult applicants aged 65 and over. Applicants suffering from a long-term illness or disability which severely restricts mobility and ability to attend language classes. Or have a mental impairment which means that they are unable to learn another language.	Adult applicants 55 or over. Adults who hold a medical certificate proving a condition that prevents them from sitting the test (Minister's decision to grant exemption). Illiterate adults may have a hearing with a citizenship judge after failing the exam.	Adult applicant 50–54 years who has lived in the US for at least 20 years as a permanent resident, and an adult applicant 55 years and over who has been living in the US for at least 15 years may be exempt from the test in English. They must still take the civics test. Any person who provides medical evidence of physical and developmental disability or mental impairment where the impairment affects the applicant's ability to learn English, US History and Government.

The handbooks for citizenship

The United Kingdom, United States and Canada each publish a handbook to assist applicants for citizenship: *Life in the United Kingdom, A Journey to Citizenship* (UK Home Office, 2007), *A Guide to Naturalization* (USCIS, 2008) and *A Look at Canada* (CIC, 2008).

Life in the United Kingdom is a self-study guide that seeks to be a useful general reference, not just a textbook for an examination. The Preface recommends that applicants read all chapters, although test questions are drawn only from chapters 2 through 6. Those chapters deal with society in the United Kingdom today, the government of the country, everyday needs and employment and 'contain all the answers to the questions that may be asked in the Life in the United Kingdom test' (Preface).[2] Additional chapters round out the picture of life in the United Kingdom, covering British history and law and offering a discussion on building better communities. The book also provides contact information for organisations that can help with further information on topics such as legal aid.

While also providing a self-study guide, Canada does not claim that all the necessary information to pass the citizenship test appears in its handbook. While test questions are based on the information pro-vided in the booklet, applicants need to source for themselves answers for regional questions on economics, geography and history. The Cana-dian booklet also does not aim to be a resource for the general public in the way that *Life in the United Kingdom* does. It was written and revised specifically for citizenship applicants and clearly lists the topics covered in the test. Topics include the following: 'The right to vote in elections in Canada; the right to run for elected office; voting procedures in Canada and how to register yourself as a voter; Canada's main historical and geographical features; the rights and responsibilities of a citizen; the structure of Canadian government; and Confederation'. Protecting the environment and sustainable development are also highlighted.

At first glance, the Canadian handbook appears less formidable than the UK handbook. It is only 47 pages long and is laid out with a sig-nificant amount of white space with supporting photographs, diagrams, tables and a map of Canada to provide an overall geographic orienta-tion. The booklet is available online as well as in hard copy and has a user-friendly format. In contrast, the British handbook is 145 pages long, must be purchased and has a very formal and official presentation. How-ever, it also uses a reader-friendly format with a non-serif font for text in a column format. There are photographs, self-study 'check' boxes and a substantial glossary. The British handbook contains all the answers to the questions that may be asked in the Life in the UK test, and those questions are drawn only from specified chapters, which constitute 58 pages of text.

The United States departs completely from the idea that citizenship questions should be based on a handbook, providing instead *A Guide to Naturalization*. This guidebook attempts to clarify the process of applying for citizenship, detailing the benefits and responsibilities of citizenship and eligibility through 'Frequently Asked Questions'. Sam-ple civics questions and sentences are given at the back of the guide and a Web address for study materials is also supplied. This format reflects the different nature of the US citizenship test. While the United King-dom and Canada provide computer-marked, multiple choice tests that directly assess reading skills, the US tests are conducted by interview to test for all four macro skills (reading, writing, listening and speaking).

Methods of testing

Methods of testing vary across all three countries. The British test is computer based, multiple choice and directly tests reading. It includes 24 questions drawn from a bank of 200 and allows 45 minutes for completion. The pass mark is around 75 per cent. The Canadian test is a paper and pencil test, although examples and practice tests are usually computer based. The test includes mandatory questions and allows 30 minutes for completion. It utilises a combination of multiple choice and short answer questions on the privileges of citizenship, history, politics, economics and geography. A pass mark of 12 out of 20 is required. In addition, there are four mandatory questions the applicant must answer on the test. The applicant must pass three out of the four mandatory questions (concerning voting, citizenship responsibilities and elections). The test directly assesses reading skills and extrapolates other skills from the test performance. As literacy is not a requirement for Canadian citizenship, illiterate applicants who fail the test may apply for an interview. The American test is by interview and directly assesses reading, writing, listening and speaking. Six out of ten questions on civics must be answered correctly, one out of three on reading and one out of three on writing.

The major advantage of multiple choice tests is that they can be scored quickly and reliably. Multiple choice questions are also an effective way of assessing a candidate's knowledge of a subject, which is the essential function of citizenship tests. However, it has now been recognised (Hughes, 2003) that it is actually very difficult to write successful items. Multiple choice questions require distractors and these are not always easy to find. It is recognised that at least four options should be presented for each question, and preferably five. Where options are limited to three, there is a 30 per cent chance that the candidate could guess the correct answer. Other common problems with multiple choice questions include there being more than one correct answer; no correct answer; clues in the options as to which is correct (the longest answer is often the right one); and ineffective distractors. Dichotomous questions, where candidates choose from only two options (yes/no; true/false), are even more problematic as they give the test taker a 50 per cent chance of guessing the correct answer.

The British test uses four versions of multiple choice questions:

a) one correct answer to be chosen from four options
b) the selection of TRUE or FALSE for a given statement
c) two correct answers to be chosen from four choices
d) selecting the correct answer from two choices

Of these, only (a) satisfies the requirements for a successful assessment item; (b), (c) and (d) are all essentially dichotomous questions and therefore highly unreliable. The Canadian test also uses four versions of multiple choice questions:

a) one correct answer to be chosen from five options
b) one correct answer to be chosen from four options
c) the selection of TRUE or FALSE for a given statement
d) three correct answers to be chosen from five choices

While options (c) and (d) are unreliable forms of multiple choice questions, options (a) and (b) are much more reliable, with (a) highly so. Analysis of a sample citizenship test showed that 40 per cent of items were type (a) questions, with a further 28 per cent of type (b). The Canadian test also uses short answer questions or gap-fill sentences, but as the options come from a short list and not an information text, these are also multiple choice questions.

Test design

The design of any test, including language tests and tests for citizenship, must address issues of practicality, reliability and validity and find an acceptable balance between them (Alderson et al., 1995; Bachman, 1990; Bachman and Palmer, 1996; Brown, 2005; Shohamy, 1985). Of those three major issues, validity can be seen as the most important. In an ideal world, practicality would not be an issue until all areas of validity have been satisfied (Weir, 2005). In reality, however, the practicality of a test is of very real and immediate concern.

Validity

Validity designates the ability of a test to assess what it purports to test. A test that aims to assess reading skills, for instance, should not require candidates to do a large amount of writing. However, as Weir (2005) has pointed out, there are several types of validity. 'Construct validity' has increasingly been used to refer to the general, overarching notion of validity, that is, including content, concurrent, predictive and face validity (Hughes, 2003, 26). A construct is 'a conceptualisation, operational definition or description of a phenomenon, such as listening or reading. Essentially, construct validity is the degree to which a test's task and topical contents operationalise, or tap into the construct as it has been described' (Moritoshi, 2001, 9). The British, American and Canadian tests all clearly indicate what material is being tested for consideration of citizenship. Topics are clearly defined even if the UK test is the only one to include all pertinent information in its handbook. The face validity for the test in all three countries is therefore very high. However, testing language skills and testing knowledge of a country are two very different objectives. Applicants with low English language skills will be handicapped in their ability to express their knowledge.

The language level is clearly defined for the British test; less so for the Canadian and American tests. Although there are alternative ways of demonstrating the required competence in the English language, the UK handbook states that 'questions [in the *Life in the UK* test] are deliberately written in a way that requires an understanding of the English language at the level (called ESOL entry 3 level) that the law requires of people becoming British citizens. So there is no need to take a separate test of knowledge of the English language' (*Life in the UK*, Preface).[3] The Canadian and American tests also aim to assess language through a test of knowledge, but given the civic, historical and legal nature of much of the content of the relevant material, the required level of English needed by candidates is in fact much higher than the 'high beginner' levels officially required, particularly for the American test.

The Canadian 'ability to speak English or French well enough to communicate with people' is less well operationalised, possibly because of the earlier practice of assessing candidates through interview. The situation is further complicated by the bilingual situation in Canada. The government-funded Language Instruction for Newcomers to Canada (LINC) can include instruction on citizenship-related topics, depending on the proficiency level of the students and the resources of the centre, but doubt has been expressed that these classes provide the necessary background knowledge for the citizenship test, even where LINC is offered to level 5 (Derwing and Thomson, 2005).

The American requirement that citizenship candidates have the ability to read, write, speak and understand words in ordinary usage in the English language is linked to the expertise of the Teachers of English to Speakers of Other Languages (TESOL) (USCIS, 2006). This association is an independent professional organisation created to bring together teachers and administrators at all educational levels with an interest in teaching English to speakers of other languages (ESOL) (TESOL, 2007). The TESOL refers to the Comprehensive Adult Student System (CASAS) (TESOL, 2003, 151) and the 'high-beginner' level specified for the US citizenship tests correlate to the CASAS skill level descriptors for ESL (CASAS, 2007). The CASAS test developers have addressed the issues of validity, reliability and fairness, and conduct ongoing research and development (Gorman and Ernst, 2004). Nevertheless, while the US

Department may use the skill level descriptors, they do not use the actual CASAS tests. Candidates' English language skills are still assessed at interview by a US-designated examiner.

Reliability

Reliability is defined as consistency of measurement (Bachman and Palmer, 1996, 19). A test should be able to obtain similar scores on any occasion for the same students with the same ability (Hughes, 2003). The use of individual interviewers for testing in the USA make the American tests very open to potentially varying and subjective decisions, and the standardisation of the procedure was a focus of the recent test redesign.

The British test also presents problems. It is based on multiple choice questions and includes questions for which more than one answer is equally valid. For example, 'In Britain, there is a well-established link between abuse of what substance and crime?' The correct answer is 'hard drugs', but it could equally as well be 'alcohol' which is one of the alternative answers given to choose from.

The UK's citizenship test randomly selects 24 questions from a pool of 200. All 200 questions should be, but are not, similar. The pool also includes dichotomous questions (true/false; yes/no). For example, 'The Queen is the Head of State of the United Kingdom – true or false?' As already discussed, dichotomous questions are problematic for a test. The Canadian test designers have addressed this issue by sorting the pool of questions from which the test is drawn, into hard and easy questions, and ensuring that each test includes a stipulated number of questions from each category. However, this raises the question of identifying what exactly is 'easy' or 'hard'.

Practicality

The United Kingdom's computer-based multiple choice citizenship test has a number of practical advantages. Testing sites can administer the test without requiring specialist staff training and results can be given to applicants quickly and economically. The Canadian test is marked by computer, which gives it a similar practical advantage. The American interviews, however, require that staff be specifically trained, which is both expensive and time-consuming. The lengthy processing of applications in the United States is a recognised issue and the subject of legal proceedings.

Literacy

Applicants for US citizenship must be able to read and write as well as speak basic English. Literacy is therefore a requirement and directly tested. The British test does not directly test speaking, listening and writing competencies, but the applicants' reading skills are considered a marker for their other English language skills. Although candidates must have writing skill to pass the test, literacy is not a requirement under the Canadian *Citizenship Act*. However, for reasons of practicality, test applicants who are not literate are still obliged to take and fail the test before being allowed an oral interview (Joshee and Derwing, 2005, 70).

Testing via computer also raises questions of literacy, in terms both of conventional reading ability and computer skills. While computer skills are clearly useful in all the countries that are being considered here given the increasing prevalence of computers in social life, they are not a requirement for citizenship. A citizenship test should therefore not also be a test of computer skills. The actual computer skills involved in taking the British test are not great, but the use of an unfamiliar technique could drastically raise the stress level for test-takers and thereby seriously reduce the reliability of the test (Bachman and Palmer, 1996). However, the increasing importance of computer skills in all three countries is reflected in the provision of Web site support for all citizenship applicants, much of which is not generally available in any other form (Table 6.2).

Table 6.2   Methods of testing

	UK	Canada	USA
Mode	Computer based	Paper and pencil. Interviews available on application after failing the test.	Interview. Reading aloud and writing.
Directly tested macro skills	Reading	Reading, pencil skills (+ listening and speaking at interview).	Reading, writing, listening, speaking.
Format of test	24 multiple choice questions from a bank of 200.	20 multiple choice and short answer questions from a bank of about 400.	10 questions on civics from a bank of 100. A separate list of questions for elderly applicants. + 3 reading items and 3 writings items.

Mandatory questions	No	Yes	No
Time allowed for test/ interview	45 minutes	30 minutes	Not specified
Assistance available for disabilities	Large-print handbook is available for people with visual impairment. Computer can read out questions if required. In some cases, it will be possible to receive assistance for data entry. Test-centres can also provide support for people with special needs.	Assistance may be available for some visual, learning or hearing disabilities, upon application.	Assistance may be available for some visual, learning or hearing disabilities, upon application.
Passmark	75%	12/20 general questions, plus 3/4 mandatory questions on voting, citizenship responsibilities and elections.	6/10 civics questions, plus 1/3 reading items and 1/3 writing items.

Analysis of text samples

As all three countries specify, to varying extents, the language level required for citizenship; (see Table 6.1) a brief content analysis was made of the sample questions provided to applicants. A readability test, designed to give a statistical analysis of the difficulty of a text based on the vocabulary used, was also made for the texts of the handbooks as well as the sample questions.

Content analysis of sample questions

The provision of sample questions varies widely across the three countries. It is worth noting that, for all countries the issues of rights and privileges are extremely important, reflecting the Bill of Rights (The United States), the Canadian Charter of Rights and Freedoms and the

Human Rights Act (The United Kingdom), and this has heavily affected the content of all the tests.

> *Canada*: Canada provides a fairly comprehensive list of 114 questions, prefaced by a clear list of topics the questions cover. Questions about Canada are context focused, clearly divided into general (Section 1) and regional questions (Section 2). Answers for questions in Section 1 can be found in the handbook, but applicants have to source answers for questions in Section 2 themselves. The list is followed by two examples of the multiple choice format of the online test.

Questions are grouped into previously defined topics that provide a clear structure for a candidate to follow. 'Who', 'what', 'when' and 'where' questions are used and there are a number of 'why' questions. There are also several 'which' questions as well as 'name', 'list' and 'give an example of' questions. Alternative formulae include the following: 'From whom are the Metis descended?'; 'One-third of all Canadians live in which province?' and 'Explain how the levels of government are different?'. Questions about Canada therefore encourage candidates to show more than just a trivial knowledge and understanding of the country of which they seek to become citizens. Questions to which answers may change – for example, 'What is the name of your mayor?' – are clearly personalised (*your* mayor) and, coming under the regional section of questions, encourage involved local knowledge.

> *USA*: The American process of testing for naturalisation has recently changed, with the new test coming into effect on 1 October 2008. The American *A Guide to Naturalization* no longer provides a list of sample questions for assessing English, but the vocabulary used in the reading and writing assessments, and the complete list of questions for the civics test are supplied separately, most easily accessed through the government Web site: http://www.uscis.gov. newtest. The list also specifies those civics-based questions asked of applicants over the age of 65 who may be exempt from the English test.

The focus of questions for US citizenship is overtly based on civics. The questions have now been restructured into sections: American Government, American History and Integrated Civics. These in turn are subdivided: into categories such as 'Principles of American Democracy', 'System of Government' and so forth. Many of the questions are similar to those previous asked, such as 'When was the Declaration of Independence adopted?' Repetitious questions have been eliminated. The new Naturalisation Test expressly states that it is neither harder nor easier than the old test, and results of piloting are given to illustrate the measures taken to ensure this. The original question, 'Who becomes President if the President dies?', has been rephrased to the more meaningful, 'If the President can no longer serve, who becomes President?', a formulation that posed little difficulty for subjects of the supplementary trial (second language students who possessed low-beginning to high-beginning levels of English comprehension). The redesigned test is intended to be understood as a vehicle for a naturalisation candidate to learn about the principles of American democracy and further identify with its civic values.

Although answers to these questions are given in the study guides provided, the interview format makes the questions more difficult to answer than the multiple choice format of the British and Canadian tests. Some questions, such as 'Who signs bills to become laws?', could be confusing as they do not specify what level of government – federal, state or local – the question relates to. Nevertheless, piloting showed a very high pass rate (98.9 per cent).

UK: The UK handbook does not provide any sample questions. However, the Web site for citizenship does offer practical help for applicants intending to take the citizenship test. This includes a range of short training sessions on using a mouse or keyboard, a short introduction to the test, a navigation tutorial and a checklist of the topics covered in the test. Only sample questions are given, and these are procedural, demonstrating the format of the online test.[4]

Lexical analysis

A lexical analysis was made using Web VP (Cobb, 1994). This is a computer-based program which can make an analysis of the words used in a text that can be uploaded by the user of the program. The analysis includes the categorisation of words in a text by the first 1000 words that a basic user of English would probably know (K1); by an additional 1000 words in a learner's vocabulary (K2); by the percentage of words of Anglo-Saxon origin, which are often the shorter and more frequently used words in the English language (Piller, 2001); by the percentage of academic words (AWL) in the text; and by the lexical density.

A contingency table (χ^2) analysis was then made of these results to assess whether there were differences in each of the three countries' use of the words. A χ^2 contingency table is a statistical procedure in which the distribution of sample data across two or more factors, each with two or more classes, is analysed to see if such distribution is purely random or not. If there were no differences between the countries, the same proportions of each type of word (K1, K2, Anglo-Saxon, AWL) would be expected. Anticipated differences, such as the likelihood that the United Kingdom might use more Anglo-Saxon words, are also confirmed or negated.

> *Handbook Texts, Including the US*: Relatively speaking, the UK handbook uses K1 words much more than the other countries. The US's *Guide* shows a mild tendency towards using K1 words (in other words, uses more K1 words than expected). Canada has a tendency not to use them. The difference between countries here is statistically extremely significant ($p = 1.2E\text{-}36$; p stands for probability). The United Kingdom is also significantly more likely to use K2 words ($p = 1.3E\text{-}5$). The United States uses them slightly less than expected and they are close to the average proportions, but Canada uses K2 words significantly less than expected. However, in an analysis of K1 + K2 words combined, the results are therefore similar to those of K1 alone as there are relatively few K2 words used overall. As expected, the United Kingdom has a very strong tendency to use Anglo-Saxon words, while Canada has a slight, and the United States a very strong, tendency not to use them. Here the statistical significance is extremely strong ($p = 4.6E\text{-}49$). The United States has a strong tendency to use academic words (words used largely in an academic, rather than everyday context). For Canada and the United Kingdom, the use of academic words does not seem significant either way. These results are statistically significant ($p = 8.1E\text{-}15$). Further analysis (separating K1 from K2 from AWL from 'other') confirms the above patterns: The United Kingdom especially, and the United States tends to use K1 words. The United Kingdom tends to use K2 words more than the other three countries. The United States is the highest user of AWL words, while Canada tends to use more off-list words than expected.
>
> *Handbook Texts, Excluding the US*: As the format and content of the USA's handbook is very different from those of Canada and the UK, an analysis was made of the latter two texts alone, the results of which confirm the tendencies previously identified: the United Kingdom tends to use K1 and K2 words significantly more than Canada. Separating K1 from K2 from AWL from 'other' further confirms these results with the United Kingdom using K1 words more than Canada, which uses slightly more words than expected

that are not listed in K1, K2 or AWL. As expected, the United Kingdom has a stronger tendency than Canada to use Anglo-Saxon words. However, omitting the USA text from the analysis results in a negligible effect and shows Canada as having a very strong tendency away from Anglo-Saxon words ($p = 1.3E-8$).

Analysis of the text of sample questions for Canada, the United Kingdom[5] and the United States: In analysing the sample questions, the first notable result is the disappearance of the United Kingdom's strong tendency towards using K1 words that had been indicated by analysis of the handbook. The significant tendency towards K1 words that the United States showed in the old sample questions is no longer evident in the redesigned naturalisation test. Canada tends to use K1 words less than expected ($p = 0.0028$). The use of K2 words in the sample questions is insignificant and again, combining K1 and K2, K1 effectively overpowers any significance of K2 usage. The redesigned United States questions, however, show a usage of K1 + K2 that is now decidedly lower than is evident in the other tests – a marked change that probably reflects the nature of the content of knowledge being assessed. In the text of the sample questions, the United States shows the same tendency as found in the analysis of the handbooks, tending away from AWL words, but this is only significant at the 5 per cent level. This also applies to the new redesigned questions. For both the United Kingdom and Canada, AWL seems irrelevant with respect to the questions. Interestingly, when looking at Anglo-Saxon word usage, the expected strong tendency for the United Kingdom disappears. The United States still uses distinctly more Anglo-Saxon words than Canada and the United Kingdom, to the extent that this is now significant at the 1 per cent level. Canada tends to use Anglo-Saxon words less than expected.

Removing the United States from this analysis of the questions, one finds that there is little difference between Canada and the United Kingdom with respect to their usage of words from each classification. This is essentially because of the small sample size; the number of words overall is very low. Removing the United Kingdom questions (an especially small sample) has no further effect. Analysis of the text of sample questions for Canada, the United Kingdom and the United States therefore indicates that the United States shows a tendency towards K1 and Anglo-Saxon words and away from academic words. Canada shows the reverse tendencies with the United Kingdom tending neither way. Noticeably, this is quite different from the analysis of the text of the handbooks where the United Kingdom stands out quite differently with a very strong usage of K1 words compared to the other two countries.

Lexical density

Lexical density measures the proportion of the content (lexical) words over the total words in a text. Texts with a lower density are more easily understood by people with low language skills. In general, written language is denser than spoken language, as it has more content words in relation to non-content words (Halliday, 1985). Analysis by O'Loughlin found that 'spoken texts had a lexical density of less than 40 per cent (24–43 per cent) and written texts a density of greater than 40 per cent (36–57 per cent)' (O'Loughlin, 1995, 221). A score above 50 per cent is therefore regarded as lexically dense. The handbooks analysed showed a range from 54 per cent (USA) to 60 per cent (Canada); and the questions all had a lexical density of 56 per cent, indicating that, while at the lower end of the difficulty range associated with written texts, all the handbooks are much more difficult than the accepted range for spoken English, and the questions even more so. The requirement that candidates be able to read these texts for citizenship therefore demands more advanced skills than those necessary for speaking and listening to the same information. It is generally accepted that the questions for any test should not be more difficult than the materials on which they are based. On this basis, with respect to lexical density, all the texts of the tests are problematic.

Impact of testing

The higher the stakes involved in a test, the more important it is that the issues of validity and reliability are seriously considered. With very high stakes, as is the case in citizenship tests, the difficulty level should be quite low. A number of citizenship applicants interviewed after taking their test for Canadian citizenship stated that they found the test quite easy (Joshee and Derwing, 2005). However, this raises a number of issues: perceived difficulty may be quite different from actual difficulty (Brindley et al., 2007) and tests may be designed to actually exclude applicants.

Conclusion

The analyses of these three case studies have revealed significant differences both in the handbooks and in the tests themselves. In summary: Britain and Canada both use multiple choice tests, but while the British test is administered by computer, the Canadian test utilises paper and pencil and candidates may request an interview should they fail. The United States uses interviews, rather than tests, to assess candidates for citizenship. The tests in each country cover many similar topics, such as social and physical geography, the rights and responsibilities of citizens and the structure of the government. However, the United Kingdom, with its long and rich history, chooses not to include historical questions, although both Canada and the United States have sections on history. The American test is overtly concerned with civics and 'American values', and Canada requires that candidates have knowledge of the specific region in which they live.

America is the only country to test all four language-based macro skills – reading, writing, speaking and listening. The United Kingdom and Canada focus on reading as an indicator of language ability, an approach which severely compromises the validity of their tests. Validity is also undermined by questions couched in language that is more difficult than the handbook texts on which they are based. The lexical analysis in this study has shown the real differences between the language used in the British, Canadian and American handbook texts and questions, and the high level of English language required of candidates, despite the fairly low standard stated by the official language requirements.

Global concerns have affected the tests, as has globalisation itself which has resulted, amongst other things, in the accommodation of dual citizenship, a state which Slade (Chapter 1) has shown does not always sit comfortably with the requirements for attaining citizenship. All the tests constitute a form of gatekeeping, however, they also reflect the common trend to make government procedure more transparent (Wright, 2008). Face validity for the tests has become extremely important and may have been the prime motivation for the revision of the American test.

The knowledge content of the tests underlines the assumption that language both reflects the cultural values of the nation and acts as a unifying force. However, the relevance and appropriateness of a test that assesses attitudes and values as much as language skills has already been questioned in Chapter 1 (Slade) and will be further queried in the Australian context in Chapter 9 (Farrell).

Notes

1. http://services.parliament.uk/bills/2008–09/borderscitizenshipand immigration.html Accessed 2 February 2010.

2. Applicants from the Channel Islands or the Isle of Man are required to pass the test or successfully complete an ESOL with citizenship course before applying for British citizenship. Tests taken on the islands are paper based and consist of 25 questions, with six questions based on local matters.

3. ESOL 3: *Speaking and listening:* At this level, adults can listen and respond to spoken language, including straightforward information and narratives, and follow straightforward explanations and instructions, both face-to-face and on the telephone. Speak to communicate information, feelings and opinions on familiar topics, using appropriate formality, both face-to-face and on the telephone. Engage in discussion with one or more people in a familiar situation, making relevant points and responding to what others say to reach a shared understanding about familiar topics. *Reading*: At this level, adults can read and understand short, straightforward texts on familiar topics accurately and independently. Read and obtain information from everyday sources. *Writing*: At this level, adults can write to communicate information and opinions with some adaptation to the intended audience. (Department for Universities Innovation and Skills, 2008). ESOL 3 also relates directly to the Common European Framework of Reference for Languages (CEFRL) and is equivalent to their B1, the lower level of independent user. This rating scale is based on communicative language ability, is 'action-oriented' (CEFRL: 9) and is widely used throughout Europe to report test scores.

4. Official practice questions and answers are now available for purchase from the government TSO (The Stationery Office). An official Study Guide is now also available.

5. Sample questions were taken from the procedural examples.

References

Alderson, J.C., C. Clapham and D. Wall (1995) *Language Test Construction and Evaluation* (Cambridge: Cambridge University Press).

Alexander, C., R. Edwards and B. Temple (2007) 'Contesting Cultural Communities: Language, Ethnicity and Citizenship in Britain', *Journal of Ethnic and Migration Studies* 33 (5): 783–800.

Bachman, L. (1990) *Fundamental Considerations in Language Testing* (Oxford: Oxford University Press).

Bachman, L. and A. Palmer (1996) *Language Testing in Practice* (Oxford: Oxford University Press).

Bedford, J., H. Marsh and D. Wright (2006) 'The National Framework for Active Learning for Active Citizenship'. Accessed 29 January, 2008. http://www.takepart.org/assets/documents/take-part-framework/

Brown, J.D. (2005) *Testing in Language Programs* (Upper Saddle River, N.J.: Prentice Hall Regents).

Brindley, G., M. Hargreaves, S. Moore and H. Slatyer (2007) *Exploring Reading Assessment Task and Item Difficulty* (Unpublished manuscript).

CASAS (2007) 'Skill Level Descriptors for ESL'. Retrieved 29 January 2008. https://www.casas.org/home/index.cfm?fuseaction=home.showContent&MapID=474

Cobb, T. (1994) 'Web Vocabprofile: An Adaptation of Heatley & Nation's (1994) *Range*'. Accessed 18 November 2007. http://www.lextutor.ca/vp/eng/

Council of Europe (2007) 'Common European Framework of Reference for Languages'. Accessed 5 November 2008. http://www.coe.int/t/dg4/linguistic/Source/Framework_EN.pdf

Citizenship and Immigration Canada (CIC) (2008) 'Applying for Citizenship'. Accessed 4 November, 2008. http://www.cic.gc.ca/english/citizenship/index.asp

Citizenship and Immigration Canada (CIC) (2008). *A Look at Canada*. Accessed 4 November 2008. http://www.cic.gc.ca/ENGLISH/resources/publications/look/index.asp

Citizenship and Immigration Canada (CIC) (2010) 'Applications Forms and Guides'. Accessed 2 February 2010. http://www.cic.gc.ca/english/index.asp

Crick, B. (2007) 'Saturday Extra Interview'. Accessed 28 April 2007. http://www.abc.net.au/rn/saturdayextra/stories/2007/1906949.htm

Department for Universities Innovation and Skills. Accessed 5 November 2008. http://www.dcsf.gov.uk/curriculum_esol/level/E3/

Derwing, T. and R. Thomson (2005) 'Citizenship Concepts in LINC Classrooms', *TESL Canada Journal* 23 (1): 44–62.

Gordon, S. (2007) 'Integrating Immigrants: Morality and Loyalty in US Naturalization Practice', *Citizenship Studies* 11 (4): 367–82.

Gorman, D. and M.L. Ernst (2004) 'Test Review: The Comprehensive Adult Student Assessment System (CASAS) Life Skills Reading Tests', *Language Assessment Quarterly* 1 (1): 73–84.

Halliday, M.A.K. (1985) *Spoken and Written Language* (Geelong: Deakin University Press).

Higham. John (1952) 'Origins of Immigration Restriction, 1882–1897: A Social Analysis', *The Mississippi Valley Historical Review* 39 (1): 77–88. Accessed 23 October 2008. http://www.jstor.org/stable/1902845

Hughes, A. (2003) *Testing for Language Teachers*. 2nd edition (Cambridge: Cambridge University Press).

Joshee, R. and T.M. Derwing (2005) 'The Unmaking of Citizenship Education for Adult Immigrants in Canada', *Journal of International Migration and Integration* 6 (1): 61–80.

Kiwan, D. (2008) 'A Journey to Citizenship in the United Kingdom', *International Journal of Multicultural Studies* 10 (1): 60–75.

Mayo, M. and A. Rooke (2006) 'Active Learning for Active Citizenship: Evaluation Report'. Accessed 29 January 2008. http://www.togetherwecan.info/files/downloads/active_citizenship/alac/ALAC%20Report_A4.pdf

McKay, A (2007) 'An investigation of strategies and programs that assist refugees and migrants into employment'. Accessed 12 July 2009. http://www.churchilltrust.com.au/content.php?id=112

Moritoshi, P. (2001) *The Test of English for International Communication (TOEIC): Necessity, Proficiency Levels, Test Score Utilisation and Accuracy* (Unpublished Manuscript: University of Birmingham).

Office of Public Sector Information (OPSI) (2002) Nationality, Immigration and Asylum Act. Accessed 5 November, 2008. http://www.opsi.gov.uk/acts/acts2002/ukpga_20020041_en_1

O'Loughlin, K. (1995) 'Lexical Density in Candidate Output on Direct and Semi-direct Versions of an Oral Proficiency Test', *Language Testing* 12 (2): 217–37.

Piller, I. (2001) 'Naturalisation Language Testing and its Basis in Ideologies of Natonal Identity and Citizenship', *The International Journal of Bilingualism* 5 (3): 259–77.

Shohamy, E. (1985) *A Practical Handbook in Language Testing* (Tel Aviv: Tel Aviv University).

Somerville, W. (2007) 'The Immigration Legacy of Tony Blair'. Accessed 4 November 2008. http://www.migrationinformation.org/feature/display.cfm?ID=600

Teachers of English to Speakers of Other Languages (TESOL) (2003) *Standards for Adult Education ESL Programs* (Alexandria, VA: Teachers of English to Speakers of Other Languages).

Teachers of English to Speakers of Other Languages (TESOL) (2007) Home page. Retrieved 18 November 2007. http://www.tesol.org/s_tesol/index.asp

US Citizenship and Immigration Services (USCIS) (2008) Home Page. Retrieved 4 November 2008. http://www.uscis.gov/portal/site/uscis

US Citizenship and Immigration Service (USCIS) (2008) 'Naturalization Test Redesign Project: Civics Item Selection Analysis'. Accessed 4 November 2008. http://www.uscis.gov/files/nativedocuments/M-693.pdf

US Citizenship and Immigration Service (USCIS) (2006) 'USCIS Naturalization Test Redesign'. Accessed 18 November 2007. http://www.uscis.gov/files/pressrelease/FactSheetNatzTest113006.pdf

US Citizenship and Immigration Service (USCIS) (2008) 'A Guide to Naturalization Handbook'. Accessed 5 November 2008. http://www.uscis.gov/files/article/M-476.pdf

US Citizenship and Immigration Service (USCIS) (2008) 'A Guide to Naturalization Web Page'. Accessed 5 November 2008. http://www.uscis.gov/natzguide

UK Border Agency (2008) Home page. Accessed 21 October 2008. http://www.ukba.homeoffice.gov.uk

UK Border Agency (2008) *The Path to Citizenship: Government Response to Consultation* (Norwich: UK Home Office).

UK Border Agency (2008) *The Path to Citizenship: Analysis of Consultation Responses*. (Norwich: UK Home Office).

UK Home Office (2003) *The New and the Old. The Report of the 'Life in the United Kingdom' Advisory Group* (Croydon: Home Office Social Policy Unit).

UK Home Office (2007a) Knowledge of Life in the UK. v.0.15. Accessed 1 January 2007. http://www.ind.homeoffice.gov.uk

UK Home Office (2007) *Life in the United Kingdom: A Journey to Citizenship*. 2nd edition (Norwich: UK Home Office).

UK Home Office, Border and Immigration Agency (2003) 'Life in the UK Test Home Page'. Accessed 5 November 2008. http://www.lifeintheuktest.gov.uk/

UK Home Office, Border and Immigration Agency (2008) *The Path to Citizenship: Next Steps in Reforming the Immigration System* (Norwich: UK Home Office).

Weir, C.J. (2005) *Language Testing and Validation, an Evidence-based Approach* (Basingstoke: Palgrave Macmillan).

Wright, S. (2004) *Language Policy and Language Planning, from Nationalism to Gobalisation* (Basingstoke: Palgrave Macmillan).

Wright, S. (2008) 'Citizenship tests in Europe: Editorial Introduction', *International Journal of Multicultural Studies* 10 (1): 1–9.

7
Civic Integration in the Netherlands

Christina Slade

It was in the home of tolerance and multiculturalism, the Netherlands, that new European forms of testing for citizenship first came into prominence. The Dutch case has received a great deal of attention, both scholarly and popular. As one commentator puts it:

> Dutch integration policy has been well documented and one can safely say that, for a medium-sized country, the Netherlands is one of the most over-studied cases in the international migration literature.

> (Vink, 2007, 337)

This chapter is not yet another study in the field. Rather, it places the Dutch case in context. The Netherlands were so widely regarded as leaders in the field of tests for civic integration that when Australia was considering introducing a test for citizenship in 2006, the Government dispatched Immigration officials to the Hague.[1] The Dutch case is particularly informative since the Netherlands were regarded as the European bastion of toleration and multiculturalism through the second half of the twentieth century. The seismic shift became most evident in the years post-9/11. Following the murder of the film maker Theo van Gogh in 2004, there was a rise of suspicion of Islamic minorities in the Netherlands, the murder sending shockwaves through Dutch society. The Dutch have prided themselves on their tolerance and acceptance of ethnic difference at least since the Golden Age. They welcomed large diasporic communities from North Africa, Turkey and their former colonies in Indonesia since the Second World War. Until the violent death of Pim Fortuyn, a flamboyant politician of segregationist views, the public and international image had been of exemplary race relations in Amsterdam. In fact, the story is more complex.

The Dutch experience

There is a characteristic Dutch flavour to the Theo van Gogh case: one much debated since the murder. One commentator remarked immediately after the murder of van Gogh:

> When Pim Fortuyn rose to (posthumous) power on an anti-immigrant agenda in 2001, and now again with the assaults on Muslim schools and mosques after the murder of Theo van Gogh, foreign commentators expressed surprise. That this could happen in the Netherlands, of all places – that cool little country where they legalised prostitution, pot and gay marriage – how could they hate foreigners?
>
> The misunderstanding here is that Dutch people have a long tradition of tolerance. This is not true. The way I would put it, is that over the ages, Dutch people have not so much learned to tolerate, as well as to ignore differences.
>
> ('Values that Shake the World', 2004)

Ian Buruma's masterly narrative, *Murder in Amsterdam: The Death of Theo van Gogh and the Limits of Toleration* (2006), explores the extraordinary circumstances of a culture which produced such neo-conservative anti-Islamic politicians as Fortuyn, Geert Wilders and the Somali-born Ayaan Hirsi Ali in the early years of the twenty-first century. He traces the history of Amsterdam in the Golden Age as a centre where Jews were welcomed and permitted to worship (2006, 18). His view is that in the twentieth century the Dutch record is more equivocal: Moroccan guest workers in particular were never really welcomed as migrants (2006, 23). Vink notes that concern about a possible 'clash of civilizations' between Islamic and Dutch values was pointed out by Frits Bolkenstein, then leader of the liberal VVD party and that there had been debate about a new 'underclass' during the 1980s (Vink, 2007, 338–9).

A historical view of Dutch tolerance is laid out by Shorto (2004) in his popular historical work, *The Island at the Centre of the World*. He argues that New York, long seen as the archetypal American mixing pot, draws not on English non-conformist models of tolerance but from the Dutch, through its beginnings as New Amsterdam. As he says:

In the 1620s a debate on the meaning of wisdom and tolerance had raged through the Dutch provinces [...]. Its climax – really a watershed in human thought – came with Arminius' follower Simon Episcopius declaring in a series of carefully reasoned arguments that the strength of the state derived not from maintaining a single, firmly held faith, but from allowing its citizens freedom of worship and intellectual inquiry.

(Shorto, 2004, 135–6)

Shorto's tale is a historical detective story, in which he identifies the shadowy Adriaen van der Donck as the prime mover of the particular political flavour of New Amsterdam, with its insistence on tolerance, representation and individual rights. But even the rather more conventional directors of the West India Company, such as Peter Stuyvesant, welcomed schismatics of all types to New Amsterdam, including Protestant dissenters rejected by the straight-laced and intolerant New England settlements. Shorto is at pains to point out that it would be an anachronism to talk of such tolerance as 'celebration of difference': it was rather both a pragmatic and intellectually motivated strategy for avoiding conflict.

'Celebration of difference' is no better as a description of modern Dutch tolerance than it was of New Amsterdam. The oddly named doctrine of pillarisation (*verzuiling*) or consociationalism as it was baptised by Arend Lijphart ('Values that Shake the World', 2004) underpins Dutch tolerance. Pillarisation was a doctrine of the legal requirement of equal treatment for those of different religious faiths – notably at the time Protestant and Catholic – and later of political orientation. In the aftermath of the bitter religious wars of the sixteenth century, and the combining of the northern Calvinist Protestant communities with the Roman Catholic south led to a policy of separation of the community into pillars which stood alone but were mutually tolerant. With the rise of socialism in the nineteenth century, socialist and liberal pillars were added. This principle played itself out in state support for religious schools of different faiths, and strong alliances between the press and particular groups. Even state housing was distributed on sectarian grounds.

When in the 1970s sizeable communities of Muslims came to the Netherlands (chiefly to work as labourers), the pillarisation principle was applied. In fact, van der Veer (2001) suggests that accommodating Islam in the Dutch East Indies was an important factor in the formalisation of the principles of pillarisation in the nineteenth century.

In the Dutch case of 'pillarization' we find a pacification of religious and ideological oppositions, but also a model for participation in a plural society. The first social science theory of plural society, formulated by Furnivall, is based on Indonesia and indeed the postcolonial *pancasila* concept has been inspired by Dutch pillarization. The idea is that religious identity is the channel through which one arrives at national identity and the two remain connected.

Pillarisation implies that different communities are separate and distinct, and that when negotiation is necessary it takes place between representatives of the communities. At this level, there must be shared canons of debate; but the pillars remained separated.

It is perhaps an over-simplification to say that pillarisation assumes that different communities are set in separate silos: the Dutch state has allowed and indeed encouraged lively debate across sectarian boundaries. Pillarisation was, as tolerance often is, associated with a claim that difference can only be tolerated if it appears in a private capacity, outside the public sphere of state jurisdiction. Difference in the private sphere is tolerable – religious difference being conceived of as private. Media outlets were considered as private spaces, remaining pillarised throughout the twentieth century, in spite of the process of depillarisation which began in the 1960s (Wintle, 2000). It is a remarkable fact of Dutch media history that television, radio and the press literally belonged to the religious and political groupings, while elsewhere in the Western world such close connections between interest groups and the media were dissolving. Only with the rise of new forms of mediated experience, and the interpenetration of the public and private spheres, the silos or pillars which sustained tolerance disappeared. As commercial television arrived in the Netherlands in the 1990s, and as the ubiquitous satellite dish spread across the country, the separation of the pillars failed. The consequence was not greater tolerance and understanding between social groups who were able to see the world from different perspectives. It was rather the rise of intolerance. Pillarisation has turned to polarisation.

Vink (2007) argues forcefully against this interpretation that pillarisation, which had been dying out over the second half of the twentieth century, was not the source of the apparent tolerance of Dutch society. Indeed he suggests that it was always something of a *façade*, and that the apparently multicultural society had long concealed deep divides. Joppke points out:

Whereas in the majority of EU countries the unemployment rate for non-EU migrants is about twice that of natives, the Dutch non-EU migrant unemployment rate, despite considerable fluctuations, has been at a minimum three times above that of natives in the past seven years. (2007, 6)

He notes figures not merely for welfare dependency, but also for school dropout rates, prison population (over 37 per cent non-Dutch) and explains that there is a greater concentration of migrants in particular areas, such as Rotterdam, than elsewhere in Europe.

Certainly the Dutch are not alone in the recent rise of anti-immigrant sentiment. In the wake of 9/11 and bombings in London and Madrid, many Western European nations have reformed and tightened procedures for immigration and granting citizenship, including the Netherlands, the United Kingdom, France, Germany and Italy, testing not merely for language capacities in prospective migrants, but also for cultural knowledge. The regimes that ensue implicitly aim to exclude security risks, and hence target Islamic groups in particular. The rhetoric of a 'clash of civilizations', popularised by Huntington (1996) with his emphasis on the forthcoming clash between Muslims and Christians in Europe, gave a veneer of academic respectability to post-9/11 fears and remains a potent factor in the development of migration policy in Europe.

Becoming Dutch

The Dutch, along with the Germans and Scandinavians, had not expected the guest workers of the post-war years to stay on. Immigration policies privileging family reunion, together with generous asylum regimes, confounded those expectations. In the later years of last century, migration to the Netherlands was overwhelmingly for reasons of family reunion. In the case of migrant populations from the former colonies of Indonesia and Surinam, where migrants were often Dutch speaking, there has been a fair degree of integration (Vink, 2007). This has not been so true of the Moroccan population with its penchant for endogamy. It is under these circumstances that the rhetoric of fear of Islamic migration was fostered. According to articles appearing in *Metro*, the popular free newspaper van Gogh wrote for, Rotterdam's population would be more than 50 per cent Islamic by 2010. The famously hospitable and tolerant Dutch began to fear that their own nation would be overwhelmed by a new citizenry who spoke no Dutch and shared few of the values that had fostered prosperity in the state. For those who already held Dutch citizenship, there was nothing that could be done. For those arriving in the country on family reunion, or to marry, there was. The privilege of Dutch citizenship not only could but should be set about with hurdles.

The origins of Dutch citizenship are charted in Prak (1997), where he explains that the forms of participation and citizenship that characterised the Dutch Republic were a specifically urban phenomenon. Prak argues that the revolutionary ideals that were a legacy of the French Revolution did not alter the fundamentally particular exclusionary flavour of urban citizenship in the Netherlands, which was tied to membership of guilds and rights within the City and was as much about excluding outsiders as about participation. The conception of citizenship as participatory in the revolutionary sense 'sat somewhat uncomfortably side-by-side with the urban citizenship', he explains (Prak, 1997, 410). This exclusionary element in Dutch citizenship has come to the fore again.

The shift in Dutch law and the underlying attitudes of the citizenry from the most liberal in Europe in the 1970s has been much discussed and its aetiology much debated (de Leeuw and van Wichelen, 2008; Entzinger, 2003; Joppke, 2007, 2007a; Koopmans & Erbe 2004 Vink, 2007). It is generally agreed that by the late 1980s there was widespread concern about the state's failure to integrate certain migrant communities, as measured by the factors noted above, such as unemployment. In 1996, the first voluntary integration programmes were introduced. In 1998, the *Wet Inburgering Nieuwkomers* (widely known as WIN) was introduced. The WIN was a law according to which new migrants were assisted by local governments to learn the Dutch language and customs and obtain employment. Newcomers were entitled to a 12-month integration course. The WIN as initially conceived was thus *inclusionary*, insofar as it aimed to assist integration. On the other hand, an exclusionary strand began to emerge in the media and was given populist voice by such politicians as Pim Fortuyn. After his murder in 2002 (not, as it happens, at the hands of an immigrant, but of a Dutch animal liberationist), and the subsequent change of government, a cabinet agreement of May 2003 emphasised the exclusionary interpretation of WIN, insofar as newcomers were now required to pass the test, and to prove their ability to integrate (Entzinger, 2003). By 2006, immigrants were required to pay for their own integration courses, and successful completion of the tests became a prerequisite for permanent residence. Joppke explains:

> This creates a linkage between the previously separate domains of migration control and immigrant integration. It also constitutes an entirely new view on immigrant integration. So far, the prevailing

view had been that a secure legal status enhances integration; now the lack of integration is taken as grounds for the refusal of admission and residence. (2007: 7–8)

In the turbulent period following the murder of van Gogh, Rita Verdonk (the minister unhappily known as 'Iron Rita' who later annulled the citizenship of Ayaan Hirsi Ali on the grounds she had misled migration officials when claiming refugee status) proposed a draconian measure: the Integration Abroad Act. This act introduced a test for particular classes of migrants to be taken abroad *before* the granting of a temporary visa. The act came into law in March 2006. The test is not required of US, Australian, New Zealand or Canadian citizens, knowledge migrants, students or self-employed visitors. It is thus aimed particularly at the category of those coming to the Netherlands under family reunion conditions. It is administered in consulates and embassies and much of the test is done by telephone connected to a computer.

The examination comprises of two parts: a test of verbal skills in the Dutch language requiring a limited degree of verbal competence (Common European Framework of Reference (CEFR), Level A 1) and a test of knowledge of Dutch society: geography, history and forms of government. Each test takes about 15 minutes. The cost of the test, 350 Euros, is sufficient to discourage some: its content others. The Education Pack and the CD, *Naar Nederland* (Ministerie van Justitie, 2005), available in a range of languages, was apparently designed to discourage migrants. The film shows dismal rainy days in Amsterdam, queues and images – much ridiculed in the local and international press – of two men kissing in front of the flag of the European Union and a well-endowed bare-breasted woman surging from the surf. With somewhat plodding literalness, the text explains that such behaviour is acceptable in the Netherlands. One assumes these images were designed to give prospective wives pause.

The Integration Abroad test is only the first stage of the civic integration process. On 1 January 2007, a new Integration Act (*Wet Inburgering*) came into effect. A further Civic Integration Test must be passed by those who have already resided in the Netherlands for 5 years or more and have a valid residence permit. Now the requirement was not that prospective citizens should attend integration courses; instead the law was outcome based and required passing the test. Prospective citizens must show that they possess listening, speaking, reading and writing skills in Dutch as a Second Language to the Level NT2. A practical (cost 104 Euros) may be passed by either offering a portfolio of evidence, by examination using role-play or both. The knowledge of Dutch society (37 Euros) is an examination of the candidate's knowledge of Dutch rules and habits, by computer. An examination of Spoken Dutch (52 Euros) by telephone involves answering questions and solving problems, while the Electronic Practical Examination (37 Euros) by computer tests abilities to deal with real-life situation questions such as how to report the birth of child to the municipality.

As with citizenship testing in other countries, there has been debate in the Netherlands about the relevance of questions about, for instance, the Dutch Royal Family; and doubt that many Dutch citizens of impeccable Low country heritage would pass the test. Nevertheless, there is a great deal of popular support for the testing regimes. Indeed a possible extension of the testing regime to those already legally in the country was only averted at the last minute (Joppke, 2007, 7).

Since the change of government in 2007, the centrist Balkenende Government has been under pressure from populist and anti-immigrant politicians such as Geert Wilders, and has in fact tightened up on standards in language testing (VROM2007a) rather than softening legislation. The Minister responsible for integration, Elsa Vogelaar, introduced a 2007–11 Integration memorandum (*Integrationota, Zorg dat je erbij hoort!* Make sure you fit in!) with the express purpose of attempting to avoid the polarisation which had developed, calling for active participation as antidote:

> Just as their native counterparts, ethnic minorities are expected to do their best to find their place in society by learning the language, completing their education, earning a living and taking responsibility for their children's upbringing, all of which are impossible without active citizenship.
>
> (Vogelaar, 2007)

While the tone is participatory, there is a strong element of exclusionary citizenship. To use the words of Joppke, the Dutch have moved towards what he calls 'repressive liberalism' (2007, 14). He goes on:

> The perceived need to master global competition is indeed one reason why old group narratives of multiculturalisms [...] are giving way to a new focus on her autonomy and self sufficiency.' (2007, 15)

Prak talked of the citizenship of the urban Dutch of the pre-Republican times as exclusionary, both protecting the guilds and enhancing trade.

It may not be to draw too long a bow to see new forms of citizenship recalling those of the past.

Assumptions of the Dutch civic integration regime

In common with civic integration tests elsewhere, the Dutch model of filtering prospective migrants shares assumptions about cultural identity and belonging that are unexamined and ill-justified. The tests are predicated on the view that certain types of cultural knowledge create 'good citizens'. The complex theorising of the relations between the state, its citizens and its laws is reduced to a set of requirements, linguistic, cultural and financial, assumed to provide the right filter for the new European.

Consider first the pre-entry immigration test, administered outside the Netherlands to prospective migrants especially for family reunion visits. The tests assume that *knowledge* of the country and of the language is a suitable filter for selecting migrants. There is evidence that linguistic skills aid integration, and there is no doubt that the cost of the test, at 350 Euros, will effectively discriminate in favour of those of certain financial means, itself an indicator of ability to integrate. This ignores, however, the equally well-evidenced correlation between successful integration and the development of community. Diasporic communities have been potent drivers for Dutch society, from the Portuguese–Jewish communities in the Golden Age onwards. Family reunion models of immigration were not the invention of soft multiculturalism late in the twentieth century. In more or less formalised terms they have existed since prehistoric times.

When it comes to detail, more questions arise. Language skills may correlate with ability to integrate, but what specific language and how should those skills be tested? What is functional literacy? If no such tests are required of students or knowledge workers (as Dutch law has it), then functional literacy skills before arrival in the country cannot be considered a *necessary* condition of integration. Indeed many knowledge workers in Rotterdam and Amsterdam use only English, and are not regarded as a threat to the nation. On the other hand, functional literacy is not *sufficient* for integration. The widespread unemployment and alienation of fluent Dutch speakers in the second or later generation of migrants is clear evidence of that.

A further assumption underpinning testing regimes takes the view that knowledge of norms is sufficient to guarantee adherence to those norms. Just because a person knows what the local culture or others say that they ought to do does not mean that they do it. So someone may understand that homosexuality is legal or bare breasts acceptable in public but that is no guarantee that that person will behave suitably. To take an extreme counter example, my knowledge that female circumcision is customary in a country I am visiting or in which I am living may not stop me from attempting forcibly to intervene should that practice be imposed on my daughter. In that case, I know local norms but reject them. Less contentiously, many of those who are well aware of practices that are legal in other nations, such as the death penalty in the United States, reserve the right to protest should they, for economic reasons, say, move to the United States. Such a protest would be regarded as a right if the incomer became a citizen.

The same lack of clarity about testing holds for the in-country examination that follows 5 years of residence in the Netherlands. Linguistic and cultural fluency do not guarantee desirable styles of integration. Broadly, immigrants are expected to accept the norms of Dutch society, not at the rather trivial level of knowing the names of the provinces, but in a much deeper fashion. The norms of religious toleration are expected to take precedence over the religious beliefs they have held heretofore, which may not respect such toleration. It is evident why that is regarded as desirable, but far less evident that successful completion of language and cultural knowledge tests is any guarantee of integration in the appropriate sense. Mohammed Bouyeri, the murderer of Theo van Gogh, was educated in the Dutch system, attending a higher level vocational school and was integrated in terms of language and cultural knowledge. The note he pinned to the body of Theo van Gogh was in Dutch rhyming couplets. Later when he was arrested, he wrote an *afscheidsbrief* or conventional Dutch farewell letter entitled *In Bloed Gedoopt/ Baptised with Blood*. It runs:

> Dit is dan mijn laatste woord...
> Door kogels doorboord...
> In bloed gedoopt...
> Zoals ik had gehoopt

> This is then my last word
> Shot through with bullets
> Baptised with blood
> Just as I had hoped.

Bouyeri had a command of such fine details of Dutch culture as the conventions of rhyming couplets composed for special occasions. His cultural knowledge proved no guarantee of the values the tests are designed to screen for.

Olivier Roy in *Globalised Islam* (2004) explains such cases with a particular focus on France. He describes the background to the rise of forms of Islam and explains the *reislamization* and *islamist* movements of modern France as a reinterpretation of Islam. Islam itself, he argues, is an essentially communal, even tribal, affair. Modern Europeanised Islam, designed as it is for disenfranchised unemployed youth who have been raised and educated in a European culture, takes over the language of the individual and of self-fulfilment. In France, with its tradition of *citoyenneté* and assimilation, the disenfranchised youths who rioted in November of 2005 were behaving in the best tradition of France. As the journalist Tom Heneghan wrote at the time:

> the rioters were unmistakably French, and not only because almost all were citizens. They have internalized French political values so well that they want France to live up to its promise of liberty, equality and fraternity. Their dream was not to overthrow the system, but to make it work so they could get ahead too. Political violence is as French as baguettes and berets. (2006)

From the bicycles ridden by murderer and murdered in the Theo van Gogh case, to the bluntness with which both Theo van Gogh and Mohammed Bouyeri expressed themselves, the murder of van Gogh had an unmistakeable Dutch flavour. It was not the notion of Dutchness celebrated in civic integration tests, that defines Dutch culture in terms of its Royal Family, traditions of thank you notes and finely pared cheese. It is instead the Netherlands of the twenty-first century, of independent globalised youth. Bouyeri joined a group of disaffected youths based in the Hague and called 'Hofstat', identifying themselves as Dutch as well as Islamic. Bouyeri and his friends followed the path of Roy's reislamisation partly because of their level of integration. Their failure to succeed in 'Dutch' terms was part of their disaffection.

At another level, civic integration regimes in the Netherlands as elsewhere draw on a mythical notion of the relation between culture, the nation state and citizens. While never made explicit, there is a notion that relation is one-to-one (ie. each legal nation has a single cultural manifestation) and onto (a different cultural identity can be associated with each nation). Both are absurd, as is the assumption that each prospective citizen should take on the one identity that already exists in the nation state. All too often the civic integration regimes appear to conceptualise migrants as disembodied *tabulae rasae*, which the nation state can fill appropriately with language, values and practices. This was never the case in Europe, where migration and power struggles changed boundaries for millennia. Even the nineteenth-century nation states have fragile and mutable identities. A reaction to pressures of globalisation and the post-9/11 world is not unexpected, but the nation states to which citizens wish to hark back were at best idealisations. As Dutch and Belgian television stations pander to national nostalgia by producing soap operas in local dialects so thick that they require Dutch subtitles, satellite dishes and cable give citizens access to hundreds, even thousands of channels. The 'imagined communities' we inhabit (to draw on Anderson's much used term) cut across national boundaries to include the communities of mother tongue, of intellectual and emotional belonging, as well as those of physical location. We all, not just migrants, live in a globalised and migratory world.

In effect, civic integration tests redefine the links from legal citizenship to its cultural components, making the cultural a pre-condition for the legal, rather than a manifestation or legitimation of the legal. As the legal structures at the level of the nation state come under pressure from increasing globalisation, the nation no longer has control of the cultural (let alone the financial). Television, language and commerce: all not only extend well beyond national borders but also are regulated beyond the national sphere. The Netherlands, as part of the EU grouping, is developing its civic integration regime in a powerful transnational regulatory bloc. The very notion of citizenship itself is in question – for all EU citizens are both citizens of a nation state and transnational citizens. What impact does this have on the tie between cultural knowledge and national belonging?

The EU context

The 2004 Dutch Presidency of the European Union was notable for Dutch initiatives to introduce EU-wide policy on immigration and integration. The Dutch initiative was a first for the Union. As Joanne van Selm puts it:

> The policy documents on which the EU has managed to agree since 1992, when the EU first decided to cooperate on migration and asylum issues, have generally taken a minimalist approach.
>
> (van Selm, 2007)

The Hague Programme, introduced in November 2004, took a new direction, introducing an ambitious 5-year agenda for policy. The Hague Programme had the support of the European Council consisting of heads of all the EU states, and was significantly subtitled 'Strengthening Freedom, Security and Justice in the European Union'. The security agenda was uppermost in the listed aims of the Programme, with the goal of fighting organised crime, and repressing the threat of terrorism made quite explicit (van Selm, 2007). Weiner talked in 1998 of a process in which European citizenship as 'identity generating and community building' had been reduced to a set of minimal political rights (1998, 11). The Hague Programme reintroduces the cultural as a hurdle for prospective immigrants rather than as a process in which new and old citizens jointly engage.

The Hague Programme must be seen in the broader context of EU policies on a range of cultural and legal issues. What it is to *be* a transnational citizen of the EU? Does such citizenship convey a further identity over and above the constitutive national identities? Is there a shared identity among European citizens and if so, is it a democratic identity? Participation as a citizen of the EU, as opposed to a citizen of the nation, is at best a vexed notion. A reaction to the so-called 'democratic deficit', the feeling that the EU bureaucracy operates without democratic constraints, has been evident in the Danish, Dutch, French and Irish referenda dealing with the EU constitution. At the very least, there is scepticism among Europeans about their shared identity.

As a concept, EU citizenship and its linkage to nation, culture and heritage has been the focus of much agonised debate and enquiry. Each entry of a new member state sets off a process of redefinition. The mantra of 'equality in diversity' is an attempt to celebrate the difference of Europeans. Smismans (2007), in a report on a 3-year project looking at active citizenship in the European Union, draws a sharp distinction between participatory and identity-based accounts, but says very little on the issue of new citizens to the union. Indeed, while there has been a great deal of debate and policy in the EU dealing with cultural diversity, Staiger (2009) notes that emphasis on cultural diversity 'aims to appeal to regional and national cultures and marks them as consistent with a unified European citizenry'. Cultural diversity is diversity *within* the Union and policies have been notably quiet on the culture of newcomers. The exclusionary force of European Union cultural policy and its impact on the non-citizen, even those resident within its borders, has also been much discussed (eg. Benhabib, 2004; Bosniak, 2006).

In fact there has been a Europe-wide shift in the discourses relating to immigration, which the Dutch merely reflect. As one theorist puts it:

> In the evolving EU framework on the integration of immigrants, a fierce struggle is taking place between the overall approach presented under the EU framework for the integration of immigrants, and the actual legally binding acts produced by a common immigration policy.
>
> (Carrera, 2006, 4)

This struggle is played out in the European policy context, and has led to tension between discourses of social inclusion, on the one hand, and exclusion, on the other.

What is evident is a widespread nervousness about migration in the nations of 'old Europe'. While 2008 was formally the European Year of Intercultural Dialogue, the year also saw a wave of new regulatory measures, such as the introduction of Civic Integration testing in Germany as of 1 September 2008, and the move of the French, during their presidency preoccupied with the shakeout in the financial sector, to revitalise issues of trans-European immigration control (Barber, 2008). Sarkozy himself was, as Interior Minister, responsible for the Loi Sarkozy of 2003 in France, drastically reducing the grounds for legal permanent residence and making the receipt of a 10-year residence card dependent on knowledge of French language and values. Sarkozy complained of the habits of the migrant groups, citing what he called 'totally clannish communalism' '(communautarisme)' (quoted and translated, Joppke, 2007a: 253).

The EU policies on migration were reviewed in the Third Annual Report on Migration and Integration (Commission of the EC, 2007, henceforth EC, 2007). New EU policies, such as the Common Basic Principles for Immigrant Integration Policies and the Common Agenda for Integration adopted by the European Council in September of 2005:

> Provide [...] supportive EU mechanisms [for concrete proposals] developing a distinctive EU approach to integration through cooperation and exchange of good practice. (EC, 2007)

The report cites networks of National Contact Points, Handbooks on Integration for Policy Makers and Practitioners (with a second edition in 2007), a conference held in 2006 in Rotterdam on 'Integrating Cities', a European Integration Forum and a Commissioner's Group on Migration

Issues. On 23 March 2007, following a meeting of Interior Ministers in Northern Germany, it was agreed that all immigrants to Europe could be required to sit a test demonstrating their knowledge of the host country.

The report talks of Common European modules for migrant integration, but begs the question of whether there is a common European identity for the various tests to assess. It is striking that the EU and its policy bodies, while self-consciously developing notions of transnational belonging and identity, fail adequately to recognise the many different sub- and supra-national forms of belonging and identity of its own citizens, let alone of those who might one day be citizens. Diasporic communities, supported by transnational media worlds, networked communities, interest groups and NGOs all serve to create forms of political identity which extend beyond the nation state; indeed beyond Europe.

While buzz terms such as 'intercultural dialogue', 'social inclusion' and 'social protection' make an appearance, throughout the report the emphasis is on the economic impact of immigration. So for instance:

> The Commission monitors the impact of national reform programmes with annual Joint Employment Reports and encourages Member States to make immigrants' labour market integration a more explicit dimension of employment.

and goes on:

> Immigrants represent an important pool of potential **entrepreneurs** in Europe. Their businesses have a significant impact on EU economic growth. An Ethnic Minority Entrepreneurship Network was set up to exchange information to overcome difficulties in setting up businesses. A study on good practice in this area will be published and a conference is planned for spring 2008. (EC, 2007)

The implicit emphasis on the economic benefits of inward migration across the EU is a reflection of the new exclusionary model of citizenship. The explicit emphasis on employment was noted by Joppke (2007a) in the statement of the original Hague Programme. He then argued that

> the strong focus on employment [...] is the one commonality in the otherwise opposite civic integration and antidiscrimination policies. On the one hand this is simply due to the fact that, unlike the classic

immigrant nations, where immigrants are generally working, immigrants to Europe often walk into welfare dependency. On the other hand, at a deeper level, it reveals that immigrants are no longer to be integrated into a self-contained nation state but are to be placed into a state engaged in global competition. (2007a: 268–9)

Whether Joppke is correct to contrast the classic nations of immigration and the EU with respect to the employability of recent migrants, he here identifies a crucial issue for citizenship testing. The nation state continues to be the vehicle of citizenship even in a transnational environment such as the EU, while at the same time the cultural and economic practices of citizenship are globalised, as are the religious and political movements civic integration is designed to undermine. Citizenship testing, civic integration and integration abroad continue to be a national matter, when the challenges faced are no longer within the control of the nation state.

Conclusion

During the 2005 UK presidency of the EU, Charles Clarke, then Home Secretary, laid out what he thought of as the common European citizenship:

> What we agreed very strongly was that the values of our societies – democracy, respect for other faiths, free speech, the rule of law, free media and so on – are values which we would expect everyone wanting to settle in these countries to respect.
>
> (Watson, 2006)

Elsa Vogelaar of the Netherlands in 2007 put it thus:

> It is important to create a society in which people feel safe and have a sense of familiarity and connectedness. In addition, integration can only be achieved if minorities and native Dutch accept this society as their own. This will not be possible without broad-based support for the freedoms, rights and duties that go hand-in-hand with life under the Dutch rule of law.
>
> (Vogelaar, 2007)

Civic integration tests developed in the Netherlands test language skills and functional cultural abilities – the abilities to get around in the

Netherlands. The values mentioned by Clarke – respect for faith, free media – and the broad-based support for freedoms, rights and duties Vogelaar herself mentions are not included in the test. It may be, as I have argued above, that such values cannot be directly tested. An appropriate *response* to a question about one's values is not necessarily an indication of how one behaves or of one's values. Testing values is a complex matter, perhaps too complex for citizenship tests. However that may be, there is at the very least a disconnect between the rhetoric of the reasons for civic integration testing and the practices of testing.

There is nothing untoward in the desire for a safe community. What Clarke calls 'the values of our societies' are indeed widely held across and beyond Europe. There is, furthermore, little surprising about the fear engendered among what Vogelaar calls 'native Dutch' when confronted by the changing nature of their society, nor of the resentment of 'minorities' if they do not feel accepted in the society. What is surprising is the widespread conviction that civic integration tests will create safe and value-driven communities. Developing strong communities requires more than a group of people with shared (and relatively low-level) language, and knowledge of bureaucratic techniques.

Perhaps it is the very lack of subtlety of such testing regimes that accounts for their adoption and general acceptance in the Netherlands. In this respect, the new Dutch testing regimes may resemble the dictation test imposed on prospective migrants to Australia described in Chapter 2. Migrants were obliged to pass a test in any European language of their choice. Originally designed to exclude Indians and Japanese who did not, naturally, speak or write any European language at all, by an unsubtle quantifier shift the requirement was transformed: the prospective migrant could be obliged to pass a dictation test in *any* European language chosen by the examiner. Egon Kisch (*ADB Online*), a multilingual central European of undesirable political background, was excluded in 1934, having passed in all languages readily available to immigration officials but finally failing in Scots Gaelic. The case was overturned on appeal, with Scots Gaelic being ruled not to be European to the chagrin of the Scottish settlers (High Court of Australia, 1935). The lesson is that instruments designed to exclude particular groups are readily transformed to serve short-term political aims. The exclusionary force of Dutch citizenship tests is scarcely disguised, and puts a powerful tool in bureaucratic hands. The cultural and linguistic knowledge deemed necessary for citizenry is not a matter to be decided lightly.

There is no doubt that these issues arouse passion. Immigration to the European Union must be understood in the broader context of a globalised market and a post-9/11 world. The civic integration testing regimes developed in the Netherlands are designed to meet two imperatives – to exclude migrants who may be a cost to the state and to restrict Islamic migration in particular. New tests across the EU and more widely have replicated those features. The question remains whether the tests achieve the sorts of society of shared values and common purposes that had been hoped for.

Note

1. Private communication, Australian Ambassador to the Hague, Stephen Brady, March 2007.

References

Anderson, Benedict (1983) *Imagined Communities: Reflections on the Origin and Spread of Nationalism* (London: Verso).
Barber, Tony (2008) 'EU Pact set to Encourage Skilled Migration and Discourage Illegals', *Financial Times*, 25 September 2008: 12.
Beck, Ulrick (2002) 'The Cosmopolitan Society and its Enemies', *Theory, Culture and Society* 19 (1–2): 17–44.
Benhabib, Seyla (1992) *Situating the Self: Gender, Community and Postmodernism in Contemporary Ethics* (London: Polity Press).
Benhabib, Seyla (2004) *The Rights of Others. Aliens, Residents and Citizens* (Cambridge: Cambridge University Press).
Bosniak, L. (2006) *The Citizen and the Alien* (Princeton, NJ: Princeton University Press).
Buruma, Ian (2006) *Murder in Amsterdam: The Death of Theo van Gogh and the Limits of Tolerance* (New York: Penguin).
Council of the European Union (2004) *Immigrant Integration Policy in the European Union*, Brussels, 19 November.
de Leeuw, Marc and Sonja van Wichelen (2008) 'Transformations of "Dutchness": From Happy Multiculturalism to the Crisis of Dutch Liberalism', in G. Delanty, R.Wodak and P. Jones (eds) *Identity, Belonging and Migration* (Liverpool: Liverpool University Press), ch 13: 261–78.
Entzinger, Hans (2003) 'The Rise and Fall of Multiculturalism: The Case of the Netherlands', in C. Joppke and E. Morawska (eds) *Towards Assimilation and Citizenship* (Basingstoke: Palgrave Macmillan).
Fraser, Nancy (1993) 'Rethinking the Public Sphere: A Contribution to the Critique of Actually existing Democracy', in B. Robbins (ed.) *The Phantom Public Sphere* (Minneapolis, MN: University of Minnesota Press): 1–32.
Heneghan, Tom (2006) 'The French Intifada that Wasn't' (Paris: Reuters).
Huntington, Samuel P. (1996) *The Clash of Civilizations and the Remaking of the New World Order* (New York: Touchstone).
Jacobs, D. & Rea, A. (2007) "OPEN FORUM: The End of National Models? Integration Courses and Citizenship Trajectories in Europe", *IJMS: International Journal on Multicultural Societies* 9 (2): 264–83.

Joppke, Christian (2007) 'Beyond National Models: Civic Integration Policies for Immigrants in Western Europe', *West European Politics* 30 (1): 1–22.

Joppke, Christian (2007a) 'Transformation of Immigrant Immigration: Civic Integration and Anti Discrimination in the Netherlands, France and Germany', *World Politics* 59: 243–73.

Koopmans, R. & Erbe, J. (2004) 'Towards a European Public Sphere? Vertical and horizontal dimensions of Europeanized political communication,' *Innovation* 17 (2): 97–118.

Ministerie van Justitie Den Haag (2005) *Naar Nederland Film, Handleiding* (Instructions) (Fotoboek: Thieme Meulenhoff, Utrecht).

Prak, Maarten (1997) 'Burghers into Citizens: Urban and National Citizenship During the Revolutionary Era (c. 1800)', *Theory and Society* 26 (4): 403–20.

Robbins, Bruce (1993) *The Phantom Public Sphere*. (Minneapolis, MN: University of Minnesota Press).

Roy, Olivier (2004) *Globalised Islam: The Search for the New Ummah* (London: Hurst and Co).

Shorto, Russell (2004) *The Island at the Centre of the World* (London: Doubleday).

Smismans, Steyn (2007) 'New Governance: The Solution for Active European Citizenship? Or the End of Citizenship?' Taskforce on Legal Issues Ia: *NEWGOV: New modes of Governance* Reports to the European Commission within Sixth Framework Programme CITI-CT- 2004–506392, Brussels.

Staiger, Ute (2009) 'New agendas: Culture and Citizenship in EU Policy', *International Journal of Cultural Policy*. 1 (15): 1–16.

Vink, M.P. (2007) ' "Dutch 'Multiculturalism" Beyond the Pillarisation Myth', *Political Studies Review* 5: 337–50.

Wiener, Antje (1998) *'European' Citizenship Practice – Building Institutions of a Non-State* (Boulder, CO: Westview Press).

Wintle, M. (2000) *An Economic and Social History of the Netherlands, 1800–1920. Demographic, Economic and Social Transition* (Cambridge: Cambridge University Press).

Young, Iris Marion (1990) *Justice and the Politics of Difference* (Princeton, NJ: Princeton University Press).

Web sites

Australian Dictionary of Biography Online (ADB) *Edwin Egon Kisch*. Accessed 7 October 2008. http://www.adb.online.anu.edu.au/biogs/A150043b.htm

Carrera, S. (ed.) (2006) The Nexus between Immigration, Integration and Citizenship in the EU Centre for European policy studies. http://www.ceps.be

Commission of the European Communities (2007) *Third Annual Report on Migration and Integration* Accessed 9 October 08. http://ec.europa.eu/justice_home/fsj/immigration/docs/com_2007_512_en.pdf

Dekker, P and Ester, P. (2004) Ideological identification and (de) pillarization in the Netherlands. Accessed 25 May 2005. www.njss.nl. http://nl.wikipedia.org/wiki/Afbeelding:Afscheidsbrief.jpg

High Court of Australia (1935) 'The King vs Fletcher and Another; ex parte Kisch' HCA1 http://www.austlii.edu.au/cases.cth/HCA/1935/1.html

'Values that shake the world: Tolerance in the Netherlands' (2004) http://www.european-democracy.org/archives/2004/11/22/values-that-shake-the-world-ii-tolerance-in-the-netherlands

Van der Veer, P. (2001) 'The Netherlands and Islam' Lecture at the Occasion of the Dr Hendrik Muller Award, Royal Dutch Academy of Sciences, Amsterdam. http://www2.fmg.uva.nl/gm/articles/pvdv01a.htm

Van Selm, Joanne (2007) 'The Hague Program reflects New European Realities', Migrant Policy Institute. http//:www.migrantinformation.org/Feature/print.cfm?ID=276

Vogelaar, Ella (2007) 'Speech my Minister Vogelaar at the informal EU conference for Integration Ministers'. Accessed 23 November 2007. http://www.sharedspace.nl/pagina.html?id=10812

VROM (2007) 'Integration Memorandum: Make sure you fit in 2007–2011'. Accessed 23 November 2007. http://www.sharedspace.nl/pagina.html?id=11094

VROM (2007) 'Minister Vogelaar to improve Civic Integration test used abroad'. Accessed 23 November 2007. http://www.sharedspace.nl/pagina.html?id=10849

Watson, R. (2006) 'EU leaders want all immigrants to take an entry exam' *The Times*. http://www.open-europe.org.uk/media-centre/article.aspx?newsid=1230

8
The Changing Scope of German Citizenship: From 'Guest Worker' to Citizen?

Martina Möllering

Introduction

According to figures from a 2005 German microcensus, 15 million of Germany's current population of 82 million have 'migration backgrounds'; that is, they are immigrants or have parents or grandparents who came to Germany from elsewhere. Despite these figures, the stance *'Deutschland ist kein Einwanderungsland'* ('Germany is not a country of immigration') has been prevalent in political discourse and the legislation regarding immigration and citizenship assisted in upholding this image. Over the last decade, there has been a major shift in German citizenship law. Up to 2000, Germany was one of the few European countries to base its citizenship laws primarily on *Ius Sanguinis*, the right to obtain citizenship on the basis of descent, rather than place of birth (*Ius Soli*).

The tension between this inflexible way of granting citizenship and the large numbers of immigrants coming to Germany since the 1950s has been noted by scholars of history and social sciences alike (Palmowski, 2008). Although there had been strong migration to Germany since the 1950s, Germany did not define itself as a country of migration and very few migrants obtained German citizenship. Large-scale migration to Germany after the Second World War was based on recruitment contracts that were signed with Italy in 1955, Greece and Spain in 1960, Turkey in 1961, Morocco in 1963, Portugal in 1964, and the former Yugoslav Republic in 1968. But despite the large numbers of migrants coming to Germany – by 1973, there were 2.6 million foreign workers, making up 11.9 per cent of the workforce, and 4 million foreigners in total, amounting to 6.4 per cent of the total population (Brubaker, 1992, 171) – Germany held on to its Empire- and State-Citizenship Law (*Reichs- und Staatsangehörigkeitsgesetz*) of 1913.

The legal definition of what it meant to be German remained unchanged and the political response regarding immigration policies was on an ad hoc basis, with a plethora of different visa categories for different groups of immigrants emerging.

> Guest workers on temporary visas were expected to go home eventually; refugees and asylum seekers were informally 'tolerated' year after year; and 'ethnic German' migrants from the former Soviet Union were already considered *de facto* citizens according to the 1913 citizenship law. A confusing array of residency categories substituted for a clear path to citizenship.
>
> (Göktürk et al., 2007, 4)

There have been attempts at reforming German citizenship laws in 1977 and in 1990, but due to the strong federalist structures determining immigration policies at the state level, no unified principles for naturalisation were set up until the newly elected Social Democrat government under Chancellor Gerhard Schröder complemented the descent-based *Ius Sanguinis* principle of German citizenship law with *Ius Soli*, the right to citizenship based on place of birth. The German rules on citizenship were thoroughly revised with the implementation of the amended Nationality Act (*Staatsangehörigkeitsgesetz*) on 1 January 2000. The rules underwent another lesser revision with the implementation of the Immigration Act (*Zuwanderungsgesetz*) on 1 January 2005.

The Naturalization Act and the introduction of *Ius Soli*

The legislation of 15 July 1999 to reform German citizenship law introduced crucial changes, such as citizenship based on place of birth and a reduced length of residence required for naturalisation. Whereas under the old legislation, at least one parent had to be a German citizen for a child to acquire citizenship by birth, under the new regulation, German citizenship is obtained by the fact of being born in Germany, if at least one parent has residency status or has (qualified) EU citizenship. As of 1 January 2000, a child born in Germany to non-German parents automatically receives German citizenship at birth, if at least one parent has lived legally in Germany for at least 8 years and has the right of permanent residence. Under the new legislation, children can keep dual citizenship – German and the nationality of their parents – but only up to the age of 23. If the child chooses German citizenship at that age, they must give up their foreign citizenship, unless it is impossible or unreasonable to do so. If the child chooses the foreign citizenship, they lose their German citizenship. By the end of 2006, 270,352 children of non-German parents had received German citizenship in addition to that of their parents (Federal Ministry of the Interior: Migration and Integration, April 2008, 112); how many will keep it when they have to decide between the two at age 23 remains to be seen.

It is a fact that Germany has been a country of immigration for a long time [...]. The assertion that 'Germany is not a country of immigration' used to be a defining political principle but has become untenable as the cornerstone of migration and integration policy.
(Government Commission on Migration, 2001)

When the new Immigration Act took effect in 2005, Germany became officially a country of immigration which it had been *de facto* since the late 50s. Since the Act was implemented, most of the provisions for acquiring German citizenship can now be found within a single law. Migrants who wish to become naturalised German citizens have to fulfill the requirements for naturalisation under the Nationality Act (*Staatsangehörigkeitsgesetz*) as last amended by the Act to Implement Residence – and Asylum-Related Directives of the European Union of 19 August 2007, which entered into force on 28 August 2008 (Bundesministerium des Inneren: Nationality Act).

Section 10 (1) of the Nationality Act outlines that immigrants are now eligible for naturalisation after 8 years of habitual residence in Germany if they have permanent residence status and provided they meet the relevant conditions, instead of the 15 years previously required. They have to declare their commitment to the 'free democratic constitutional system enshrined in the Basic Law of the Federal Republic of Germany' and declare that they do not pursue or support any activities opposed to it. Furthermore, they have to be able to financially support themselves and their family and they cannot have been convicted of a crime. The Act further stipulates that an applicant for citizenship has to possess an adequate knowledge of German and knowledge of the legal system, the society and living conditions in the Federal Republic of Germany.

'Adequate knowledge of German' is defined as follows:

The conditions specified in sub-section 1, sentence 1, no. 6 are fulfilled if the foreigner passes the oral and written language examinations leading to the *Zertifikat Deutsch* (equivalent of level B 1 in the Common European Framework of Reference for Languages). Where a minor child is under 16 years of age at the time of naturalization the conditions of sub-section 1, sentence 1, no. 6 shall be fulfilled if the child demonstrates age-appropriate language skills.

(Nationality Act, Section 10/4)

Provisions are made for a reduction of the required 8 years of residence for spouses and children (Section 10/2) and for those applicants demonstrating their efforts at integration (Section 10/3):

Upon a foreigner confirming successful attendance of an integration course by presenting a certificate issued by the Federal Office for Migration and Refugees, the qualifying period stipulated in sub-section 1 shall be reduced to seven years. This qualifying period may be reduced to six years if the foreigner has made outstanding efforts at integration exceeding the requirements under sub-section 1, sentence 1, no. 6, especially if he or she can demonstrate his or her command of the German language.

The aim of avoiding multiple nationality remains a key feature – becoming a naturalised German citizen also requires renouncing one's previous citizenship, although that requirement can be waived under special circumstances, applying for example to elderly persons and victims of political persecution. Applicants may also keep their nationality if it is legally impossible for them to renounce it or if they cannot be expected to do so, for example, because of the excessive cost or degrading procedures used. The same is true if renouncing the foreign nationality would bring serious disadvantages, especially economic disadvantages or problems with property and assets. The rules have also been relaxed for the citizens of most EU countries. These politics of dual nationality have been heavily criticised and they have been described as an impediment to obtaining German citizenship. Green (2005) for example, describes the opposition between the stated ideology of opposing dual citizenship on the one hand and the pragmatic approach of allowing for dual citizenship under a variety of circumstances on the other hand as effectively discouraging naturalisation, thereby continuing to adhere to an exclusive concept of citizenship that might be reflected in the small numbers of non-Germans taking up citizenship (for a discussion, see also Faist, 2007).

From the late 1980s, the number of non-Germans residing in the country had increased sharply from 4.2 million (6.9 per cent of total population) in 1987 to 7.3 million (8.9 per cent) between 1998 and 2004 (Green, 2004 in Palmowski, 2008, 547). Yet, the number of naturalised citizens remains relatively small after the changes in citizenship law were introduced, with a peak in 2000, the year the new law took effect, and declining numbers thereafter:

Naturalised citizens in Germany, 2000–2006

Year	Persons naturalised
2000	186,688
2001	178,098
2002	154,547
2003	140,731
2004	127,153
2005	117,241
2006	124,566
Total	1,029,024

Source: Federal Statistical Office, 30 August 2007, in: Federal Ministry of the Interior: Migration and Integration, April 2008, p. 117.

Another hurdle to taking up German citizenship might be the relatively high standards set for language competence, for example, in comparison to the Netherlands: Level A2 (Chapter 7) or US and Canadian levels described in Chapter 6. As outlined above with reference to the *Nationality Act*, one necessary condition for obtaining German citizenship is 'an adequate knowledge of German', which is defined with reference to the Common European Framework of Reference (CEFR) as level B1. Piet Van Avermaet (2009) in a discussion of testing regimes across Europe describes a range of required levels of language proficiency for immigration and entry (pp. 23–25) as well as in the context of integration and residency policies (pp. 27/28) (for a discussion of different European case studies, see also Extra et al., 2009). Germany's requirement for language proficiency at level B1 sits at the high end in comparison to the countries included in his study. [1] The general descriptors for Level B1, which is labelled the 'Threshold' level as the third of six defined levels, read as follows:

Can understand the main points of clear standard input on familiar matters regularly encountered in work, school, leisure, etc. Can deal with most situations likely to arise when travelling in an area where the language is spoken. Can produce simple connected text on topics which are familiar or of personal interest. Can describe experiences and events, dream, hopes and ambitions and briefly give reasons and explanations for opinions and plans.

A closer look at the different language skills and the abilities described at level B1 reveals that the following skills are of significance:

Reading	Listening	Writing	Spoken Interaction	Spoken Production
• understand texts that consist mainly of high frequency everyday or job-related language.	• understand the main points of clear standard speech on familiar matters regularly encountered in work, school, leisure, etc. • understand the main point of many radio or TV programmes on current affairs or topics of personal or professional interest, when the delivery is relatively slow and clear.	• write simple connected text on topics which are familiar, or of personal interest. • write personal letters describing experiences and impressions, as well as semi-formal letters and formal letters, such as enquiries or complaints.	• deal with most situations likely to arise whilst travelling in an area where the language is spoken. • enter unprepared into conversation on topics that are familiar, of personal interest or pertinent to everyday life (e.g. family, hobbies, work, travel and current events).	• connect phrases in a simple way in order to describe experiences and events, my dreams, hopes and ambitions. • briefly give reasons and explanations for opinions and plans. • narrate a story or relate the plot of a book or film and describe reactions and interpretations.

Applicants can show that they have the requisite language requirements by providing one of the following documentations:

- Successful attendance of an integration course by presenting a certificate issued by the Federal Office for Migration and Refugees/ Successful completion of a language course as part of an integration course; as certified by BAMF (*Bundesamt für Migration und Flüchtlinge*);
- Completion of *Zertifikat Deutsch* (equivalent of level B 1 in the Common European Framework of Reference for Languages) or above;

- Four years of successful schooling in German;
- School Certificate from German school;
- Admitted to Year 10 of a German school (Realschule, Gymnasium oder Gesamtschule);
- University degree from German-speaking University;
- Completed vocational training.

In case none of these can be provided, an applicant for citizenship might be asked to take a language test at an adult education centre (*Volkshochschule*). Applicants can be exempted from having to prove their German language skills in case of illness or disability or due to their age.

The introduction of formal naturalisation tests

The legislation implementing far-reaching changes to German citizenship law as described above was not without controversy, as was to be expected given the insistence on the stance that 'Germany is not a country of immigration' under the Christian Democratic Union (CDU) Government up until the Centre-Left Government of the Social Democrats (*SPD*) and the Green Party came to power in 1998. In 2000, the CDU/CSU posited *Ausländerpolitik* (policy on foreigners) as a major issue in the forthcoming elections, initiating what has become known as the *Leitkulturdebatte*. The term *Leitkultur*-which can be literally translated as 'guiding culture' or 'leading culture', but in this political debate is often taken to mean 'core culture' – was first introduced by Bassam Tibi, professor of political science in Tübingen, who used the term to summarise a set of norms and values characterising the European cultural community (Pautz, 2005, 43). From 2000 onwards, the term became a key feature of the political debate surrounding immigration and integration and it took on connotations of cultural assimilation and a monocultural vision of German society. Tibi (1998) had referred to a European *Leitkultur*, based on Western values, advocating cultural pluralism based on value consensus, a point which he stressed in later media releases (Tibi, 2000).[2]

The term entered the national political debate in October 2000, when Friedrich Merz, then chairman of the CDU parliamentary group in the Bundestag, in a newspaper interview rejected multiculturalism, advocated the restriction of immigration, and called for compulsory assimilation into a German core culture, claiming that immigrants had a duty to adopt the basic cultural values of Germany – the *Leitkultur*.

His comments sparked a heated debate, with Bassam Tibi protesting that his proposal had been appropriated by politicians for their own purposes. The majority of reactions to Merz's proposals were negative with a debate that was split along party lines, with the *SPD* and *Grüne* Government coalition rejecting a German *Leitkultur*.

The *Leitkulturdebatte* has, however, strongly influenced the debate about citizenship tests in Germany and, not surprisingly, the first models for such testing were developed in the CDU/CSU-governed states of Hessen (*Leitfaden Wissen und Werte*, 2006) and Baden-Württemberg (*Gesprächsleitfaden für Einwanderungsbehörden*, 2006). These models for questions to be asked of applicants for citizenship reflect the debate about common values as outlined above as they contained not only detailed questions on German geography, history, and law but also embedded cultural values by asking attitudinal questions such as follows:

> A woman should not be allowed to be in public or to travel without being accompanied by a male relative. What is your opinion on this?
>
> (*Gesprächsleitfaden für Einwanderungsbehörden*,
> *Hessen*, my translation)

The introduction of such guidelines at state level was hotly debated, again very much along party lines (Spiegel online, 23 March 2006), with the strongly opposed view of the *SPD/Grüne* fraction slowly softening (Spiegel online, 24 and 26 March 2006). A compromise position was reached that saw the introduction of a compulsory integration course (*Orientierungskurs*) of 30 hours duration focusing on German language and law, history, and culture. The integration course was to be attended by all future applicants for citizenship and presupposed an intermediate level of German language skills (CEFR B1). It was funded by the Government; applicants for citizenship had to contribute 1 Euro per class, the same as for the language classes offered, with a maximum of 600 hours leading up to level B1 (CEFR).

The decision to refrain from formal testing at a national level was revoked in 2008, and a formal citizenship test was introduced across all German states from 1 September 2008. Currently, applicants for naturalisation are required to pass a formal citizenship test, which is based on an amendment to the Nationality Act in 2007. The tests are carried out by the Federal Office for Migration and Refugees on behalf of the German states (*Länder*) and in conjunction with adult education centres (*Volkshochschulen*) which serve as test centres.

The current German citizenship test: Procedures and preparation

The responsibility for and administration of naturalisation procedures rest with the *Länder* (states). Therefore, applications are submitted to local naturalisation authorities, which also decide on the applications. They inform applicants about the necessary conditions for receiving citizenship, that is, the necessary language skills and proof of civic knowledge, which can be proven by having a leaving certificate from a German school of general education or by having passed a naturalisation test. The naturalisation authorities inform applicants who need to take a naturalisation test of the test centres available.

The actual tests are administered by naturalisation test centres, a list of which is available for each state on the Web site of the Federal Office for Migration and Refuges (*Bundesamt für Migration und Flüchtlinge – BAMF*). The test centres are not in government offices, but in adult education centres (*Volkshochschulen*), which are spread across each state with coverage at the local level (in North-Rhine-Westphalia, for example, 135 centres are listed). Applicants register for a test with the local centre and pay 25 Euro to participate in the test.

The test is a paper-based multiple choice test and it consists of 33 questions, of which the applicant needs to answer 17 correctly in order to pass. The questions are to be answered within 60 minutes and the test papers are then marked centrally. Test candidates receive a certificate from the Federal Office with their personal test result. If they have passed the test, they can prove the required civic knowledge to the naturalisation authorities using this certificate. Candidates who have not answered the required number of questions correctly may resit the test. Applicants are exempted from the test if they are unable to take it 'on account of a physical, mental or psychological illness or disability or on grounds related to age' (*BAMF*).

Out of the 33 questions for the test, 30 are related to three areas of civic knowledge, which the description of the test on the *BAMF* Web site outlines as: 'Living in a Democracy', 'History and Responsibility', and 'People and Society'. Three test questions will relate to the *Bundesland* in which the test is taken. The database with all 300 general and ten *Länder*-related questions is available to applicants via the web pages of the Federal Ministry of the Interior (*Bundesministerium des Innern*) as a printable document. Applicants can also prepare for the test through an interactive online sample test or via an interactive questionnaire that provides access to and feedback on all of the 300 possible general questions.

As outlined earlier, the shift in citizenship legislation to include naturalisation on the basis of *Ius Soli* was based on a shift in perception of the role of immigration in the German context. The report of the Independent Commission on Migration to Germany states in 2001:

> Germany needs immigrants. An overall plan defining clear goals is needed to structure immigration to Germany as well as integration: in order to meet its humanitarian responsibilities, to contribute to the safeguarding of economic prosperity, to improve the co-existence of Germans and immigrants to Germany as well as to foster integration. (1)

In subsequent years, the Government allocated substantial amounts of funding to what it perceived to be a way of fostering integration: the introduction of so-called integration courses:

> The main thrust of state integration measures and efforts is an integration course consisting of a language course aimed at giving participants a good command of German together with an orientation course in which immigrants learn about the German legal system, history and culture. First and foremost the integration course aims to smooth the integration of immigrants into German society by enabling them to participate in German social life and giving them the same opportunities as their fellow citizens. A further aim is to encourage migrants to think positively about their new home by familiarizing them with German culture, history, the political values of the Constitution, the legal system and the political institutions of the democratic constitutional state.
>
> (*Concept for a nation-wide integration course*, October 2005, 4)

These integration courses were implemented at federal level in 2005 and initially funded with 208 million Euro. They consist of two components: a) language courses of up to 600 units (45 minutes each) leading to the CEFR level B1 described above in a modular structure, so that learners can choose an entry point in correspondence with their existing language skills, and b) an orientation course that presupposes B1 language skills and aims at teaching civic knowledge, now to be tested in the citizenship test. The orientation courses, which are based on a curriculum set nationally, have been extended from 30 to 45 units' duration. Course material is available through commercial publishers (e.g. Klett, Hueber).

The listed objectives of these orientation courses do not only aim at imparting knowledge ('Develop an understanding of the German State',

'Provide information on migrants' rights as residents and citizens') but they are clearly aiming at attitudinal goals ('Develop a positive attitude towards the German State') as well as at competences ('Develop the ability to inform oneself (method competence)', 'Enable participation in social life (ability to act)', 'Acquisition of intercultural competence').

The content of the orientation courses can be summarised as follows:

Legal System	History	Culture
• State structure of the Federal Republic of Germany; democracy; political influence; electoral law; and standing of the federal states and communities	• Birth and development of the Federal Republic of Germany	• Image of people • Concept of time • Rule orientation • Religious diversity
	Optional:	Optional:
• Constitutional state • Welfare state principles • Basic rights • Duties of citizens	• European integration • Reunification • History of migration in Germany • Regional history	• Cultural and regional diversity • Division of home and work spheres • Symbols
Optional: • Europe • Social market economy		

German citizenship: A reward for integration?

The political discourse regarding immigration and integration in Germany – as very briefly outlined in this chapter with regards to the *Leitkulturdebatte*, the introduction of the Citizenship Act, and the citizenship testing that followed it – leaves no doubt about the fact that integration and citizenship rights are closely tied to one another in the German context. As the report by the Independent Commission on Migration to Germany stated in 2001 (1):

> At present, 7.3 million foreigners are living in the Federal Republic of Germany; that is 8.9 percent of the entire population. Almost 40 percent of these people have been living here for more than 15 years. However, up to now, there has been no up-to-date and future-oriented overall concept for the structuring of immigration to Germany and the integration of these immigrants in place – two areas which are inseparably linked.

This statement expresses very clearly the linking of immigration policy on the one hand and migrant policy on the other. The changes to

German citizenship and immigration laws and the introduction of integration courses and citizenship testing at federal level show how this linkage is played out. Immigration and integration policies in Germany, which was traditionally considered as following a collectivist-ethnic model (Wright, 2008) or in Joppke's (2007a) words, 'a segregationist model of nationhood', now resemble those of other European countries, such as the Netherlands, which was traditionally considered to sit at the other end of the spectrum, promoting multiculturalism within a pluralistic-civic model of nationhood (Wright, 2000). In fact, Joppke (2007b) goes so far as to state: 'And "segregationist" Germany has adopted the (hitherto) least control-minded, most "Canadian" variant of civic integration', although it must be said that he arrived at this conclusion before the introduction of formal citizenship testing in Germany. What seems at play here is a convergence of immigration and integration policies beyond national models at a European level, but the verdict is still out on how much EU member states are influencing one another in the sphere of citizenship (Green, 2007; Joppke, 2007 a and b; Wright, 2008).

In her contribution on the relationship between naturalisation language testing and ideologies of national identity and citizenship, Piller stated in 2001 that 'Germany espouses a national ideology in which citizenship cannot be divided from national identity' (268). Language features strongly as part of this national identity. Wright (2000, 15ff) in her description of ethno-linguistic nationalism stresses the roots of this form of nationalism in the German *Sturm und Drang* movement and she refers to Herder's argument that 'each nation was unique and that for a group to preserve its specificity and survive as a discrete entity it must preserve its own language and culture' (15) as a precursor to the importance of language in the nineteenth-century project of nation building. Coulmas (1995 in Piller, 2001) sees the continued vitality of linguistic nationalism confirmed through German reunification where the principle that one nation with one language should be united in one state was adhered to without questioning.

It seems that language continues to play this identity-building role in the current citizenship regime. Where the *Nationality Act* makes reference to integration, it is the German language that is identified as the strongest marker of successful integration. As I have outlined earlier in this chapter, special provision is made for an early application to citizenship – after 6 or 7 instead of 8 years of residence in Germany – where 'the foreigner has made outstanding efforts at integration [...] especially if he or she can demonstrate his or her command of the German language'

(*Nationality Act,* Section 10/13). Civic knowledge – as it is taught in the orientation course and tested in the citizenship test – assumes a sufficient level of language proficiency (B1, CEFR) without which the course materials and test questions cannot be understood.[3]

It is therefore not surprising that the German government has committed a substantial amount of funding to the integration courses, which are, in the main, language courses (600 out of 645 units). Stevenson and Schanze speak of a 'significantly more differentiated and sophisticated approach to language learning which is the cornerstone of the new integration strategy' (2009, 103). The financial contribution for immigrants taking these courses is minimal and can be waived upon application if the applicant proves that they do not have the financial means to pay (cf. Van Avermaet, 2009 for a range of other European countries). Joppke (2007a, 253) comments on the paradox of entitlement and obligation in regards to integration courses, where newcomers are entitled to and at the same time obliged to attend a course if they want to apply for permanent residency and do not have the prerequisite language skills, but he concedes that this is not a major issue as the majority of newcomers arrive as family migrants and therefore are entitled to a residency permit. It is interesting to look then at the uptake of integration courses and their make-up. So far, about half a million migrants have taken up an integration course as the following figures from a report on the implementation of integration courses (BAMF, 2008, 4) since their introduction in 2005 show:

	2005/6	2007	2008 (1. half year)	Total
Number of participants	248.682	114.365	59.045	422.092

The same report provides figures based on the nationality of participant for the first half year 2008 and the following picture emerges:

	1. Half 2008	In %
Turkey	6.168	19.2
Russian Federation	2.515	7.8
Ukraine	1.461	4.5
Poland	1.363	4.2
Iraq	1.077	3.3
Serbia	744	2.3

(Continued)

Kazakhstan	719	2.2
Thailand	698	2.2
Vietnam	659	2.0
Iran	625	1.9
German	1.450	4.5
Other nationals	12.908	40.1
Total	30.387	94.5
Plus ethnic Germans	1.782	5.5
Grand total	32.169	100

Two figures here are particularly striking: the large percentage of Turkish nationals in the overall enrolment figures and the 4.5 per cent of participants categorised as 'Germans'. Immigrants of Turkish background are the largest grouping in Germany and in any discussion about integration this group is strongly implied, in particular in discussions about education as outlined below. The fact that 'German' is given as a nationality category for 1450 participants indicates that those are naturalised Germans that have enrolled for the integration course after having received German citizenship.

The refusal to acknowledge that migration to Germany since the 1950s was of a permanent rather than a transitory nature has led to serious shortcomings in the education of second and third generation migrants. This is borne out in the large number of youths with a migration background who either do not obtain a school leaving certificate – 16.4 per cent vs. 6.9 per cent with German background(Granato, 2003) – or obtain one of the lowest category. In comparison to children of German background, far fewer children of migrant background gain university entrance qualifications – 15.4 per cent vs. 31 per cent (ibid.), thus severely limiting access to tertiary education and the employment prospects that it brings. Gogolin (1994) refers to the 'monolingual habitus' of the German education system (*Monolingualer Schulhabitus*)[4] as a cause for these shortcomings, where individual bilingualism or multilingualism is seen as a hindrance rather than as an asset – and Gogolin and Neumann (2008) argue that the introduction of integration courses with a very strong focus on language skills – directed at newcomers as well as those who have been living in Germany for a long period of time – is to be seen as an attempt to make up for the lack of integration measures in the past.[5] The fact that, according to the 2008 statistics, 4.5 per cent of participants in integration courses are naturalised citizens lends weight to their argument.

In the German context, then, integration is largely measured in accordance to a degree of linguistic integration, as very clearly indicated in the National Integration Plan, issued by the government in 2007, which states that 'language is the prerequisite for integration' (*Sprache ist die Vorraussetzung für Integration*) (*Nationaler Integrationsplan*, 2007, 16). This definition of integration has been much criticised as 'social integration that depends on a unilateral effort of the incoming minority to learn the "national" language of the state' (Stevenson, 2006) and it has been referred to as a societal view of integration that assumes a *Bringeschuld der Zuwandernden* (Gogolin and Neumann, 2008, 39) – a duty that migrants owe to the receiving country. Stevenson and Mar-Molinero (2006, 159) quote a *faux pas* delivered by Otto Schily, then Federal Minister of the Interior, in an interview with the *Süddeutsche Zeitung* where he stated 'the best form of integration is assimilation' (*die beste Form der Integration ist die Assimilierung*) as the involuntary revelation of an assimilation ideology that can be described as follows:

> According to this view, reducing the observable evidence of otherness (as an irritant or affront to the singularity of the dominant monolingual majority) and re-asserting the authority of the majority through the sole legitimacy of 'its' language are more important than enabling or empowering the multilingual minority and fostering social integration based on reciprocal accommodation of indigenous and immigrant populations. (Ibid., 158)

Brubaker (2001) argues that a 'modest return of assimilation' is to be seen not only in Germany but also in other immigration countries such as France and the United States, but his use of the term has a much more positive ring to it when he states with regards to the changes of citizenship legislation in Germany:

> The new practices, policies, and discourses surrounding citizenship are assimilationist, rather, in the sense of politically recognizing, legally constituting, and symbolically emphasizing *commonality* rather than difference.
>
> (Brubaker, 2001, 539)

The current citizenship legislation in Germany is new and its implications are still evolving. The strong emphasis on language skills as a prerequisite for integration seems to bear out for the German context Piller's (2001, 271) conclusion that 'Ideologies of national identity are a central facet of modern social identities and they are intricately bound up with linguistic identity. Furthermore national identity is crucially implicated in citizenship.' The immigrant aspiring to German citizenship has to provide proof that s/he subscribes to this national identity by acquiring German language skills to a relatively high level of proficiency and by engaging with German culture, history, and civics. Citizenship is not awarded as part of this process but as an end point to integration.

The integrative process is helped, however, by generously funded integration courses that allow for the acquisition of linguistic skills at different levels and in a variety of different settings. Civic knowledge is taught in the same framework in an environment geared at adult education, and testing of both – language skills and civic knowledge – is transparent and easily accessible. If we agree with Wright's (2000, 3) position: 'Whether individuals have particular linguistic skills or not is always one of the factors of inclusion or exclusion in a number of spheres: access to knowledge; employability; participation in the democratic process; active citizenship', the availability of these integration courses – on a voluntary basis – has to be seen as a positive development in the context of German migrant policy, which for a long time has been marred by a neglect of educational opportunities for migrants and their children. Whether this perception is shared by those concerned warrants further research.

Notes

1. The European countries involved in his comparative study of immigration policies are: Austria, Belgium, Bulgaria, Denmark, Estonia, Finland, France, Germany, Greece, Hungary, Ireland, Italy, Latvia, Lithuania, Luxembourg, Netherlands, Norway, Poland, Portugal, Russia, Slovenia, Spain, Sweden, and United Kingdom.
2. 'Ich meine damit nichts anderes als einen Wertekonsens westlicher Prägung als Gegenprogramm zu multikultureller Wertebeliebigkeit. Natürlich ist innerhalb Europas ein Dialog zwischen Europäern und nicht-europäischen Migranten, die Platz für ihre Kultur Europas beanspruchen, notwendig.'
3. Whether the bank of 300 test questions, that serve as a basis for each individual test, are in fact situated at the B1 level in terms of their semantic, syntactic, and pragmatic features would warrant a closer linguistic analysis.
4. C.f. Clyne (2005) for a discussion of a 'monolingual mindset' in the Australian context.
5. Es ist in das politische Bewusstsein gerückt, dass die lange Phase der Enthaltsamkeit bei der Steuerung und Gestaltung von Zuwanderung zu einigem Nachholbedarf in der Förderung von Integrationsprozessen geführt hat. Dass die Nachsteuerung vorranging im sprachlichen Bereich gesehen wird, wird

etwa daran kenntlich, dass im Zuwanderungsgesetz 'Integrationskurse' für neu Einwandernde ebenso wie für solche Menschen vorgesehen sind, die schon lange in Deutschland leben (Gogolin and Neumann, 2008, 48).

References

Baden-Württemberg: Das Landesportal (2006) Gesprächsleitfaden für Einwanderungsbehörden. Accessed 30 January 2007. http://www.badenwuerttemberg. de/de/Meldungen/111612.html?referer=88525

Brubaker, Rogers (1992) *Citizenship and Nationhood in France and Germany* (Cambridge, MA: Harvard University Press).

Brubaker, Rogers (1996) *Nationalism Reframed. Nationhood and the National Question in the New Europe* (Cambridge: Cambridge University Press).

Brubaker, Rogers (2001) 'The return of assimilation? Changing perspectives on immigration and its sequels in France, Germany and the United States', *Ethnic and Racial Studies* 24 (4): 531–48.

Bundesamt für Migration und Flüchtlinge (BAMF) (2009) Integrationsportal – Naturalization Test. Accessed 4 April 2009. http://www.integration-in-deutschland.de/nn_1344996/SubSites/Integration/EN/02__Zuwanderer/ Einbuergerungstest/einbuergerungstest-inhalt.html

Bundesamt für Migration und Flüchtlinge (BAMF) (2008) Bericht zur Integrationskursgeschäftsstatistik für das 1. Halbjahr 2008. Accessed 3 December 2008. www.bamf.de

Bundesministerium des Innern (2000) Staatsangehörigkeitsgesetz. Accessed 5 June 2008. www.bmi.bund.de

Bundesministerium des Innern (2005) Zuwanderunsgesetz. Accessed 15 June 2008. www.bmi.bund.de

Bundesministerium des Innern – Gesamtfragenkatalog, Accessed 4 April 2009. http://www.bmi.bund.de/cln_144/SharedDocs/Downloads/DE/Themen/ MigrationIntegration/Einbuergerungstest/Einburgerungstest_Allgemein. html?nn=104078

Die Bundesregierung (2007) Der nationale Integrationsplan. Neue Wege – neue Chancen. Berlin. Accessed 16 June 2008. www.nationaler-integrationsplan.de

Extra, G., M. Spotti and P. Avermaet (eds) (2009) *Language Testing, Migration and Citizenship: Cross-National Perspectives on Integration Regimes* (London: Continuum).

Faist, Thomas (2007) 'Dual citizenship: Change, prospects and limits', in Thomas Faist (ed.), *The Politics of Dual Citizenship in Europe: From Nationhood to Social Integration* (Avebury: Aldershot), 171–200.

Federal Ministry of the Interior (2005) 'Nationality Act. Unofficial Translation of the Federal Ministry of the Interior'. Accessed 16 June 2008. www.bmi.bund.de

Federal Ministry of the Interior (2008) 'Migration and Integration', Accessed on 16 November 2008. http://www.en.bmi.bund.de/nn_148138/Internet/ Content/Broschueren/2008/Migration__und__Integration__en.html

Federal Office for Migration and Refugees (2005) *Concept for a Nation-Wide Integration Course* (Nürnberg: The Fedarl Office).

Göktürk, Deniz, David Gramling and Anton Kaes (2007) *Germany in Transit. Nation and Migration 1955–2005* (Berkeley, CA: University of California Press).

Gogolin, Ingrid (1994) *Der monoliguale Habitus der multilingualen Schule* (Münster and New York: Waxmann Verlag).

Gogolin, Ingrid and Ursula Neumann (2008) 'Regionale Bildungs – und Sprachplanung – Die Beispiele Sheffield und FörMig', in Angelika Redder and Konrad Ehlich (eds), *Mehrsprachigkeit für Europa – sprachen- und bildungspolitische Perspektiven. Osnabrücker Beiträge zur Sprachtheorie*, 74: 39–54.

Granato, M. (2003) 'Jugendliche mit Migrationshintergrund in der beruflichen Bildung' WSI-Mitteilungen 8, S. 474–83.

Green, Simon (2004) *The Politics of Exclusion: Institutions and Immigration Policy in Contemporary Germany* (Manchester: Manchester University Press).

Green, Simon (2005) 'Between ideology and pragmatism: The politics of dual nationality in Germany', *International Migration Review* 39 (4): 921–52.

Green, Simon (2007) 'Divergent traditions, converging responses: Immigration and integration policy in the UK and Germany', *German Politics* 16 (1): 95–115.

Hessisches Ministerium des Innern und für Sport (2006): Leitfaden Wissen und Werte. Accessed 30 January 2007. http://www.hmdi.hessen.de/irj/HMdI_Internet?cid=572f2377e386d21a6dd018aa0ad8b0b5

Independent Commission on Migration to Germany (2001) *Structuring Immigration, Fostering Integration.Summary* (Berlin: Zeitbild Verlag).

Joppke, Christian (2007a) 'Transformation of immigrant immigration: Civic integration and anti discrimination in the Netherlands, France and Germany', *World Politics* 59: 243–73.

Joppke, Christian (2007b) 'Beyond national models: Civic integration policies for immigrants in Western Europe', *West European Politics* 30 (1): 1–22.

Palmowski, Jan (2008). 'In search of the German nation: Citizenship and the challenge of integration', *Citizenship Studies*, 12 (6): 547–63.

Pautz, Hartwig (2005) 'The politics of identity in Germany: The Leitkultur debate', *Race & Class* 46 (4): 39–52.

Piller, Ingrid (2001) 'Naturalization language testing and its basis in ideologies of national identity and citizenship', *The International Journal of Bilingualism* 5 (3): 259–77.

Spiegel Online 23 March 2006. CSU: Stoiber fordert Einbürgerungstest nach US Vorbild. Accessed 31 October 2008. www.spiegel.de

Spiegel Online 24 March 2006. Testfall für die SPD. Einbürgerungstests. Accessed 31 October 2008. www.spiegel.de

Spiegel Online 24 March 2006. Auch SPD Politiker wollen einheitliche Einbürgerungstests. Accessed 31 October 2008. www.spiegel.de

Stevenson, P. and C. Mar-Molinero (2006) 'Language, the National and the Transnational in Europe', in C. Mar-Molinero and P. Stevenson (eds), *Language Ideologies, Policies and Practices. Language and the Future of Europe* (New York: Palgrave Macmillan).

Stevenson, Patrick and Livia Schanze (2009) Language, Migration and Citizenship In Germany: Discourses on Integration and Belonging, in Extra, G., M. Spotti and P. Avermaet (eds), *Language Testing, Migration and Citizenship: Cross-National Perspectives on Integration Regimes* (London: Continuum), 87–106.

Tibi, Bassam (1998) *Europa ohne Identität. Leitkultur oder Wertebeliebigkeit* (München: Econ).

Tibi, Bassam (2000) 'Deutschland braucht eine Leitkultur. Gegenprogramm zu multikultureller Wertebeliebigkeit', *Focus* 44. Accessed 31 October 2008. http://www.focus.de/politik/deutschland/standpunkt-deutschland-braucht-eine-leitkultur_aid_184384.html

Van Avermaet, Piet (2009) 'Fortresss Europe? Language Policy Regimes for Immigration and Citizenship', in Gabirelle Hogan-Brun, Clare Mar-Molinero and Patrick Stevenson, *Discourse on Language and Integration* (Amsterdam/Philadelphia, PA: John Benjamins), 15–44.

Wright, Sue (2000) *Community and Communication. The Role of Language in Nation State Building and European Integration* (Clevedon: Multilingual Matters).

Wright, Sue (2008) 'Citizenship Tests in Europe – Editorial Introduction. Citizenship Tests in a Post-National Era', *International Journal on Multicultural Societies* 10 (1): 1–9.

9
'Do I feel Australian? No You Tell Me': Debating the Introduction of the Australian Formal Citizenship Test

Emily Farrell

1 Introduction

The Australian Citizenship Amendment (Citizenship Testing) Bill (2007) states: '[t]he introduction of a citizenship test is a key part of the Government's ongoing commitment to help migrants successfully integrate into the Australian community' (1). How does a test assist migrants to become a part of a community? Furthermore, how is the 'Australian community' defined, and what signifies successful integration? This chapter is concerned with how such concepts are defined, who is defining them, and how they appear in the final citizenship test materials.

I will address these questions through an examination of submissions responding to the 2006 Discussion Paper and to the 2007 Senate Inquiry into the test, as well as media responses to the introduction of the test during the same period. In addition, voices of migrants themselves are heard through an examination of a corpus of data from individual interviews and focus groups consisting of people who had migrated to Australia as adults. Some of the participants had chosen to take up Australian citizenship and others had chosen not to. The combination of these data sources gives a perspective from government, media, and community levels, and adds insight from insiders who have gone through the process of migration to Australia. The analysis shows the complex networks of national identity negotiation that occurred around the introduction of the test and the silencing of these complex negotiations in the subsequent test resources.

The debates surrounding the test's introduction conflated citizenship, national identity, and the notion of belonging, placing particular stress on the idea that citizenship necessarily entailed subscription to a set of national values. It can be said that citizenship, by its nature, is always a mechanism of exclusion:

> Nations are not only 'Imagined Communities', that is, systems of cultural representation whereby people come to imagine a shared experience of identification with an extended community, but also exclusionary historical and institutional practices to which access is restricted via citizenship.
>
> (Piller, 2001, 259)

While someone may be 'included' if they pass a formal citizenship test, this cannot simply be equated with shared values. In the debates surrounding the introduction of the formal citizenship test an imagined, shared experience is inextricable from the discussions of Australian citizenship. This is stressed particularly through the use of 'values' as central to defining who should be able to take up Australian citizenship. To examine the entextualisations of these debates in the test materials (that is, 'the process by means of which discourses are successively or simultaneously decontextualised and metadiscursively recontextualised' (Blommaert, 2005, 47)), it is relevant to first review the timeline of events surrounding the citizenship test introduction and the requirements of the current test, before introducing the data and analysis.

2 The path to the new formal citizenship test

Australia has had a problematic history in regard to the use and abuse of testing to restrict migration. The Immigration Restriction Act (1901) is infamous in its application of a language dictation test that allowed officials to administer the test in whichever European language they desired, whether it was a language the applicant spoke or not, in order to keep out 'undesirable immigrants' (Chesterman and Galligan, 1999, 50). The dictation test was abandoned in 1958 and replaced with an informal test whereby applicants' knowledge of 'basic' English was assessed in an immigration interview (for a detailed discussion, see Part 1 of this book). The possible introduction of a new formal citizenship test stirred up debate regarding the relationship between the new test and the former test, as well as more recent discourses surrounding discriminatory practices concerning migration (Clyne, 2005).

On 17 September 2006, the Parliamentary Secretary to the Minister for Immigration and Multicultural Affairs, Andrew Robb, released the Discussion Paper *Australian Citizenship: Much More than a Ceremony* in order to 'seek the Australian community's views on the merits of introducing a formal citizenship test' (Department of Immigration and Multicultural Affairs, 2006a, 7). The paper asked individuals and organisations to comment on the introduction of a formal citizenship test. Contributors could choose whether their submission would be public or not and were given until 17 November 2006 to respond.

The Government issued a summary report of the 1644 responses received, with a cursory statistical analysis of all responses concluding that 60 per cent of responses were in favour of the test (Department of Immigration and Multicultural Affairs, 2006b) (for further discussion see Section 5.2). On 11 December 2006, the Government announced that it would indeed be introducing a formal citizenship test the following year. The Australian Citizenship Act (2007) was introduced, followed by the Australian Citizenship Amendment (Citizenship Testing) Bill (2007), which included the following aspects to be tested:

- Applicant understands their application
- Has a basic knowledge of English
- Has an adequate knowledge of Australia and Australian citizenship. (Section 21(2), Australian Citizenship Amendment (Citizenship Testing) Bill, 2007)

On 13 June 2007, the Minister for Immigration and Citizenship, Kevin Andrews, did a second reading of the Australian Citizenship Amendment (Citizenship Testing) Bill (2007), which was then referred to the 'Standing Committee on Legal and Constitutional Affairs' to provide an inquiry and produce a report on the test.

In comparison to the large number of responses to the Discussion Paper in 2006, the Senate Inquiry received only 59 responses, many of which were authored by people and organisations that had submitted responses earlier in the process. Six of those responses did not address the citizenship test, instead requesting reviews of individual cases.[1] The Senate published a report of its findings in July 2007. The report included the recommendations that the test be reviewed 3 years after its implementation, that the questions be made public, and that the Bill 'specifically require that the test relate to the eligibility criteria' in the legislation (Senate Standing Committee on Legal and Constitutional Affairs, 2007, ix). The test, however, was introduced without the questions being tabled in parliament (discussed further in Section 5.2, below).

August 2007 saw the release of the draft handbook, from which the questions for the test were to be drawn, with the first people sitting the test on 1 October 2007. The final copy of the resource booklet was published in November 2007, after testing had begun. Following the introduction of the test, the newly elected Rudd Government called for a review of the test, sooner even than the time frame recommended in the Senate Inquiry. Before the release of the report, the head of the committee, Mr Richard Woolcott, was quoted as saying: 'The standout recommendation would be that the present test is flawed and seen by some as intimidatory and needs substantial reform' (Australian Associated Press, 2008, August 29).

On 22 November 2008, the Government released the Woolcott Review's Report, which included 34 recommended major changes to the test (for further discussion of the report, see Möllering and Silaghi in this book). The Government's response to the Report supported 27 of these changes, including the recommendations that 'educational experts' be responsible for the development and quality assurance of the test questions, and that there be a clearer implementation of 'basic English', although it is still unclear in linguistic terms how this level of English is being defined.

The test will be retained, and thus far, the timeline for implementation is vague with the Citizenship test Web site stating in early 2009 only that '[i]t will be sometime before any changes to the citizenship test are implemented' (Department of Immigration and Citizenship, 2008), while the report itself suggests the new resource book and test will be available by August 2009. In the following section, I will provide an overview of the current testing regime, in place in early 2009, including eligibility and test format.

3   The current test

In order to be eligible to sit the citizenship test, applicants must be permanent residents of Australia and have legally resided in the country for a minimum of 4 years. Test exemptions are allowed for those under 18 or over 60 years of age, and those with physical or mental disabilities that will prevent them from understanding the nature of the test, noted as a requirement in the legislation. Special assistance is offered to people with low levels of English literacy, including staff to read aloud test questions. This assistance is only available to applicants who have completed a minimum of 400 hours of English language classes through the Government-run Adult Migrant English Program (AMEP). The Government also specifies that no childcare will be offered to test takers.

The test is administered via a computer-based multiple-choice test. It is comprised of 20 questions drawn at random from a pool of 200 questions. Three of the questions, on the 'rights and responsibilities of citizenship' (Australian Government, 2007a, 43), are compulsory and must be answered correctly to pass the test. The pass mark is currently set at 60 per cent. Once the 2008 amendments to the test are brought in, the pass mark will be raised to 75 per cent (Australian Government, 2008).

The test resource booklet, *Becoming an Australian Citizen*, includes all possible information that might appear in the actual multiple-choice test. The booklet is comprised of 46 pages from which the test's 20 questions are derived. There has been much debate surrounding the decision to withhold the test questions, despite the recommendations of the Senate Inquiry and the 2008 Review that the questions be made public (see Section 5 for further discussion). The resource book for the citizenship test is available in 29 community languages, although the test must be taken in English. The community languages include some of the more commonly spoken languages in Australia such as Amharic, Greek, Hindi, and Italian.

Sample test questions are available in the resource booklet, and a five question practice test appears on the Citizenship test Web site. The sample questions include the following:

Which of these is a responsibility for every Australian citizen?

a) Renounce their citizenship of any other country
b) Serve in Australian Diplomatic Missions overseas
c) Join with Australians to defend Australia and its way of life, should the need arise

in addition to:

Which one of these Australians is famous for playing cricket?

a) Rod Laver
b) Sir Donald Bradman
c) Sir Hubert Opperman[2]

The changes, once implemented, will hone the focus of the test to questions on civics, rather than 'notable Australians', which will instead be the focus of a non-examinable section of the new resource booklet.

In addition to sample questions, applicants can access a test tutorial that familiarises them with the layout and general procedures of the computerised test. Applicants are able to sit the test both within Australia and in selected offshore sites. Currently, there is no fee for sitting the test, a fee is instead administered after passing the test and paid in conjunction with the citizenship application.

4 Data and approach

Having discussed the background of the citizenship test and current testing procedures, it is relevant to now turn to a discourse analysis of the debates surrounding the test. Who was saying what about the introduction of the test, and whose voices appeared in the resulting test and materials? In order to gain an understanding of the ways, these debates are entextualised in the test and study resources, a wide range of data were gathered from across the spectrum of debate (at varying levels: from individual to organisational and institutional). The analysis draws on the following resources:

1. The Government Discussion Paper (released September 17, 2006)
2. Responses to the Discussion Paper (submitted by November 17, 2006)
3. Summary Report on the Discussion Paper submissions (December 2006)
4. Submissions to the 2007 Senate Inquiry
5. Senate report on the inquiry (July 2007)
6. Media reports on the 2008 Review
7. Australian newspaper articles from January 26, 2006 to October 28, 2008
8. Data from an interview study conducted from 2003 to 2004 with people who had migrated to Australia as adults.

There is a dialogic, intertextual relationship between the source materials. The importance of intertextuality, or the notion 'that every text is embedded in a context and is synchronically and diachronically related to many other texts' (Blackledge, 2005, 10), can be seen in the ways that the data form a network of dialogues. The Government reports and submissions draw on public debates, such as newspaper polls, while the media refers both to governmental releases, historical precedent and broader public discussion.

The interview data also draw on similar discursive networks. It comes from a longitudinal study conducted from 2003 to 2004 with 16 participants who had migrated to Australia as adults and had lived in Australia for a minimum of 5 years.[3] All were highly advanced second language speakers of English and all participated in individual and focus group interviews over the course of the year. Exactly half of the participants had chosen to take up Australian citizenship. Of the 16, only one was eligible for dual citizenship and had kept his Portuguese passport. During the course of the study, participants were asked questions regarding their citizenship status and why they had or had not taken up Australian citizenship. The interviews show the complexity of personal discussions about what citizenship means, particularly to those who have gone through the process of migration.

5   Debating citizenship

The first issue that this analysis addresses is the notion of belonging to the nation (Section 5.1). Much of the debate surrounding the introduction of the test dealt with the conflation of citizenship and national identity, the question of where belonging to the nation starts, how it is defined, and who defines it. Section 5.2 addresses how secrecy was used as a strategy during the test development to manage the criticisms of the test. Section 5.3 looks at the test and resource booklet to see how debates about belonging and secrecy are, or are not, entextualised in the test materials.

5.1   Defining 'belonging' and Australian citizenship

Throughout the debates, Australian citizenship was conflated with 'Australian values'. The official test resource booklet states that, '[i]n particular, new citizens are asked to embrace the values of Australia' (Australian Government, 2007a, 4), defining such 'values' as:

- respect for the equal worth, dignity, and freedom of the individual
- freedom of speech
- freedom of religion and secular government
- freedom of association
- support for parliamentary democracy and the rule of law
- equality under the law
- equality of men and women

- peacefulness
- tolerance, mutual respect, and compassion for those in need. (5).

Prior to the publication of the list, there had been much public debate about the meaning of Australian values and how they could be tested. Certainly the above-mentioned values are not *Australian* only? One line of argument was that there was no way to 'objectively' define these 'values' (Senate Submission 32, New South Wales Council for Civil Liberties). Professor Tim McNamara, in his submission to the Senate, stressed that:

> While it is true that formal tests, if they are properly managed, can be fairer than informal assessments, they are not automatically fair, as they necessarily involve subjective judgements about test content and test format on the part of test developers.
>
> (Senate Submission 33, Professor Tim McNamara, 3)

Contradicting such submissions, the Government sources claimed, '[t]his bill delivers an objective way of assessing whether prospective citizenship applicants meet the legal requirements for citizenship by conferral under the general eligibility provisions via a test' (Senate Submission 30, Department of Immigration and Citizenship).

Arguments about the problem of objectivity are more clearly seen in the wider debates about the test and how Australian values are defined. There were conflicting statements about what subscribing to 'Australian values' meant and how a test was to show this. In an article published in the *Sydney Morning Herald* the day after the release of the Discussion Paper, Prime Minister Howard was quoted as saying: 'we require everybody to be part of the mainstream community' (*Sydney Morning Herald*, 2006, September 18). In contrast, the citizenship resource booklet says, immediately following the list of responsibilities, privileges, and values:

> This statement of values and principles should not be seen as a quest for conformity or a common set of beliefs. On the contrary, respect for the free-thinking individual and the right to be different are foundations of Australian democracy.
>
> (Australian Government, 2007a, 5)

The set of values are, then, set up as something that is necessary for mainstream membership, and yet, not something that should be conformed to necessarily.

In his speech of 13 June 2007 the Minister, Kevin Andrews, stated:

> The test will encourage prospective citizens to obtain the knowledge they need to support successful integration into Australian society. The citizenship test will provide them with the opportunity to demonstrate in an objective way that they have the required knowledge of Australia, including the responsibilities and privileges of citizenship, and a basic knowledge and comprehension of English.
>
> (Senate Standing Committee on Legal
> and Constitutional Affairs, 9)

There is not space enough in this chapter to explore the problems associated with the notion that testing will result in success. However, Andrews constructs 'successful integration' as a responsibility placed in the hands of those who wish to migrate *into* the already formed Australian society. The burden of belonging and the ability to 'integrate' being placed on the outsider is a common marker of discriminatory discourses. As Liu and Mills (2006) find in their study of discourses of racism in New Zealand newspapers, nationalist discourse is used primarily to promote and defend the interests of the majority, with minorities referred to only indirectly in relation to 'the well-being of the nation' (84–5). Belonging, though, is not one-sided or one-directional. Belonging to something as large and protean as a national community depends less on objective definition than on the authority to claim the Australian national space (Hage, 1998). Belonging is always co-constructed, with the ability to claim belonging always being unequal. Such notions find support in the interview data. Paulo, an adult migrant from Portugal who had taken up Australian citizenship, when asked whether he feels Australian responded: 'Do I feel Australian? No you tell me'. Whoever is the object of Paulo's 'you tell me' request, his response demonstrates his belief that citizenship and feelings of belonging are separate, and that belonging is interpersonally constructed.

The idea propagated by the Government rhetoric is that one acquires the adequate knowledge of the country, attains citizenship, and is thereby 'successfully integrated'. Does belonging to Australia then follow from obtaining citizenship? One answer comes from another study participant, Eva, who had lived in Australia for nearly 20 years at the time of interview and had also chosen to become an Australian citizen. Unlike Paulo, Eva had to give up her Chilean passport and offers a different view of how citizenship pertains to feelings of belonging:

Because here? We are the foreigners, no matter what the papers say. I mean you are foreigner and- and you feel it most of the time. [...] Unfortunately? In silly things people make you feel it.

Would sitting a formal citizenship test have aided Eva in understanding and affiliating with 'Australian values' in such as way that feelings of being an outsider were dissipated? It is difficult to see how memorising an official list of values would assist, when feeling at home is challenged by others, even in the 'silly things', even after gaining citizenship. As Eva's utterance attests, this identity is still being formed, long after the paperwork says 'Australian'.

Some submissions to the Senate Inquiry point to the notion that belonging would likely be felt most strongly after acquiring citizenship, particularly for refugees and humanitarian entrants. For instance, the submission from the Premier of Victoria, Steve Bracks (Senate Submission 53) raises the concern that: 'If this Bill is passed it will allow for the potential exclusion of valuable members of the Australian community from gaining the sense of belonging they deserve' (3). Belonging is something you gain after citizenship. National Legal Aid (Senate Submission 57) also links the notion of belonging with citizenship, saying, 'Citizenship provides a sense of "belonging" to a supportive nation' (2). Along similar lines, Senator Lundy, at the second reading of the testing amendment, said:

> There has to be adequate funding for settlement services so that people who come to Australia with the least opportunity and the least advantage do not find themselves in circumstances where it will always be extremely difficult for them to take on their roles as full members of Australian society.
>
> (Lundy, 2007)

Rather than national membership coming from the knowledge one must acquire in preparation for citizenship, it is after citizenship that this feeling a part of the nation will grow. The Forum of Australian Services for Survivors of Torture and Trauma (Senate Submission 8) in their Senate submission expresses the concern that the test may:

> serve as a barrier to social cohesion and increased identification with Australia as a new homeland as our clients may feel like 'outsiders' and that their permanent settlement is delayed. (2)

In the examples cited above, citizenship can be seen as something that promotes social belonging after it is acquired, rather than something that must be preceded by belonging. While the Government documents do not acknowledge the complexity of this process, the dialogues of people like Paulo and Eva, who have undergone the process of migration and acquiring citizenship, show this quite clearly.

In responding to both the Government's Discussion Paper and to the Senate Inquiry, many of the public submissions also address the issue of test exemptions, laying special emphasis on the disadvantage the test would most likely pose for those arriving in Australia as refugees. A submission from the Refugee Council of Australia, for instance, relates citizenship to social inclusion, with citizenship being identified as the first step:

> The sense of inclusion that many refugees who have come to Australia feel can be partly attributed to their early opportunity to publicly declare their commitment to Australia through gaining citizenship. (2006, 1)

This claim for inclusion in light of citizenship in the case of refugees can be seen in a parallel example from the interview corpus.

Another participant in the interview study, Katja, had fled Poland for Denmark, where she met her husband Nicolas (a fellow Polish refugee) and lived for 15 years. She and Nicolas migrated to Sydney in 1989. Although it is unlikely she would ever move back to Denmark, Katja expresses a strong emotional affiliation for her Danish citizenship, due to the symbolic nature of its bestowal. Because of that, it is unlikely she would take up Australian citizenship unless it were possible to gain dual citizenship, despite the fact that her residency in Australia is of longer duration. Nevertheless, Katja feels involved in and connected to Australian society, at one point noting: 'I feel more home here than in Denmark'. In our age of mobility, the likelihood that those considering becoming Australian citizens have prior affiliations with more than one other country is increasingly likely.

The example of Milena, a 28-year-old migrant from the Czech Republic who had been in Australia for 10 years at the time of interview, also directly counters the notion that citizenship is symbolic of emotional affiliation. She constructs herself as an 'internationalist', viewing mobility as the most important thing, with her EU passport more suited to her desires as a mobile individual. She also separates emotional affiliation to a place from citizenship: 'so I don't feel like I need to have a passport to feel at home'. At another point, in response to being asked whether she feels Australian and would take up an Australian passport, Milena said, 'it'd make me feel only more Australian if I had one, [...] but no I don't feel Australian'. Concerns that formal citizenship tests prove little more than the ability to take tests – rather than any intention to subscribe to Australia's values – are supported by the complex construction of citizenship and belonging expressed by Milena.

Utility is another idea that is prominent in participants' discussions of citizenship, but absent from the Government publications. For instance, the test resource booklet begins with the following reader-directed statement:

> You have chosen to live in Australia and to make a contribution to its future by seeking to become an Australian citizen. Becoming a citizen gives you the opportunity to call yourself an Australian. It is the final and most important step in the migration journey.
>
> (Australian Government, 2007a, 1)

What of those who have and do contribute to Australia, but who see a greater utility in another citizenship? The data from the interview corpus show that frequently citizenship is viewed through the lens of utility. A commonly expressed sentiment by those in the interview study with EU passports that were not eligible for dual citizenship was the loss of privileged access to European employment markets. Mobility is a concern, and for those with access to the EU, their original citizenship remains more desirable and overrides the potential benefits of taking up Australian citizenship.

Participants in the study linked different sides of the discourse of citizenship with utility. Paulo found Australian citizenship appealing because it meant decreased university fees. Kara, however, a participant who had been in Australia for 15 years at the time of interview, frames her relationship to citizenship through an emotional affiliation. She does this, not only through speaking of her struggle in deciding to take up Australian citizenship and relinquish Korean citizenship, but also by distancing herself from citizenship as utility. She did not take up Australian citizenship until she had been in the country for 10 years, and offers the explanation that she was unsure if she could see herself 'as part of Australia', making her process different from those who 'get their citizenship as soon as they are eligible'.

For Kara taking up Australian citizenship involves more than just gaining access to the benefits it offers, especially as she is ineligible for dual citizenship. While Paulo can more readily take up Australian citizenship without feeling that he is losing a part of his home or upbringing, Kara must consider things from a perspective of loss. These two differing sides of citizenship as utility are important to note in regard to the complexity of the citizenship debate.

For the three young Korean men in the study, Joo Man, Patrick, and Ki Dae, Australian citizenship is appealing as a way of avoiding military service. All three of them are Australian citizens. While Australian citizenship in the case of these young men serves a pragmatic purpose, their individual relationships to emotional belonging and citizenship are different. Ki Dae, for instance, says that he is 'officially Australian' and 'unofficially Korean'. He also mentions his brother, who claims he would return to fight for Korea in wartime.

Kara also notes the spectre of war in her decision-making process:

> Imagine if there is a war between Korea and Australia, which country are you gonna choose? [...] If I choose to be a citizen of Australia [...] you got this duty as an Au- Australian citizen to defense [*sic*] Australia! If there is a war between Korea and Australia, I can't say, I couldn't say yes! I'll fight for Australia.

Her decision ultimately is that war between the countries is unlikely enough that she will not need to consider it in actuality. The conflict is imagined and therefore the burden of choosing Australian citizenship is lighter; however, it still plays a central part in Kara's process.

Something that is agreed upon across the corpus is that the test stands as a gate-keeping mechanism, keeping people outside of the national community and belonging. On the side of those supporting the test, for example, the *Australia for Australians'* submission in response to the Discussion Paper states:

> In view of multicultural debacle the 3 major parties have got Australia into over the last 40 years the time has come for a much harsher approach to immigration requirements and just who we want to let into our country. [...] It is time to say No, No, No, not you, not you, not you, yes you are eligible, but you are only on probation.

In this case, there is a positive attachment to the gate-keeping prospective of the test. The historical context for the argument is recent, though unspecified, 'multicultural' policy. On the other side, the submission from the *Chinese Australian Forum* also discussed the gate-keeping issue, but relates the discussion to the context of the *Immigration Restriction Act* (1901), noting the problematic nature of the abuse of language testing in Australia for the purpose of keeping out people on the basis of race.

Ultimately, many of the commentaries on the test argued about the difficulty of defining national belonging. In addition, returning to the quote from Kevin Andrews at the start of this section, a central question is also who is defining belonging? If being a good citizen is defined by active engagement and commitment to the community, how can this be proven through testing? The Australian Council of TESOL Associations argued that multiple-choice tests are inappropriate for this purpose (Senate Submission 34). Other arguments against the appropriateness of the test include the fact that it merely encourages rote learning (Senate Submission 7). The final test remains a multiple-choice test, with the voice of the Government most prominent in determining its content.

5.2   Shrouded in secrecy

How did the prominent voice remain that of the Government, despite widespread criticism? In addition to the debates surrounding what it means to be an Australian citizen and belong to Australian society, secrecy became a central theme. The details of the test questions were kept confidential. As such, secrecy was used as a strategy from the release of the Discussion Paper in 2006 all the way through to the Rudd Government's handling of the 2008 Woolcott Review's Report. The Immigration Minister, Senator Chris Evans, said in response to questions about why the report had not yet been made public by the end of October 2008, despite being submitted 2 months earlier, that 'anyone who wants to make their submission public can do so, I haven't had any involvement in hiding submissions' (Bird, 2008). The Minister denied secrecy and suppression, yet also acknowledged that secrecy has been an integral part of the citizenship test debate. This section of the chapter deals with the ways secrecy was used, from the legislation (Section 5.2.1) to the circulation of imprecise statistics in support of the test (Section 5.2.2), and the content of the test (Section 5.2.3).

5.2.1   Legislating secrecy

One aspect of secrecy raised in the debates was concerned with the stipulations of the testing legislation. Both the Premier of Tasmania in his submission to the Senate Inquiry (Senate Submission 52) and Senator Lundy (2007) of the Australian Capital Territory refer to the bill as 'shell legislation'. Other submissions were concerned with 'the ongoing lack of transparency that this legislation will entrench' (Senate Submission 46, Canberra Multicultural Community Forum, 1). The lack of transparency involved in the 2008 review by the Rudd Government could be taken to be a consequence of continued secrecy from the initial stages of the test introduction.

As outlined in Section 2, one of the three parts of the legislation to be tested is 'Has a basic knowledge of English', but no indication is given about who defines 'basic', how it will be tested, or who will ensure that the test and study materials are in fact only assessing 'basic knowledge'. While the test questions remain confidential (see also Section 5.2.3), the test resource booklet is well above a language level that could be labelled basic and in fact 'would present difficulties for many native speakers of English with limited education and/or limited familiarity with texts of this type' (Piller and McNamara, 2007, 1).

Another major concern in the debates, tied also to the issue of language level, was the lack of detail about the content of the test in the legislation. Senate Submission 26 (Australia/Israel & Jewish Affairs Council), for example, states: 'I am foremost concerned about the Bill's delegation of power to the Minister for Immigration and Citizenship to set the content of the citizenship test. The Bill provides no guidance whatsoever on what the test is designed to include or to achieve' (1). In their submission, the Ethnic Communities' Council of Victoria note: 'There is no mention of the content, length, standard or severity of the test in the Bill. This will be left to a written determination by the Minister which we are advised will not be a disallowable instrument or reviewable by Parliament' (Senate Submission 31, 2). How can the language level of the test be assessed when the questions are confidential and are not clearly detailed in the legislation?

5.2.2 *Support by numbers*

Secrecy was further entextualised through the circulation of the notion of majority support for the test. Following the Discussion Paper, the Government, in the *Summary Report on the Outcomes of the Public Consultation on the Merits of Introducing a Formal Citizenship Test*, claimed that 60 per cent of submissions in response to the Government Discussion Paper were in favour of the test introduction (Department of Immigration and Multicultural Affairs, 2006b, 2). The report provides a review of the 1644 submissions for and against the test. While the report offers a number of statistical breakdowns – for instance, the number of applications in support or against the introduction of the test and the number of organisations versus individuals in support of or against the test – the information provided allows no way for a finer statistical analysis of the data to be undertaken. Further, not all of the responses to the paper were made public, which means it is not possible to assess the accuracy of the statistics.

The calculation of majority support is problematic and lacks transparency. In the summary report all responses are divided into 'brief responses' (66 per cent of respondents), 'which simply answered one or more of the questions posed in the discussion paper' (3), and 'submissions' (34 per cent of respondents), 'which sought to engage with the issues raised in the discussion paper in at least some detail' (3). The report also makes the distinction between 'individual' (90 per cent of responses) and 'organisation' submissions (10 per cent of responses), including 'State and Territory Governments and government bodies, political parties, community organisations, religious groups, ethnic groups, business groups, peak bodies and a range of interest groups' (3). The summary states that: 'Overall, there was strong support for the introduction of a formal citizenship test' (2), with 60 per cent reportedly in favour, 25 per cent against, and 15 per cent unclear. While it is the case that a majority of submissions favour the introduction of the test, these statistics conflate the distinctions, made in the report itself, between 'brief response' and 'submission', as well as 'individual' and 'organisation'.

Of the 16 questions presented in Section 4 of the report, *Responses to Key Questions*, only one question, Question 1 'Should Australian introduce a formal citizenship test?' was directly answered by the majority of respondents. The 15 remaining questions were not directly answered by the majority, ranging from 60 per cent for Question 3, 'What level of English is required to participate as an Australian citizen?', to 91 per cent for Question 11, 'What form should a commitment to Australian values take [for permanent and long term temporary residents]?'.

Particularly problematic is the way in which the report addresses some of the specific questions posed by the Discussion Paper. Heading 4.3, *Level of English to participate*, for example, includes Question 3: 'What level of English is required to participate as an Australian citizen?'. The tabulated data divide the responses into four categories: English is very important; English is important; English is not important; and Didn't Address. In the first instance, the framing of the responses in this table does not answer the question posed as to the *level* of language needed to participate in Australian society. The report acknowledges the wide range of responses meaning they were only coded as 'an opinion' in three ways:

> that English is very important (where the opinion was expressed strongly), important (where the opinion was not expressed strongly), or not important.
>
> (Department of Immigration and
> Multicultural Affairs, 2006b, 6)

While the report states that 90 per cent of the responses write that 'English is very important', its relevance to the introduction of the citizenship test is unclear, as nearly all respondents who addressed English in their submission agree. Arguing that English is important is by no means arguing in favour of the test. These statistics further blur the distinct arguments made by respondents, and ignore both the common arguments against the test and the complexity of individual responses.

As important as this claim to majority support is where the numbers reappear and are further entextualised. The Senate inquiry, for example, uses this report, stating that it 'reported that there was overall support for the introduction of the formal citizenship test, with 60% of respondents supporting a test' (Senate standing committee on legal and constitutional affairs, 2007). The statistic was also reproduced in newspaper reports on the debate, for example, '60% were supportive' (Lim, 2007), 'about 60 per cent favoured a formal test' (Shanahan, 2006). Although both of those newspaper articles used the statistic as part of their arguments against the test, the entextualisation of majority support remained an important argument for the Government's introduction of the test.

5.2.3   What is the test?

Alongside the secrecy embodied in the legislation (Section 5.2.1), and the surety in majority support for the test (Section 5.2.2), is the debate surrounding the test's composition. For example, Senate Submission 14 from Monash University 'Castan Centre for Human Rights Law' notes the difficulty of commenting on the 'validity of the test when very little is actually known about the content of the test itself' (Senate Submission 14, 2).

The secrecy surrounding the test content fuelled discussion of what might be on the test. Relating to the notion of 'values', these discussions were tied very closely to what and who defines national belonging or membership. Without transparency in regard to the test content, public discussion extended to the absurd in framing what could potentially be tested. One example of suggested test content comes from an 'alternative citizenship test' that circulated widely via email around the time of the introduction of the test. The test question below challenges the notion that 'Australian values' exist as anything more than stereotypes and caricatures:

> Explain the following passage: In the arvo last Chrissy the relos rocked up for a barbie, some bevvies and a few snags. After a bit of a Bex and a lie down we opened the pressies, scoffed all the chockies, bickies and lollies. Then we drained a few tinnies and Mum did her block after Dad and Steve had a barney and a bit of biffo.
>
> ('The Real Australian Citizenship Test', 2007)[4]

In this mock question example, Australian values and being Australian are tied primarily to a lexicon of shortenings like arvo (afternoon), Chrissy (Christmas), relos (relatives), and barbie (barbeque). The rest of the alternative test, made up of similar questions as the above, implies the irrelevancy of a test that will surely only be a test of exaggerations. The secrecy surrounding the test introduction provided fertile ground for these satirical treatments of potential test questions. The notion of 'Australian' as only existing as stereotypes also appears in the interview data, with Paulo saying, directly after his earlier example on whether he feels Australian, that there is no 'Australian', only 'some travesties and some exaggerated kind of, you know like the crocodile man and stuff like that'. What then was to be on the test? How were values going to be tested?

One of the major recommendations of the Senate Inquiry (as noted in Section 2) was that the test questions be tabled in Parliament for the sake of transparency. Senator Lundy in her second reading speech to Parliament stated:

> Given the level of community disquiet about the questions that might be included in a citizenship test, the government should make the test questions public [...]. It would also help to ensure accountability of the proposed regime. [...T]he government making the questions available is completely in the interests of citizenship being a process of unifying Australians.
>
> (Lundy, 2007)

Lundy stresses the 'community disquiet', focusing on the importance of a democratic process. This runs counter to the argument of the Government, who state in their senate inquiry submission that the secrecy:

> will help to encourage prospective citizens to develop an adequate knowledge of Australia and the rights and privileges of citizenship as required by the legislation, rather than simply rote learning the answers.
>
> (Senate Submission 30, 3)

The argument cited above discredits the voices of the community, favouring secrecy as a necessary protector of 'rights and privileges of citizenship'. For Lundy, moving towards the transparency called for by 'Australians' is a 'unifying' factor. As the many Web sites that have sprung up since the test's introduction attest (see for instance, www. australiancitizenshiptest.net, www.australiantest.com, and www. aussietest.com), rote learning occurs regardless, and frequently places a further financial burden on the potential test taker.

In addition, the secrecy of the content led to questions of why the test was being introduced at all when the prior test, an informal immigration interview, did not appear to have been problematic. This discourse of 'why fix it when it isn't broken' appears both in the press (Summers, 2006) and in Parliamentary debate: 'There is already a test and it has never been controversial' (Lundy, 2007). Although the informal interview, where assessment of 'basic spoken English' was to some degree in the subjective hands of immigration officials, it was not without bias, as Piller (2001) notes in her discussion of the Australian immigration interview 'the purposes, the procedure, and the passing standard are clearly stated in the relevant legislation' (p. 266).

Finally then, returning to the central aim of this chapter, if the citizenship test remains shrouded in secrecy, how is it possible to assess which voices have and have not been incorporated into the final test? As the test questions remain confidential, the access point to the test is through the resource material, out of which the questions are formulated.

5.3   The test and resource booklet

As noted in Sections 2 and 3, the test questions are drawn from the resource booklet, *Becoming an Australian Citizen*, which was initially released in draft form immediately prior to the introduction of the test in August 2007. The final version of the booklet was released in

November 2007, a month after testing began. Of particular interest are some of the differences between the draft and final editions. One discourse of note that is further stressed in the final edition is that of sharing 'Australian values' as the central tenet of citizenship. The draft edition, for example, offers:

> **The responsibilities and privileges of citizenship provide the everyday guideposts for living in Australia,** for participating fully in our national life and for making the most of the opportunities that Australia had to offer. New citizens are also asked to embrace the values of Australia.
>
> (Australian Government, 2007b, 4, emphasis added)

In the revised final edition, however, the paragraph reads differently:

> In particular, new citizens are asked to embrace the values of Australia. As important as the responsibilities and privileges of citizenship, **these values provide the everyday guideposts for living in Australia,** for participating fully in our national life and for making the most of the opportunities that Australia has to offer.
>
> (Australian Government, 2007a, 4, emphasis added)

The voices that insisted that values were difficult to define and difficult to test, for example, are not present in this change in focus. The wider debates are silenced further in shifting emphasis from 'responsibilities and privileges' to 'values'.

As noted in Section 5.1, many of the submissions to the Discussion Paper and Senate Inquiry raised the concern that the test would be discriminatory. Some submissions particularly pointed to the high likelihood that the test would discriminate against women as the literacy rates and prior access to education for women from some countries of origin is much lower than for men. One of the ten Australian values, as noted earlier (in Section 2), is the 'equality of men and women'. As a 'value', it is something that could be included in one of the three mandatory questions included in the test. There is, however, an unequal treatment of men and women in the history of Australia provided by the booklet. The draft includes no information on famous Australian women. A major change from draft to the final resource booklet is that there are five additional paragraphs about famous Australians. Only one of the new paragraphs refers to an Australian man, the remainder are about women. Whereas the draft resource booklet refers to no influential women, the final booklet refers to Caroline Chisolm, Nancy Bird Walton, Dame Nellie Melba, Edith Cowan, Enid Lyons, and Louisa Lawson. While the draft resource book stressed the equality of men and women in Australian society as a central 'value', something that if answered wrongly would fail the applicant, important women in Australia's history were entirely forgotten.

What it means to be an Australian citizen and how this can be proven by a test were constructed in the texts surrounding the test introduction and, as this section has examined, silenced by the strategy of secrecy. The voices that argued that legislation lacked sufficient detail, the complexity of the criticisms of the test, and test questions themselves were all blurred by the insistence that secrecy protects the validity of the test. The changes from the draft resource book to the final book reveal that the concerns relating to the possibility of defining 'values' were not entextualised. In fact, values became a greater focus.

6   Conclusion

This chapter has analysed in detail the multiple voices that contributed to the debates surrounding the introduction of the Australian citizenship test. An examination of the official releases relating to the test, the individual, community, and media responses, as well as the test itself through the resource materials, reveals that the primary voice that appears in the test is that of the Government. The complexity and finer detail of individual ways of understanding citizenship are not heard. The interview data, in the utterances of Eva, Paulo, and Kara, show that belonging to a nation is constantly in negotiation, both before and after the acquisition of citizenship. All three participants hold Australian citizenship, and yet all three have differing and complex relationships to what this means in terms of their belonging in Australia. For Eva, feeling Australian can be challenged, despite 'the papers', in day-to-day interactions. Kara, while making the decision to take up Australian citizenship, acknowledges the difficulty of black and white national allegiance. The voices entextualised in the citizenship process are not organic or flexible in their understanding of what citizenship means to the people sitting the test. The complexity of defining and testing 'values' are instead navigated through the use of secrecy.

There is no acknowledgement in the test that, with dramatically increasing international migration and people flows, we have access to transnational or multiple national affiliations that do not pose a threat to perceived social cohesion. Migration creates upheaval and a need to rewrite and realign oneself in relation to social belonging. As evidenced in my interview data, while my participants make positive contributions to their communities and Australian society, it is not straightforward or easy making the decision to take up citizenship. It remains unclear how a formal values test encapsulates the complexity of these processes and how passing such a test actually shows how and whether potential citizens are contributing to society or, in the Government's words, are successfully integrating. Silencing the multiple voices explored in this chapter resonates instead with a history of discrimination in the context of Australian immigration.

Acknowledgement

I am deeply indebted to Ingrid Piller for initiating this chapter and providing insight and guidance in its development.

Notes

1. http://www.aph.gov.au/Senate/committee/legcon_ctte/completed_inquiries/ 2004–07/citizenship_testing/submissions/sublist.htm, accessed 31 October 2008). See submissions 1, 5, 6, 11, 15, and 21.
2. The correct answers are c and b.
3. The study was conducted as part of an Australian Research Council (ARC) Discovery Grant 2003–2004 entitled 'Success and failure in second language learning' (Grant number P0343604) awarded to Professor Ingrid Piller.
4. A translation of the alternative test question can be found at http://www.efl. ru/forum/threads/21878/Accessed 4 November 2008.

References

Australian Associated Press (2008) 'Citizenship Test to be Overhauled'. Accessed 27 October 2008. http://www.news.com.au/story/0,23599,24260095– 29277,00.html

Australian Citizenship Test (2007). Accessed 22 October 2008. http://www.efl.ru/ forum/threads/21878/

Australian Government (2007a) *Becoming an Australian Citizen*. Accessed 28 June 2008.http://www.citizenship.gov.au/test/resource-booklet/citz-booklet-full-ver. pdf

Australian Government (2007b) *Becoming an Australian citizen: August 2007 draft.*

Australian Government (2008) *Moving forward…Improving pathways to citizenship: Government response to the report by the Australian citizenship test review committee.* http://www.citizenshiptestreview.gov.au/_pdf/government_ response_to_the_report.pdf

Bird, J. (2008) 'Australian Citizenship Test Review to be Released within Weeks'. Accessed 28 October, 2008. http://www.visabureau.com/australia/news/27–10–2008/australian-citizenship-test-review-to-be-released-within-weeks.aspx

Blackledge, A. (2005) *Discourse and Power in a Multilingual World* (Amsterdam and Philadelphia, PA: Benjamins).

Blommaert, J. (2005) *Discourse* (Cambridge: Cambridge University Press).

Chesterman, J. and B. Galligan (eds) (1999) *Defining Australian Citizenship: Selected Documents* (Melbourne: Melbourne University Press).

Clyne, M. (2005) 'The Use of Exclusionary Language to Manipulate Opinion: John Howard, Asylum Seekers and the Reemergence of Political Incorrectness in Australia', *Journal of Language and Politics* 4 (2): 176–96.

Department of Immigration and Citizenship (2006) *Summary Report on the Outcomes of the Public Consultation on the Merits of Introducing a Formal Citizenship Test*.

Department of Immigration and Citizenship (2008). 'Overview of the Citizenship Test'. Accessed 5 January 2009. http://www.citizenship.gov.au/test/

Department of Immigration and Multicultural Affairs (2006a) *Australian Citizenship: Much More Than a Ceremony*. Accessed 26 June 2008. http://pandora.nla.gov.au/pan/64133/20061005–0000/www.citizenship.gov.au/news/DIMA_Citizenship_Discussion_Paper.pdf

Department of Immigration and Multicultural Affairs (2006b) *Summary Report on the Outcomes of the Public Consultation on the Merits of Introducing a Formal Citizenship Test*.

Hage, G. (1998) *White Nation: Fantasies of White Supremacy in a Multicultural Society* (Sydney: Pluto Press).

Lim, N. (2007) 'Citizenship Tests: Mateship – or Racism?', *The Courier Mail*, 12 November. http://www.news.com.au/couriermail/story/0,23739,22743166–27197,00.html

Liu, J. H. and D. Mills (2006) 'Modern Racism and Neo-Liberal Globalization: The Discourses of Plausible Deniability and their Multiple Functions', *Journal of Community and Applied Social Psychology* 16: 83–99.

Lundy, K. (2007) Australian Citizenship Amendment Bill 2007 – Second Reading Speech. Retrieved 24 October 2008. http://www.katelundy.com.au/citizenshipspeech.htm

Piller, I. (2001) 'Naturalization Language Testing and its Basis in Ideologies of National Identity and Citizenship', *The International Journal of Bilingualism* 5 (3): 259–77.

Piller, I. and E. Farrell (2006) 'Submission to DIMA in Response to the Discussion Paper Suggesting the Introduction of a Formal Citizenship Test'. Unpublished Discussion Paper Submission.

Piller, I. and T. McNamara (2007) 'Assessment of the Language Level of the August 2007 Draft of the Resource Booklet "Becoming an Australian Citizen"'. Unpublished Report.

Refugee Council of Australia (2006) Response to Australian Government Discussion Paper: 'Australian Citizenship: Much More than a Ceremony'.

Senate Standing Committee on Legal and Constitutional Affairs (2007) Australian Citizenship Amendment (Citizenship Testing) Bill 2007 [Provisions]. Accessed 31 October 2008. http://wopared.parl.net/Senate/committee/legcon_ctte/completed_inquiries/2004–07/citizenship_testing/report/index.htm

Shanahan, A. (2006) 'Citizenship Cane'. Accessed 24 October 2008. http://www.theaustralian.news.com.au/story/0,20867,20774740–28737,00.html

Summers, A. (2006) 'New Language Barrier No Way to Build a Tolerant Society'. Retrieved 30 September 2008. http://www.smh.com.au/news/opinion/downside-of-citizenship-tests/2006/05/01/1146335669337.html

Sydney Morning Herald (2006) 'Citizenship Test not "Targeting Muslims" '. September 18. Accessed October 31, 2008. http://www.smh.com.au/news/national/citizenship-test-not-targeting-muslims/2006/09/18/1158431640493.html

'The Real Australian Citizenship Test' (2007). Accessed 22 October 2008. http://www.rugbynetwork.net/boards/read/s97.htm?99,8382951

Part III

Citizenship Tests Under Revision: Philosophical Implications and Popular Attitudes

10
Citizenship, Identity, and Immigration: Contemporary Philosophical Perspectives

Catriona Mackenzie

Introduction

Over the last two decades there has been increasing recognition amongst political philosophers that 'the health and stability of a modern democracy depends, not only on the justice of its institutions, but also on the qualities and attitudes of its citizens' (Kymlicka and Norman, 2000a, 6). At a minimum, at least the majority of citizens must endorse liberal democratic values, demonstrate tolerance towards those from different cultural or ethnic backgrounds, or with different religious beliefs than their own, be willing to participate in the political process even if for some this participation is limited to voting, and have some commitment to the redistribution of economic and social resources to support public services and to assist those in need. Of course liberal states have coercive means at their disposal to ensure citizen compliance – anti-discrimination laws, compulsory taxation, and, in Australia, compulsory voting. But state coercion in the absence of citizen commitment to liberal democratic principles, institutions and processes, attitudes of tolerance, or some sense of obligation to support fellow citizens in need, is unlikely to secure the conditions necessary for a stable society.

This recent recognition of the importance of 'civic virtue' (Galston, 1991; Macedo, 1990) marks a shift from the more passive, rights-based conception of citizenship that became dominant in the middle of the twentieth century to a more active conception of citizenship.[1] Despite considerable agreement concerning the need for such a shift, in both the theory and practice of liberal democracy, there is considerable disagreement amongst contemporary political philosophers about the capacities and virtues necessary for active citizenship, and about the proper role of the state in their development and exercise. There is also disagreement about whether civic virtue requires a commitment to notions of national identity and about whether multiculturalism poses a threat to the sense of social cohesion that is necessary for active citizenship. These questions are not merely of theoretical interest. How they are answered has implications for public policy and the law in a range of areas including immigration and naturalisation, education, language policy, indigenous rights, and religion.

This chapter provides a brief overview of recent philosophical debates concerning citizenship, focusing specifically on conceptions of active citizenship and their implications for multiculturalism and immigration. I will argue that a flourishing democracy does require citizens to be committed to the polity, to feel they belong, and to exercise certain civic virtues. However, this does not require a commitment to a strongly defined and exclusive national identity and is quite consistent with multiculturalism. I will also consider the implications of this argument for naturalisation policy, with specific reference to the current Australian citizenship test and the Australian government booklet, *Becoming an Australian Citizen* (2007), which immigrants seeking citizenship must study in preparation for the test. The booklet emphasises the importance for new citizens to understand the 'core values that have helped to create a society that is stable yet dynamic, cohesive yet diverse' (2007, 5), and the citizenship pledge requires new citizens to pledge their 'loyalty to Australia and its people' and to affirm their commitment to its 'democratic beliefs', to respect its 'rights and liberties', and to 'uphold and obey' its laws. The booklet and the pledge thus seek to inculcate in new citizens at least a minimal sense of active citizenship. The booklet also aims to construct and foster a specific conception of shared national identity. While I agree with the importance of active citizenship, I question the necessity of understanding social cohesion and belonging in terms of shared national identity. I also question whether citizenship testing is at all adequate to the task of fostering active citizenship, assuming for the sake of the argument that this is the aim of such tests.[2]

Active citizenship

Will Kymlicka and Wayne Norman (2000a, 30–1) usefully distinguish three notions of citizenship: legal status, citizenship identity, and active citizenship or civic virtue. In modern liberal democracies the legal status of citizenship entitles citizens to a range of rights: civil rights, such as freedom of speech and association, freedom of religion, property rights, and equality under the law; political rights, such as the right to vote and stand for public office; and social rights, such as state-funded public education, health care, and welfare benefits (although the nature and extent of social rights differ considerably among the liberal democracies).[3] These rights confer extensive protections and benefits on citizens of liberal democracies compared with citizens living under many other political regimes, and the importance of these rights should not be underestimated.[4] Legal citizenship also entails certain duties. In addition to the duty to uphold the law, the duties specifically mentioned in *Becoming an Australian Citizen* are the duty to vote, jury duty, and the duty to 'defend the nation and its way of life' should the need arise (2007, 4).

Citizenship identity refers broadly to a person's membership of a political community. In some political communities, citizenship identity is grounded in shared ethnic, cultural, linguistic, or religious identities. For the first 150 years of European settlement, Australian citizenship identity was bound up with a sense of 'British' identity, despite the persistence of some ethnic and religious divisions among those with English, Irish, and Scottish heritages. Over the last 40 years, however, Australia has become a multicultural nation and Australian citizenship identity may be just one of a number of identities – for example, ethnic, national, religious, or linguistic – in terms of which citizens conceive themselves. This raises the question of whether social cohesion requires Australian citizenship identity to be grounded in a common sense of national identity, of 'belonging together', having shared characteristics, or shared values that unifies Australians as a 'people' despite their diversity. *Becoming an Australian Citizen* seeks to promote such a conception of national identity. Among political philosophers, liberal nationalists (eg. Miller, 1995; Tamir, 1993) also argue that social cohesion in a multicultural liberal democracy requires a common national identity. I will return to this question in the final section of this chapter.

Many contemporary political philosophers agree that the rights-based, legal status conception of citizenship, despite both its historical importance and its importance for individual citizens, is insufficient to meet the challenges of sustaining flourishing liberal democratic institutions in large, pluralistic societies. In addition, citizens must exercise distinctive civic virtues or active citizenship. I will focus on two influential accounts of active citizenship, the liberal virtue view articulated by William Galston (1991), and theories of deliberative democracy.

Galston distinguishes a liberal conception of virtue from the Aristotelian civic republican conception. Briefly, the Aristotelian view is based on a specific conception of human nature: that human beings (or, more accurately men for Aristotle) are political animals and thus that political participation is the highest form of social relationship and a necessary condition for a good and flourishing human life. In 'From Virtues to Values' (this volume), Ian Tregenza argues that this Aristotelian conception, articulated in the modern era by T.H. Green, informed conceptions of Australian citizenship in the early years of Australian nationhood, as evidenced in the writings of Walter Murdoch. Contemporary liberals, such as John Rawls, reject the Aristotelian conception as incompatible with pluralism about the good, arguing that the promotion of civic virtue must be justified by the demands of justice rather than on the grounds of a specific conception of what constitutes a good and flourishing human life (Rawls, 1972). In contrast to the Aristotelian view that civic virtue is an end in itself, the liberal conception is instrumentalist. Civic virtue, and in particular, the exercise of certain political virtues, is instrumentally necessary for sustaining just institutions.[5] As Galston puts it, 'the viability of liberal society depends on its ability to engender a virtuous citizenry' (1991, 217). Nevertheless, Galston notes that elements of an Aristotelian conception of civic virtue are present in the views of many liberal theorists, such as J.S. Mill, and also in Rawls's view that a well-functioning and just liberal society enables its citizens to express their natures 'as free and equal rational beings who have realised their innate capacity for justice' (1991, 219).

Liberal civic virtues are also substantively different in kind from Aristotelian virtues. Galston suggests that there are certain *general* virtues that any polity must promote in its citizens: courage and the willingness to defend one's country, law-abidingness, and loyalty to one's political community and its core principles. However, because of their distinctive character, liberal polities require of their citizens distinctive economic, social, and political virtues. Galston describes the distinctive character of liberal polities in the following terms: 'popular-constitutional government; a diverse society with a wide range of individual opportunities and choices; a predominantly market economy; and, a substantial, strongly protected sphere of privacy and individual rights' (1991, 220). Galston characterises the *economic* virtues required of citizens in a liberal market economy as having a strong work ethic, the capacity for delayed gratification, and adaptability to economic and technological change. However, I would suggest that these qualities are required of citizens in most modern economies, whether their polities are liberal or not.

Of most interest is Galston's account of the *social* and *political* virtues. The central *social* virtues are independence and tolerance. Galston argues that the emphasis on individual rights requires citizens to be independent and willing to take responsibility for their lives.[6] However, the development of capacities for independence requires strong family relationships. Hence family solidarity is a virtue that is critical for the development of independence and other virtues in children and hence for the success of liberal societies.[7] The diverse character of liberal societies requires that citizens develop the virtue of tolerance. According to Galston, tolerance does not entail relativism about ways of life, but it does require disagreements about value to be settled using reasoned persuasion rather than coercion.[8] A related social virtue, although not one discussed by Galston, is civility, which Kymlicka, drawing on the work of Jeff Spinner, characterises as 'treating others as equals on the condition that they extend the same recognition to you' (Kymlicka, 2002, 302; Spinner, 1994). Kymlicka suggests that civility is the extension of anti-discrimination legislation in our interactions with non-intimates. Just as anti-discrimination legislation prohibits employers from refusing to hire employees on grounds on race, gender, or sexual preference, so the norms of civility rule out rudeness on such grounds towards other citizens in public contexts.

The central *political* virtues required of citizens are respect for the rights of others, self-restraint in demands made on the public purse, and the ability and willingness to question political authority, that is, to seek justifications for the decisions and judgments of elected representatives and to hold public officials to account. Liberal democratic polities also require their leaders to exercise specific virtues: 'to work within the constraints on action imposed by social diversity and constitutional institutions'; 'to forge a sense of common purpose against the centrifugal tendencies of an individualistic and fragmented society'; and to make decisions based on the public interest rather than popular sentiment (Galston, 1991, 226). Citizens, leaders, and public officials must also develop the disposition, and exercise the capacity, to engage in public discourse, a political virtue that overlaps considerably with the social virtue of tolerance: 'This virtue includes the willingness to listen seriously to a range of views which, given the diversity of liberal societies, will include ideas the listener is bound to find strange and even obnoxious. The virtue of political discourse also includes the willingness to set forth one's own views intelligibly and candidly as the basis of a politics of persuasion rather than manipulation or coercion' (Galston, 1991, 227). As I shall discuss shortly, for theorists of deliberative democracy, the capacity to engage in public discourse is central to democratic legitimacy.

Galston's account of liberal social and political virtues is echoed in a number of the values listed in *Becoming an Australian Citizen* as important 'Australian values'. These include 'respect for the equal worth, dignity and freedom of the individual', 'tolerance, mutual respect and compassion for those in need', and 'peacefulness'. The latter is characterised in terms of the politics of persuasion as the belief 'that change should occur by discussion, peaceful persuasion and the democratic process. We reject violence as a means of changing a person's mind or the law' (2007, 7).

Galston's conception of liberal virtue does not require that all citizens participate actively in political life, or subordinate their personal interests to the common good. Nor does it require that all citizens exercise the liberal virtues. However, it is premised on the hypothesis that 'as the proportion of nonvirtuous citizens increases significantly, the ability of liberal societies to function successfully progressively diminishes' (Galston, 1991, 220). Galston regards the promotion of civic virtue as a particular challenge for liberal societies. As he puts it, 'the liberal virtues are the traits of character liberalism needs, not necessarily the ones it has' (1991, 217). In his view, this challenge arises from tensions endemic to liberalism between, on the one hand, individualism and self-interest, and, on the other, the necessity of civic virtue for the viability of liberal societies, tensions which are only exacerbated by their increasing diversity. The underlying anxieties generated by this sense of the challenge facing liberal societies have surfaced particularly post-9/11, as the internal challenge has combined with a perceived external threat. In my view, these anxieties are given expression in the growing concern among liberal democracies about immigration and citizenship.

Galston's political virtue of being able and willing to engage in reasoned public discourse, which is often referred to as the virtue of 'public reasonableness', has been emphasised most forcefully by theorists of deliberative democracy, whose central concern is to articulate the conditions necessary for democratic legitimacy.[9] Such theorists agree that the legal status conception of citizenship is inadequate to sustain healthy democratic institutions, but are also motivated by other concerns about the political practices of liberal democracies: in particular, that the political process has become overly focused on polling and voting, and that it has become captive to the interests of powerful individuals, corporations, and lobby groups. Deliberative theorists argue that vote-centred democracy is really just a form of majority rule, in which voting decisions are driven too much by self-interest, prejudice or ignorance, while the influence of powerful interests can subvert the political process. Deliberative theorists also aim to give voice to minority or marginalised social groups who are outnumbered by majority voting contests and whose only hope of influencing the political process is through public debate and by influencing the formation of public opinion. Thus, deliberative theorists, such as Joshua Cohen (1997), argue that the legitimacy of the democratic process depends on whether it meets certain requirements, specifically, that it involves free and reasoned decision-making among equals deliberating about the public good.

The notion of free decision-making implies that, although participants in the deliberative process might come to it with certain starting values, interests, and views, they must be open to others' expressions of their views and prepared to revise their views in the light of debate, discussion, and dialogue. The notion of reasoned decision-making emphasises that collective choices must be the outcome of reasoned debate. As Cohen argues, 'the mere fact of having a preference, conviction, or ideal does not by itself provide a reason in support of a proposal' (1997, 76). In order to persuade others that my views are worth considering or must be taken seriously, I must provide reasons for those views, reasons that others who may not share my worldview will nevertheless find persuasive. Justifying one's views according to religious dictates, for example, is unlikely to persuade in a pluralist society where many citizens do not share one's religious convictions. The notion of equality involves both formal and substantive aspects. Everyone capable of deliberating must be given a voice in the decision, and their ability to put an item on the political agenda or to contribute to the decision-making process must not be determined by factors such as their ability to wield social power or command resources. Finally, the focus of deliberation must be the public good, not each individual's self-interested concerns and preferences. This does not mean that people are expected to discount their own interests, but rather to focus the debate on matters concerning the common good: 'the interests, aims, and ideals that comprise the common good are those that survive deliberation, interests that, on reflection, we think it legitimate to appeal to in making claims on social resources' (Cohen, 1997, 77). An implication of this account is that the common good is actually decided by the deliberative process, not by a particular conception of the good, as in Aristotelian republicanism, nor by prior considerations, such as the interests of powerful groups, religious convictions, or narrow economic concerns.

Theories of deliberative democracy have provoked debate on a range of issues. One set of issues concerns how deliberative processes might be implemented in large, pluralistic societies. Proposals include reforms to existing political processes (eg. to make candidate selection more representative; to limit or abolish private funding for political parties and election campaigns), and setting up a variety of publicly funded forums (eg. citizen juries; pre-polling deliberative assemblies) in which citizens can deliberate and debate about matters of public concern. Recently, the Internet has been used, for example by the Australian organisation Get Up, to provide an extremely effective deliberative forum for citizens. Another set of issues concerns whether theories of deliberative democracy require an overly demanding conception of active citizenship. As Kymlicka puts it: 'Democratic citizens must be not only active and participatory, critical of authority, and non-dogmatic, but also committed to seeking mutual understanding through deliberation rather than exclusively seeking personal benefit through bargaining or threats' (2002, 293). The concern is not only that this conception of citizenship is overly idealistic, but also that it requires of citizens capacities for critical reflection and articulacy that may favour the well-educated and middle class and may thus end up being exclusionary of members of minority or marginalised groups.[10]

This criticism certainly poses a challenge that theorists of deliberative democracy must meet, and raises questions concerning how to ensure that deliberative processes are genuinely inclusive, and what institutional structures are best able to develop in citizens the capacities and social virtues, such as tolerance, that are necessary for 'public reasonableness'. There has been considerable debate about the role and responsibility of the education system to promote the development of these capacities and virtues in children and about the legitimate extent and limits of civic education. Amy Gutmann, for example, argues that education for democratic citizenship requires that school curricula develop in children the intellectual and critical capacities to question authority, including the authority of political, religious, and cultural traditions, and to 'evaluate ways of life different from their parents' (Gutmann, 1987, 30). These capacities, in her view, are a precondition for meaningful choice in a liberal society. Galston rejects this conception of civic education as a coercive intrusion on legitimate parental authority and as enforcing a conception of the good, centred on the value of autonomy, that is incompatible with diversity (1991, 253–5).[11]

This debate points to deep underlying tensions within liberal democratic theory about the value of autonomy. The ideals of deliberative democracy and political virtues such as public reasonableness are premised on a conception of citizens as autonomous, that is, as able to critically reflect upon and reason about their own beliefs and values, as well as those of others, and, potentially, to revise their beliefs and values in light of reflection. Furthermore, a traditional tenet of liberalism is not just that citizens are capable of autonomy but that they have a right to exercise it and that the state must protect that right. This idea underpins other important liberal rights, such as freedom of religion, freedom of speech, and freedom of association.[12] Kymlicka argues persuasively that it also underpins the liberal conception of tolerance. What distinguishes liberal tolerance from its non-liberal forms, such as the 'millet system' of religious toleration that regulated relations between Muslims, Christians, and Jews under the Ottoman Empire, is that liberal tolerance has historically been bound up with the exercise of individual freedom of conscience, which is premised on the notion of autonomy (Kymlicka, 2002, 229–40). However, the exercise of autonomy can pose a threat to a range of traditional religious and cultural beliefs, as well as ways of life and conceptions of the good founded upon them. This raises the question of whether a commitment to autonomy is consistent with liberalism's professed commitment to diversity. Galston argues that it is not, and seeks to defend a form of liberalism based on the value of diversity rather than the value of autonomy.[13]

In his later work, Rawls (1985, 1993) tries to deal with this difficulty by distinguishing 'political' from 'comprehensive' liberalism, and our identities as citizens from our identities as private individuals. Comprehensive liberalism is committed to the value of autonomy and individuality, and thus to the idea that all our beliefs and values, including those arising from religious or cultural traditions, are, in principle, revisable in light of rational reflection. Gutmann's conception of the kind of education necessary for democratic citizenship is underpinned by such a comprehensive liberalism. Political liberalism seeks to secure agreement, or an overlapping consensus, on the fundamental political principles of liberalism while allowing that different groups in society will hold quite diverse comprehensive conceptions of the good. Political liberalism requires that citizens must have the capacity and willingness to exercise 'public reasonableness' on political questions – issues of justice, rights, and public responsibilities. However, Rawls holds that the exercise of this capacity in the political sphere is quite compatible with citizens *qua* private persons being committed to diverse comprehensive conceptions of the good, some of which will prohibit critical reflection and questioning, for example on matters of faith. There is extensive debate in the literature, which I cannot engage with in any detail here, concerning whether Rawls' strategy is successful. Suffice to say that Kymlicka, for example, raises serious questions about the plausibility of Rawls's claim that the exercise of autonomy in the context of public reason will have no 'spillover effects' for citizens' non-public identities (2002, 236) and be without cost for those groups in society that do not value autonomy. It is difficult to see how the capacity to question one's own and others' beliefs in the political sphere and to engage in reasoned public discourse can be quarantined from the exercise of that capacity when it comes to religious belief or cultural traditions.[14] It is also difficult to see how a sharp distinction between comprehensive and political liberalism can be maintained in practice, given that, in liberal societies, governments are obliged to inform citizens of their basic rights and liberties (including rights to freedom of association, speech, and religion) and to ensure that individuals have the capacity (through the public education system, for example) and the liberty to exercise those rights.

To sum up the discussion so far, despite considerable agreement among contemporary political philosophers that the rights-based notion of legal citizenship needs to be bolstered by a more active conception of citizenship, there are significant differences of view concerning the capacities and virtues necessary for active citizenship, and the role the state should play in promoting these capacities and virtues. These differences are connected to deep disagreements within liberalism concerning the value of autonomy. Although I have not developed a detailed argument for this claim here, in my view the capacity for autonomy is crucial for the exercise of the social and political virtues required in a liberal polity. The relevant question is not whether autonomy is central to liberalism, but what conception of autonomy liberalism presupposes. The different responses to this question proposed within contemporary political philosophy reflect some of the tensions and diversity of philosophical and political views within liberalism.[15] A further question concerns whether governments have a duty not only to protect autonomy, but also to promote the social conditions necessary for the development and exercise of this capacity in citizens.[16]

As we have seen, while stressing the importance of civic virtues for liberal societies, Galston thinks liberal societies face considerable challenges in producing a virtuous citizenry, challenges that are exacerbated by their increasing diversity. One of the main anxieties about multiculturalism is that it threatens to erode the sense of social cohesion and commitment to the polity that is necessary for a virtuous citizenry. In the following two sections of the chapter, I consider several responses to this worry in contemporary political philosophy. In the next section, I discuss Kymlicka's liberal defence of multiculturalism. In the final section, I address the question of whether the social cohesion necessary for the realisation of liberal values requires a commitment to a notion of shared national identity.

Multiculturalism and social cohesion

In several important and highly influential books (Kymlicka, 1989, 1995, 2002), Kymlicka develops a powerful defence of multiculturalism appealing to liberal principles. His aim is to argue that multiculturalism, including certain group-differentiated rights, is necessary for promoting the liberal values of autonomy, equality, and inclusive citizenship. Kymlicka distinguishes between a number of different multicultural groups, which, in his view, have different rights claims against the state: national minorities, indigenous peoples, immigrants, isolationist ethno-religious groups, and African–Americans (2002, ch. 8, section 4). My discussion in this section and the next will focus primarily on the claims of immigrants.

Kymlicka develops three main arguments in defence of multiculturalism: the arguments from autonomy, equality, and citizenship.[17] The argument from autonomy connects the value of cultural membership with the value of autonomy and involves two main claims: first, that cultural heritage and membership of a cultural community play a constitutive role in the formation of individual identity, or more simply, that our sense of who we are is inextricably bound up with our sense of place and belonging within a broader cultural structure; and second, that this cultural structure – in the form of language, heritage, history, culturally intelligible patterns of activities, and cultural narratives – provides the context within which we develop and exercise our capacities for agency and autonomy. We become agents already embedded and participating in particular ways of life and the decisions and choices we make are structured and made meaningful by the culturally available options. For both these reasons, it is crucially important to individual identity formation and to the development of a person's capacity for autonomy that their cultural identity is recognised and respected by the broader community.

Joseph Raz argues along similar lines. In his view, the exercise of freedom depends on the availability of options. Options are those complex and multi-dimensional activities, practices, and relationships that make our lives meaningful, such as pursuing a career in a particular profession, being a parent, being a member of a religious community, or participating in sport, cultural activities, or politics. Because options are complex and depend on implicit rules, conventions, and shared meanings, they 'are available only to those who master them [...] who have or can acquire practical knowledge of them, that is, knowledge embodied in social practices and transmitted by habituation' (1994, 177). Cultures, in Raz's view, are constituted by complex networks of interlocking social practices, and individuals only gain access to any culture's constitutive range of options through a process of socialisation. Thus, 'by and large one's cultural membership determines the horizon of one's opportunities' (1994, 177). This is why Raz thinks that 'individual freedom and prosperity depend on full and unimpeded membership in a respected and flourishing cultural group' (1994, 174).

The argument from autonomy has been the subject of extensive subsequent debate. One criticism claims that it assumes and perpetuates a false conception of cultures as static and homogenous.[18] Another influential criticism suggests that it bases the value of culture on a controversial and specifically liberal value, which many cultures do not endorse.[19] In the case of such non-liberal communities, the autonomy argument would therefore seem to justify cultural interference, rather than cultural protection, requiring those communities to liberalise. But this requirement would undermine the very basis of many cultural communities, and is in fact inconsistent with the liberal value of respect for diversity. This criticism targets in particular Kymlicka's distinction between external protections and internal restrictions (1995, ch. 3).

Kymlicka defends cultural rights that take the form of 'external protections' against economic, political, and cultural domination. Such external protections (eg. land rights for indigenous people) are justified, he argues, because they 'reduce the vulnerability of minority groups to the economic pressures and political decisions of the larger society' (1995, 38). Further, these kinds of external protections are consistent with the protection of the individual rights of community members. However, group-specific cultural rights that take the form of 'internal restrictions' cannot be justified by a liberal theory. These are restrictions imposed by communities on their own members in the name of 'tradition' or 'cultural integrity', and that function to quash dissent and limit the ability of individuals within those communities to 'question, revise, or abandon traditional cultural roles and practices' (Kymlicka, 1999, 31). Kymlicka argues that groups seeking cultural rights on the grounds of internal restrictions are seeking to curtail the basic civil and political liberties of group members. A liberal theory of minority rights thus cannot consistently accept such restrictions because they conflict with the protection of individual rights.

It is beyond the scope of my concerns in this chapter to engage with the complex issues raised by this debate. Suffice to say that it raises pressing issues for liberal societies, specifically concerning the limits of tolerance and questions of gender justice. As many feminist commentators have pointed out, 'internal restrictions' are most often imposed on women and girls, often within the context of the family, effectively curtailing their basic freedoms and in some cases subjecting them to serious injustice and harm.[20] I concur there are good grounds for arguing that such restrictions are not consistent with gender justice and I would argue that feminists have good reason for upholding the importance of autonomy.[21]

The argument from equality is that group rights are necessary to secure substantive equality for members of minority cultural communities. This argument translates feminist arguments against 'gender-blind' conceptions of equality as sameness to minority groups. Just as feminists have argued that women's equality, and genuine justice for women, cannot be secured simply by granting women the same formal individual rights as men but rather requires gender-specific rights that redress the inequalities arising from women's circumstances and from the structure of the workplace and the family, so liberal multiculturalism argues that justice and equality for minority ethnic or aboriginal communities in a culturally plural society require culture-specific rights. However, the kinds of group-based rights required by different groups will be different and involve different justifications. In the case of indigenous groups, for example, group-based rights, such as land rights, are required to protect indigenous cultures from disintegration, fragmentation or assimilation. Other group-specific rights, such as special entry schemes to universities, indigenous health care services, and so on are required in order to redress inequalities in their circumstances arising from historical disadvantage and cultural marginalisation. In the case of immigrant groups the justification, as I shall discuss shortly, is to enable integration and a sense of social inclusion and belonging.

In his recent work, Kymlicka articulates a citizenship-based argument for multiculturalism (2002, 343–65), which centres on notions of social inclusion and belonging, responding to what he regards as an inaccurate conception of the liberal state as indifferent to, or adopting an attitude of benign neglect towards, issues of ethno-cultural identity. That conception is based on the false claim that liberal states treat culture in the same way as religion – as a private matter, which thereby precludes an official state religion and requires a strict separation of church and state.[22] As Kymlicka points out, liberal states do not treat culture as a private matter; rather, they engage in activities of 'nation-building' which attempt to integrate citizens into a particular societal culture, with a common language and social institutions; to get citizens to identify with the nation-state.[23] Citizenship policies, 'official' national language(s), education policies, national media, symbols, and public holidays are all aimed to promote the societal culture of the nation. As I will argue in the following section of this chapter, such a nation-building agenda is evident in *Becoming an Australian Citizen*. Kymlicka does not reject such nation-building efforts as inherently normatively problematic, but suggests that they are problematic if they function by assimilating, excluding, or disempowering minorities. Kymlicka thus argues for a 'differentiated' conception of citizenship that grants 'certain groups or their members rights or opportunities that are not available to other groups of citizens' (Kymlicka and Norman, 2000a, 31).

What does differentiated citizenship mean for immigrant groups? Kymlicka and Norman (2000a, 20–2) distinguish three kinds of immigrant groups: immigrants with rights of citizenship; immigrants without rights of citizenship; and refugees and asylum seekers.[24] Immigrants with rights of citizenship have voluntarily chosen to emigrate, usually under an immigration policy that entitles them to citizenship after a short period of residence, subject to minimal conditions. As Kymlicka points out, until fairly recently liberal states have adopted assimilationist policies towards immigrant groups, discouraging them from using their native languages, requiring them to abandon traditional customs and practices, and failing to recognise the worth of their cultural or religious identities within the broader culture. Assimilation was certainly the norm in Australia until at least the 1970s, and during the years of the conservative Howard Government, there was a decided retreat from explicitly multicultural policies to a more assimilationist stance. Kymlicka argues that such policies are unjust and impose unfair costs and disadvantages on immigrant groups. On grounds of justice, liberal polities must accommodate and integrate immigrants on fairer terms.[25]

Kymlicka suggests two main kinds of claims against the state to which immigrant groups are entitled. First, liberal states have an obligation to minimise the costs of integration, for example through the provision of free language classes to migrants as well as a range of other special services, such as specialised migrant support services in areas such as health, education, and legal rights. Second, immigrant groups have a right not only to maintain their ethnic heritage, but also to have their identities respected and recognised. Such respect and recognition 'requires a systematic exploration of our social institutions to see whether their rules and symbols disadvantage immigrants' (2002, 355). Where necessary, it also requires institutional changes, enabling reasonable accommodation of diverse identities. For example, schools should allow students to respect religious dress codes, such as wearing the hijab,[26] and schools and employers should accommodate religious holidays and make it possible for students and employees to observe requirements for prayer (for example, by providing prayer rooms). Kymlicka nevertheless argues that while immigrant groups should not be expected to forsake their heritage and cultural practices, they should be expected to integrate with the dominant societal culture. Thus multiculturalism in the sense of polyethnicity does not involve the creation of separate societal cultures alongside the dominant culture, but rather the inclusion of diverse ethnic groups within it. Of course, such inclusion will not leave the dominant culture unchanged but will gradually transform it in the process, as has happened in Australia.[27]

Tariq Modood (2000) also argues that, for immigrant groups, the focus and political significance of notions of differentiated citizenship, or hybridity, is exclusion and inclusion. In other words, the political demands made by such groups are aimed at redressing inequalities in the worth of legal citizenship and creating the social and political conditions under which members of immigrant groups may fully participate in society as active citizens.[28] He argues that the empirical evidence 'suggests that this is a movement of inclusion (at least from the side of those excluded) and social cohesion, not fragmentation' (2000, 186).

Immigrants without rights of citizenship include an array of different groups, including illegal migrants, workers on temporary visas, and guest workers.[29] Members of such groups face a range of legal, political, economic, social, and psychological obstacles to integration and are socially marginalised (Kymlicka, 2002, 358). What they seek is to be treated as immigrants, but because of the routes through which they ended up in a country, many liberal states have resisted their demands to be accepted as citizens. Kymlicka argues, rightly in my view, that immigrants in this category have been treated unjustly by the policies and practices of many liberal states. The result has been the creation of a 'permanently disenfranchised, alienated, and racially defined underclass' (2002, 359), which may pose real dangers to social cohesion and stability. Recently liberal states have also begun adopting increasingly punitive and unjust policies towards refugees and asylum seekers. In Australia under the Howard Government, such policies included mandatory detention and temporary protection visas that denied asylum seekers who had been released from detention access to the usual range of migrant services, such as accommodation assistance and free English language classes. In many well-documented cases, the impact of these policies on the physical and mental health of individual refugees and asylum seekers has been devastating. In the case of both these categories of immigrant groups, it seems evident, as Kymlicka argues, that the threat they potentially pose to social cohesion is the result of unjust policies, social stigmatisation, marginalisation, and failures to provide members of these groups the opportunity to integrate.

National identity or belonging?

Some citizens might not conceive of citizenship as central to their identity: ethnic, national, religious, or linguistic identities may figure more importantly in their self-conceptions. Or, a person's self-identity may be a complex hybrid – Chinese–Australian, Indigenous–Australian (or more specifically Noongar or Koori Indigenous–Australian), Jewish–Australian, Muslim–Lebanese–Australian – the different aspects of which may sometimes be in conflict. This notion of differentiated citizenship raises the question of whether liberal states that adopt multicultural policies also need to foster a sense of common national identity amongst citizens. The claim that they do is based on the assumption that, in a multicultural society, a sense of shared national identity is necessary for social cohesion and active citizenship. This assumption is evident in *Becoming an Australian Citizen*, for example in the statement that 'modern citizenship...rests on sentiments of nationhood and enduring attachment to what Australians hold in common' (2007, 1). The booklet aims to foster such a sense of common national identity, based on a shared national language (English), a commitment to 'Australian values' – which are an amalgam of liberal principles and liberal virtues inflected with notions of 'mateship' – national symbols and holidays, the system of parliamentary democracy, the territory of Australia, and a story about the history of the nation.

Amongst political philosophers, this conception of national identity has become known as liberal nationalism (Miller, 1995; Tamir, 1993). Liberal nationalists hold that a sense of national identity is a necessary condition for the realisation of liberal values. In particular, they argue that a shared national identity is necessary in a liberal polity for citizens to identify with their political institutions; to maintain social stability; to foster social trust; and to elicit a commitment to a politics of the common good and support for distributive justice, both of which require a sense of solidarity with one's co-nationals.[30] To have a sense of national identity is to have a sense of 'belonging together', to identify oneself as part of a 'people'. Shelley Wilcox (who does not endorse liberal nationalism) characterises this sense of identification as involving 'mutual and exclusive feelings of solidarity, sympathy, and obligation for one's fellow nationals over and above a sense of patriotism for one's country' (2004, 569). David Miller understands national identity as a sense of belonging together arising from shared characteristics, which are reflected in the public culture – in shared political principles, social norms, and ideals (1995, 25–6). Kymlicka endorses the liberal nationalist conception of national identity, which he characterises as a 'sense of belonging to an intergenerational society, sharing a common territory, having a common past and sharing a common future' (2002, 264). He gives reasons, such as those just cited, for thinking that a common national identity is a condition for social cohesion in a multicultural polity, arguing that the liberal nationalist conception of national identity is sufficiently 'thin' to be inclusive.

However, Kymlicka acknowledges that the 'tendency to "thicken" notions of national identity is a permanent danger in any regime that tries to build unity through notions of nationhood' (2002, 267). This is indeed the worry that was expressed by many Australians, particularly from non Anglo-Celtic ethnic backgrounds, about the introduction of the citizenship test and the specific conception of national identity that is constructed in *Becoming an Australian Citizen*, through its story of a common Australian history. This story seems to perpetuate certain national myths – about the significance of the Anzac tradition in forging an Australian national identity;[31] that colonisation in Australia was 'peaceful'; the hagiography of sporting idols. These myths are exclusionary, most notably of Aboriginal people, through a silence about the violent history of Aboriginal dispossession and other practices of attempted cultural genocide, but they are also exclusionary of other groups, most notably Australians of non Anglo-Celtic or European backgrounds (women also do not figure prominently in this history). In many ways, this history functions to undermine the claims elsewhere in the booklet about the way Australia values its cultural diversity.

This raises the question of whether attempts to found a cohesive multicultural society on notions of a common 'national identity' have a tendency to bolster an assimilationist agenda. Andrew Mason (1999) raises this concern, drawing on Iris Young's politics of difference (1990). He suggests that notions of common national identity can have moral costs for members of some groups, leading to disadvantage and inequality in the worth of citizenship. These costs might be justifiable, he concedes, if a common national identity is indeed necessary for the realisation of liberal values. However, Mason argues that the alleged benefits of national identity could be secured by a sense of what he calls 'belonging to a polity'. Mason characterises this sense as follows:

> [A] person has a sense of belonging to a polity if and only if she identifies with most of its major institutions and some of its central practices and feels at home in them. When a person identifies with those institutions and practices, she regards her flourishing as intimately linked to their flourishing [...]. When a person feels at home in a practice or institution, she is able to find her way around it, and she experiences participation in it as natural. In order to be able to feel this way, she must not be excluded from the practice or institution or be marginalized in relation to it. (1999, 272)

Mason thinks citizens might have this sense of belonging to a polity even if they do not agree with the policies of their government, do not identify with or endorse the historical processes that led to the formation of their institutions (or the myths that are told about these processes), or have any deep shared sense of 'belonging together', that is, any deep sense of national identity. He argues that the sense of belonging to a polity might be sufficient for citizens to forge a sense of sharing a common fate that enables the maintenance of a stable liberal society; for social trust; and for a commitment to a politics of the common good and support for distributive justice. Mason suggests this notion of belonging to a polity as one interpretation of Charles Taylor's proposal that Canada 'might become a polity held together by the acceptance of a "deep diversity" in which a plurality of ways of belonging were acknowledged' (Taylor, 1993, 183, as cited by Mason, 1999, 273). Whether a stable liberal polity could be maintained on the basis of a widespread acceptance of 'deep diversity' is an empirical hypothesis that has yet to find confirmation in any contemporary society. But Mason's notion of 'belonging to a polity' may be an apt characterisation of the sentiments of those Australians who feel a sense of belonging but who are alienated by constructions of national identity that do not connect with their cultural backgrounds, experience, or sentiments.

Mason suggests two main ways that a sense of 'belonging to a polity' might be fostered: first, by ensuring that public institutions and policy-making bodies are inclusive of members of diverse cultural communities and that their perspectives and identities are socially recognised;[32] second, accommodation through group differentiated laws and policies. Although he does not discuss naturalisation, or address the question of how naturalisation policies might also foster this sense of belonging, Wilcox (2004) does address this question with reference to Mason's distinction between the nationalist notion of 'belonging together' and the notion of 'belonging to a polity'. The focus of Wilcox's discussion is naturalisation policies in the United States; so many of her concrete proposals do not apply to the Australian context. However, she makes two central points in response to liberal nationalist claims that the primary goal of a naturalisation policy should be to encourage new citizens to embrace the national identity, which can relevantly be applied to the Australian context. First, she questions the idea that the formal aspects of the naturalisation process – whether in the form of civics classes, language and citizenship testing, or naturalisation ceremonies – are sufficient to instil the sense of national identity, and in particular emotional identification with a 'people', that liberal nationalists advocate. With reference to 'the strong fellow feelings of solidarity, sympathy, and mutual obligation associated with such national identification', she says 'surely no formal naturalisation process, no matter how substantive and symbolic, can produce such social solidarity' (2004, 573). Second, she questions on two grounds the normative desirability of a naturalisation policy that aims to foster such nationalist sentiments: that it is implicitly assimilationist; and that it 'could be used to justify restrictive immigration policies' (2004, 574).

It was precisely those worries that underpinned concerns about the introduction of the citizenship test by the Howard Government in Australia in 2007, though they have lessened to some extent over the past year under the new Labor Government, due to a range of substantive changes to immigration policy, including a review of the citizenship test and the booklet *Becoming an Australian Citizen*, both of which will be revised.[33] The new booklet will be divided into testable and non-testable sections and the test will focus primarily on the commitments in the pledge, democratic principles, and the responsibilities and privileges of citizenship, rather than 'knowledge of Australia'. However, the political context in which the Australian test was introduced, as discussed in Lloyd Cox's chapter in this volume, does suggest that concerns about the assimilationist tendencies of liberal nationalism are not without foundation. Further, given that the virtues and capacities necessary for democratic citizenship are complex and are acquired through education and social and political participation, it is unclear how they can be 'tested' in anything but the most superficial way.

Following Mason, Wilcox argues that a naturalisation policy that aims to foster a sense of belonging to a polity may be just as effective, if not more, in promoting liberal virtues as a policy that aims to promote a shared sense of national identity. Having a sense of belonging to a polity may also be associated with affective attitudes such as 'feelings of loyalty to one's country, pride in its political institutions and practices, and the sense of a shared future that can develop when individuals participate together as equals in democratic practices' (2004, 576). However, this sense of belonging need not involve the belief that one belongs together with one's co-nationals as a 'people', nor does it require special sentiments of relatedness or sympathy with one another. Rather, it involves a sense of inclusion and participation in a political community with which citizens regard their fate as bound. The aims of a naturalisation policy should thus be to foster such a sense of inclusion by making new citizens feel welcome, and to enable participation as active members of the society by providing the social resources necessary for participation.

If citizenship testing were a means of fostering such a sense of inclusion and enabling participation, then this might count as an argument in its favour. Whether citizenship testing could have these beneficial effects is an empirical question that needs to be tested against the evidence. In the current political contexts in which citizenship testing is being introduced in various countries, however, the evidence often seems to point in the other direction, suggesting that the aim of such tests is to exclude certain categories of migrants who are perceived as a threat to social cohesion. The question liberal states must address is whether this exclusionary agenda actually contributes to the social fragmentation and alienation that they are seeking to prevent.

Acknowledgement

I would like to thank Sue Dodds, Duncan Ivison, and Jeremy Moss for their participation in the panel I chaired on 'Philosophical Perspectives on Citizenship' at the conference 'From Migrants to Citizens: Testing Language, Testing Culture', held at Macquarie University, December 3–5, 2008. Their presentations and the ensuing discussion were extremely useful in helping me to clarify the focus of this chapter.

Notes

1. For more detailed discussion, see Ian Tregenza, 'From Virtues to Values', Chapter 4, this volume.
2. For an analysis of the political context in which the Australian citizenship test was introduced that questions this assumption, see Lloyd Cox, 'The Value of Values?', Chapter 5, this volume.
3. Kymlicka and Norman's analysis of the legal status concept of citizenship draws on the work of T.H. Marshall. For further discussion, see Tregenza, 'From Virtues to Values', and Kymlicka (2002, 287–8).
4. Despite its nationalistic tone, there is thus considerable truth in the description of Australian citizenship (in *Becoming an Australian Citizen*), as 'a privilege that offers enormous rewards to all those who strive to uphold its obligations' (2007, 1).
5. For a more detailed discussion of the philosophical disagreements underlying the differences between the Aristotelian and the liberal conceptions of civic virtue, see Kymlicka (2002: 294–302). It should be noted that although Galston's conception of liberal virtue is largely instrumentalist, Galston rejects Rawls' view that liberalism should be neutral between competing conceptions of the good, arguing that liberalism is committed to a particular conception of the good.
6. Feminist critics have criticised the assumption of many liberal theorists that all citizens are capable of independence. Kittay (1997) points out that all citizens are dependent and vulnerable at various times and argues forcefully that an assumption of independence excludes many groups of citizens, especially those with disabilities, and leads to serious flaws in liberal conceptions of justice and citizenship. For a related argument, see also Nussbaum (2006).
7. Galston claims that 'the family is the critical arena in which independence and a host of other virtues must be engendered. The weakening of families is thus fraught with danger for liberal societies' (222). Since Rousseau, liberal theorists have long recognised the importance of the family for the development of a virtuous citizenry and the stability of liberal society. For example, the role of the family in developing citizens' moral capacities is discussed extensively in Rawls' *A Theory of Justice* (1972). However, traditional liberal conceptions of the family have historically been premised on a sharp, gendered, distinction between the public and the private spheres. For this reason, they have been subject to extensive critique by feminists. For a feminist critique of liberalism that uses liberal principles to argue for gender justice, see Okin (1989).
8. There has been extensive discussion in the literature about both the complexities and limits of tolerance. It is beyond the scope of my discussion here to address this literature, but see for example, T.M. Scanlon's essay 'The Difficulty of Tolerance' in Scanlon (2003). It is also important to distinguish tolerance from respect (eg. Taylor, 1994, 21–2) and recognition (eg. Fraser, 1997, ch. 1). It is worth pointing out that although liberal states discourage citizens from using coercive means to settle disputes about value, governments use coercive means, such as sedition laws and anti-terrorism legislation, to deal with those citizens whose views they are not prepared

to tolerate. The extent to which such measures are justifiable is a highly contentious question in liberal societies.

9. For an influential statement of the ideal of deliberative democracy, see Cohen (1997). See also the essays in Bohman and Rehg (eds) (1997) and Macedo (ed.) (1999). A number of important recent essays are reprinted in Fishkin and Laslett (2003).

10. Iris Young, for example, raises this concern. While also arguing for a form of deliberative democracy, she is critical of deliberative theorists' focus on rational debate, appeals to the common good and the ideal of consensus, arguing that this focus privileges certain cultural styles and values and can exclude marginalised social groups and individuals. For a succinct statement of her critique, see the essay 'Communication and the Other: Beyond Deliberative Democracy' in Young (1997).

11. The differences between the views of Gutmann and Galston regarding civic education are also reflected in more recent debates about whether, or under what conditions, liberal states should fund religious schools. See for example Callan (2000) and Spinner-Halev (2000).

12. In *Becoming an Australian Citizen*, these rights are included in the list of Australian values. One of the problems with this list of values, apart from the fact that they are not specifically 'Australian', is that it conflates rights and virtues.

13. See Galston (1991) and, for an extension of this argument in the context of debates about multiculturalism and rights of exit for minority group members, Galston (1995).

14. Galston, drawing on Macedo (1990), also rejects Rawls' conception of a purely political liberalism on these grounds (1991, 291–6).

15. For a sophisticated recent discussion that addresses this question, see the essays in Christman and Anderson (eds) (2005).

16. For a liberal perfectionist argument that governments *do* have a duty to promote the social conditions necessary for autonomy, see Raz (1986). For a related argument from a more communitarian perspective, see Charles' Taylor essay 'Atomism' (in Taylor, 1985).

17. The arguments from autonomy and equality are developed in Kymlicka (1989) and (1995). The citizenship-based argument is developed in Kymlicka and Norman (2000) and Kymlicka (2002, ch. 8).

18. See for example Kukathas (1992). I think this criticism is quite inaccurate. Kymlicka makes it clear that he regards cultures as internally differentiated and constantly changing.

19. See for example Kukathas (1992) and Galston (1995). See also Kymlicka's (1992) trenchant and in my view, persuasive, response to Kukathas.

20. For a provocative and controversial argument to this effect, see Okin (1999). For critical responses to Okin, see the essays in Cohen et al. (1999). For a more considered analysis of gender justice in relation to multicultural policies, particularly relating to religious and family law, see Shachar (2000, 2000a). For a critique of the feminist position, see Spinner-Halev (2001).

21. I develop this argument in detail in Mackenzie (2007).

22. As far as religion is concerned, however, many liberal states, particularly the US, do not treat religion as a private matter and on some matters, such as abortion, there is not a clear separation between the state and religion.

23. Kymlicka defines a societal culture as 'a culture which provides its members with meaningful ways of life across the full range of human activities, including social, educational, religious, recreational, and economic life, encompassing both public and private spheres. These cultures tend to be territorially concentrated, and based on a shared language' (1995, 76). Kymlicka argues that societal cultures are an effect of modernisation, which 'involves the diffusion throughout a society of a common culture, including a standardized language, embodied in economic, political, and educational institutions' (1995, 76).

24. While Kymlicka and Norman have a point in wanting to distinguish the different claims of these immigrant groups, in the current global context the reasons for migration may often be complex and multifarious – economic, political, environmental. As a consequence, the distinction between voluntary and forced migration on which this categorisation depends, is often not clear-cut.

25. I follow Kymlicka in distinguishing assimilation from accommodation and integration.

26. As is well-known, the French legislation banning the wearing of the hijab in schools has prompted fierce debate. For an illuminating philosophical analysis of the French controversy, see Benhabib (2002, 94–100). In Australia, wearing the hijab in schools is not particularly controversial and the practice is reasonably common in schools with a high proportion of students from Muslim backgrounds.

27. Kymlicka distinguishes the character of a society from its basic institutional structure (1989, 166–72). On the basis of this distinction, it could be argued that while immigration has certainly changed (in overwhelmingly positive ways) the character of Australian society, it has not transformed in any detrimental way its basic liberal democratic institutional structure.

28. This focus on the political significance of inclusion and exclusion and inequalities in the worth of legal citizenship are also of central concern to the politics of recognition (Taylor, 1994) and to 'difference' theorists such as Iris Young (1990). For an influential analysis of the distinction between a 'politics of redistribution' and a 'politics of recognition', see Fraser (1997, ch. 1).

29. In Australia, some international students who want to use the qualifications obtained through their studies in Australia to gain citizenship would also count as immigrants without citizenship.

30. This summary is drawn from Mason (1999, 263).

31. Anzac Day, a national holiday on 25 April, commemorates the landing of Australian and New Zealand troops in Gallipoli in 1915. Twenty-five thousand Australian troops died during the 8-month Gallipoli campaign. The political significance of this campaign and its commemoration is that it is seen to mark the emergence of an Australian (as distinct from British) national identity. Over the last few decades, in particular, the commemorations have been increasingly linked to nationalist sentiments. *Becoming an Australian Citizen* describes Anzac Day as 'the unofficial national day' (2007, 21).

32. Mason distinguishes the inclusion of members of diverse cultural groups in policy-making bodies from the idea of 'group representation', which he

argues could result in group representatives making decisions solely on the basis of the interests of their group, rather than the interests of the polity as a whole. For extended discussions of the complexities of group representation, see Phillips (1997), Mansbridge (2000), and Williams (2000).

33. See http://www.citizenshiptestreview.gov.au/content/read-report.htm for the report of the review committee. Accessed 2 January 2009.

References

Bohman, J. and W. Rehg (eds) (1997) *Deliberative Democracy: Essays on Reason and Politics* (Cambridge, MA: MIT Press).

Benhabib, S. (2002) *The Claims of Culture: Equality and Diversity in the Global Era* (Princeton, NJ: Princeton University Press).

Callan, E. (2000) 'Discrimination and Religious Schooling', in W. Kymlicka and W. Norman (ed.), *Citizenship in Diverse Societies* (Oxford: Oxford University Press).

Christman, J. and J. Anderson (eds) (2005) *Autonomy and the Challenges to Liberalism* (Cambridge: Cambridge University Press).

Cohen, J. (1997) 'Deliberation and Democratic Legitimacy', in R. Goodin and P. Pettit (eds), *Contemporary Political Philosophy: An Anthology* (Oxford: Blackwell).

Cohen, J., M. Howard and M. Nussbaum (eds) (1999) *Is Multiculturalism Bad for Women?* (Princeton, NJ: Princeton University Press).

Commonwealth of Australia (2007) *Becoming an Australian Citizen*, November reprint, available at: http://www.ag/gov.au/cca. Accessed 28 November 2008.

Kittay, E. (1997) *Love's Labor* (New York: Routledge).

Fishkin, J.S. and P. Laslett (eds) (2003) *Debating Deliberative Democracy* (Malden, MA and Oxford: Blackwell).

Fraser, N. (1997) *Justice Interruptus: Critical Reflections on the 'Post-Socialist' Condition* (New York: Routledge).

Galston, W. (1991) *Liberal Purposes: Goods, Virtues, and Diversity in the Liberal State* (Cambridge: Cambridge University Press).

Galston, W. (1995) 'Two Conceptions of Liberalism', *Ethics* 105: 516–34.

Gutmann, A. (1987) *Democratic Education* (Princeton, NJ: Princeton University Press).

Kukathas, C. (1992) 'Are There Any Cultural Rights?', *Political Theory* 20 (1): 105–39.

Kymlicka, W. (1989) *Liberalism, Community and Culture* (Oxford: Oxford University Press).

Kymlicka, W. (1992) 'The Rights of Minority Cultures: Reply to Kukathas', *Political Theory* 20 (1): 140–5.

Kymlicka, W. (1995) *Multicultural Citizenship: A Liberal Theory of Minority Rights* (Oxford: Oxford University Press).

Kymlicka, W. (1999) 'Liberal Complacencies', in Cohen, Howard and Nussbaum (eds), *Is Multiculturalism Bad for Women?* (Princeton, NJ: Princeton University Press).

Kymlicka, W. (2002) *Contemporary Political Philosophy: An Introduction*. 2nd edition (Oxford: Oxford University Press).

Kymlicka, W. and W. Norman (eds) (2000) *Citizenship in Diverse Societies* (Oxford: Oxford University Press).

Kymlicka, W. and W. Norman (2000a) 'Citizenship in Culturally Diverse Societies: Issues, Contexts, Concepts', in Kymlicka and Norman (eds), *Citizenship in Diverse Societies* (Oxford: Oxford University Press).

Mason, A. (1999) 'Political Community, Liberal-Nationalism, and the Ethics of Assimilation', *Ethics* 109: 261–86.

Macedo, S. (1990) *Liberal Virtues: Citizenship, Virtue and Community* (Oxford: Oxford University Press).

Macedo, S. (ed.) (1999) *Deliberative Politics: Essays on Democracy and Disagreement* (Oxford: Oxford University Press).

Mackenzie, C. (2007) 'Relational Autonomy, Sexual Justice and Cultural Pluralism', in B. Arneil, M. Deveaux, R. Dhamoon and A. Eisenberg (eds) *Sexual Justice, Cultural Justice* (New York: Routledge).

Mansbridge, J. (2000) 'What does a Representative Do?', in Kymlicka and Norman (eds), *Citizenship in Diverse Societies* (Oxford: Oxford University Press).

Miller, D. (1995) *On Nationality* (Oxford: Oxford University Press).

Modood, T. (2000) 'Anti-Essentialism, Multiculturalism, and the "Recognition" of Religious Groups', in Kymlicka and Norman (ed.), *Citizenship in Diverse Societies* (Oxford: Oxford University Press).

Nussbaum, M. (2006) *Frontiers of Justice: Disability, Nationality, Species Membership* (Cambridge, MA: Harvard University Press).

Okin, S. (1989) *Justice, Gender and the Family* (New York: Basic Books).

Okin, S. (1999) 'Is Multiculturalism Bad for Women?', in Cohen, Howard and Nussbaum (ed.), *Is Multiculturalism Bad for Women* (Princeton, NJ: Princeton University Press).

Phillips, A. (1997) 'Dealing with Difference: A Politics of Ideas or a Politics of Presence?', in R. Goodin and P. Pettit (eds) *Contemporary Political Philosophy: An Anthology* (Oxford: Blackwell).

Rawls, J. (1972) *A Theory of Justice* (Oxford: Oxford University Press).

Rawls, J. (1985) 'Justice as Fairness: Political Not Metaphysical', *Philosophy and Public Affairs* 14 (3): 223–51.

Rawls, J. (1993) *Political Liberalism* (New York: Columbia University Press).

Raz, J. (1986) *The Morality of Freedom* (Oxford: Clarendon Press).

Raz, J. (1994) 'Multiculturalism: A Liberal Perspective', in *Ethics in the Public Domain: Essays in the Morality of Law and Politics* (Oxford: Clarendon Press).

Scanlon T.M. (2003) *The Difficulty of Tolerance: Essays in Political Philosophy* (Cambridge: Cambridge University Press).

Shachar, A. (2000) 'On Citizenship and Multicultural Vulnerability', *Political Theory* 28 (1): 64–89.

Shachar, A. (2000a) 'Should Church and State Be Joined at the Altar?: Women's Rights and the Multicultural Dilemma', in Kymlicka and Norman (eds), *Citizenship in Diverse Societies* (Oxford: Oxford University Press).

Spinner, J. (1994) *The Boundaries of Citizenship: Race, Ethnicity and Nationality in the Liberal State* (Baltimore, MD: John Hopkins University Press).

Spinner-Halev, J. (2000) 'Extending Diversity: Religion in Public and Private Education', in Kymlicka and Norman (ed.), *Citizenship in Diverse Societies* (Oxford: Oxford University Press).

Spinner-Halev, J. (2001) 'Feminism, Multiculturalism, Oppression and the State', *Ethics* 112: 84–113.

Taylor, C. (1985) *Philosophical Papers 2* (Cambridge: Cambridge University Press).

Taylor, C. (1993) 'Shared and Divergent Values', in G. LaForest (ed.), *Reconciling the Solitudes: Essays on Canadian Federalism and Nationalism* (Montreal, QC: McGill-Queen's University Press).

Taylor, C. (1994) 'The Politics of Recognition', in A. Gutmann (ed.), *Multiculturalism: Examining the Politics of Recognition* (Princeton, NJ: Princeton University Press).

Tamir, Y. (1993) *Liberal Nationalism* (Princeton, NJ: Princeton University Press).

Williams, M. (2000) 'The Uneasy Alliance of Group Representation and Deliberative Democracy', in Kymlicka and Norman (eds), *Citizenship in Diverse Societies* (Oxford: Oxford University Press).

Wilcox, S. (2004) 'Culture, National Identity, and Admission to Citizenship', *Social Theory and Practice* 30 (4): 559–82.

Young, I. (1990) *Justice and the Politics of Difference* (Princeton, NJ: Princeton University Press).

Young, I. (1997) *Intersecting Voices: Dilemmas of Gender, Political Philosophy and Policy* (Princeton, NJ: Princeton University Press).

11
Nativism as Citizenship: Immigration, Economic Hardship, and the Politics of the Right

Murray Goot and Ian Watson

In a society of migrants what makes someone 'truly Australian'? For most, the answer to this question has to do with whether someone is an Australian citizen, the feelings they have about the country and its institutions, and whether they speak English. For others – those with a 'nativist' disposition – the only 'real' Australians are those who not only meet all these criteria; they are those whose connections to the country are long established. For most Australians, migrants can be 'truly Australian'. For those with a nativist outlook, migrants can never be 'one of us', a sentiment that lends itself to manipulation by political parties; in our time, parties of the Right – especially the far Right. Clearly, the influence of nativism in public life deserves serious attention.

In this chapter, we use data from the Australian Survey of Social Attitudes (AuSSA), conducted in 2003, to explore three things about the nativist disposition: the extent to which nativism explains attitudes to the number of migrants coming to Australia; whether the number of respondents who subscribe to nativist views is boosted by the struggle many Australians have to go through to make ends meet; and how nativism shapes the way Australians vote. Our analysis shows that nativism does help explain the attitudes of Australians to immigration, that the financial difficulties of day-to-day living do not drive Australians to embrace nativist beliefs, but that nativism does make a difference politically – nativist views favour parties of the Right including the most politically potent party of the extreme Right, Pauline Hanson's One Nation. In this sense, Australian nativist beliefs work in much the same way as they do in the United Kingdom, Europe, and the United States (Mudde, 2007).

Measuring nativism

According to a series of national surveys conducted in Australia from 1995 to 2003, there is overwhelming agreement that what makes someone 'truly Australian' is 'feeling Australian', 'having Australian citizenship', 'respecting Australia's political institutions and laws', and 'speaking English'. Each of these ideals was endorsed by roughly 9 respondents out of 10 (Goot and Watson, 2005, table 4); no fewer than 74 per cent endorsed all four. Importantly, these are qualities that anyone, in principle, can *achieve* – migrants included; they are not ascribed characteristics that one is either born with or has to live without (McAllister, 1997, 14).

However, survey respondents also endorse attributes that would rule out many – even most – of their compatriots. Two-thirds (68 per cent in 2003) believe that having lived 'mostly in Australia' is at least 'fairly important' to being 'truly Australian'. How many of these respondents, one wonders, recognise that nearly a million Australians live overseas (Fullilove and Flutter, 2004)? More than half the respondents (58 per cent in 2003) think it is at least 'fairly important' for 'true' Australians to be born in Australia; this despite the fact that in mid-2004 almost a quarter (24 per cent) of the population had been born overseas – the highest proportion of Australians born overseas since Federation (ABS, 2005). And a third of the respondents (37 per cent in 2003) said that to be thought of as 'truly Australian' it was at least 'fairly important' to have 'Australian ancestry', a phrase which probably implied Australian birth and may or may not have encompassed the idea of forebears who went back more than one generation. Those who rejected the proposition for reasons other than these may have been mindful of the fact that more than a quarter of the Australian population are of migrant stock, the biggest groups tracing their roots back to the United Kingdom or New Zealand. Importantly, two of these characteristics – being born in Australia and having Australian ancestry – are *ascribed* characteristics; they are not things that anyone who fails to posses them can set out to achieve.

In addition, more than a third of the respondents said that to be 'truly Australian' a commitment of some kind to Christianity should be considered either 'very important' or 'fairly important'. On this criterion, even if we include those who are Christian in name only, we would have to disqualify more than a third of the population – those who identify with no religion as well as those who identify with a religion other than Christianity. However, unlike place of birth or ancestry,

Christianity is not exclusionary in an absolute sense; it is a characteristic that non-Christians, in principle, could adopt.

To grasp how these eight items are interrelated, and to see how they inform respondents' understandings of what makes someone 'truly Australian', we need to express support for them in a metric of a different kind. We do this by applying factor analysis, a technique that isolates the underlying factors, giving similar weights to those items that are most similar and dissimilar weights to those items that are least similar. We do this by using principal components analysis, which produces a rather different view of the similarities and differences to that which might be gleaned from raw scores or percentages. The less similar the weights, the more likely it is that the items in question tap different dimensions.

The analysis shows that three characteristics – being born in Australia, having lived most of one's life there, and having Australian ancestry – are very similar: they contributed the highest scores to the scale: few respondents who thought Australian ancestry was a necessary characteristic for anyone to be 'truly Australian' failed to say that being born in Australia or living one's life in Australia were also prerequisites. This means that on our scale, those respondents who most strongly endorse birthplace, longevity, and ancestry as aspects of Australianness score most strongly. We call the scale a nativism scale. Christianity, English-speaking ability, citizenship, and 'feeling Australian' were also similar to one another, but contributed lower scores and loaded less heavily. The other characteristic – respect for Australian political institutions and laws – was quite distinct: it contributed the lowest score and loaded least heavily (Table 11.1).

Table 11.1 Nativism scale: Factors contributing to score

Factors	Loadings
Important to have been born in Australia	−0.447
Important to have lived in Aust for most of one's life	−0.443
Important to have Australian ancestry	−0.430
Important to have Australian citizenship	−0.332
Important to be able to speak English	−0.329
Important to be Christian	−0.325
Important to feel Australian	−0.278
Important to respect Aust political institutions & laws	−0.135

Notes: Uses principal components analysis. The negative values occur because the original questionnaire scored most important 1 and least important 5.
Source: The Australian Survey of Social Attitudes 2003.

The proportion of the respondents (34 per cent) that endorsed all three 'nativist' propositions as requisites for being considered 'truly Australian' was large, even if the proportion that thought it is 'very important' that 'true Australians' be born in Australia, have lived most of their life there, and have Australian ancestry was only half as great (17 per cent). However, we should stress that in the factor analysis 'nativism' is not a category, where some respondents are nativists and others aren't. Rather, nativism is a disposition, to which some respondents are attracted more strongly than others. Seeing it as a spectrum of sentiments – something our nativism scale sets out to capture – is not only more realistic, but also lends itself, as we shall see, to more useful types of analysis.

The demography of nativism

A number of characteristics are strongly associated with support for nativism. Those respondents who are older, less educated, or working in the private sector are more inclined towards nativism than those who are younger, better educated, or working in the public sector. Strength of religious belief and of class identification also predict support for nativism; for example, respondents who were atheists or who said they had no class identification achieved scores on the nativism scale considerably lower than those who were Catholics or who identified as working class, and also much lower than those who were Anglicans or identified as middle class. Surveys in the United Kingdom and the United States, conducted in 2003, showed relationships of a similar kind between nativism, on the one side, and education, age, and religion, on the other (Tilley et al., 2004, 156–7, for the United Kingdom; and Davis, 2007, 183–4, for the United States). However, the best predictor of nativism is place of birth. Respondents born overseas are very cool towards nativism, those who are second generation migrants are warmer, with respondents who were born in Australia and whose parents also were born in Australia being warmest of all (see Table 11.2). Since the overseas born and to a lesser extent second generation migrants are inherently handicapped in the nativism stakes, their lack of enthusiasm is hardly surprising.

Rather more puzzling are the results we get when we look at the way the influence of birthplace is affected by education. As one would expect, and as Figure 11.1 shows, the effect of higher levels of education on reducing attachment to nativism is quite pronounced among Australian-born non-migrant respondents. It is evident, too, if not as clearly, among respondents who are second generation migrants.

However, among the overseas born, the relationship between education levels and nativism is the reverse: the better educated they are, the *more* attracted they are to nativist beliefs.[1] While the slope of the line is not as steep as it is in relation to second generation migrants – and at all levels of education the overseas born continues to eschew nativism – education brings them closer to endorsing nativist views rather than taking them further away. We shall speculate on the implication of this in our conclusion.

Table 11.2 OLS regression on nativism score

Intercept	−4.949
	(0.511)
Age	0.026
	(0.003)
Years of education	0.033
	(0.033)
Managers & administrators	−0.320
	(0.141)
Associate professionals	−0.126
	(0.133)
Tradespersons	0.303
	(0.153)
Advance clerical, sales & service	0.315
	(0.186)
Intermediate clerical, sales & service	0.239
	(0.130)
Intermediate production & transport	0.266
	(0.182)
Elementary clerical, sales & service	0.162
	(0.175)
Labourers	0.031
	(0.181)
Private sector	0.168
	(0.082)
Immigrant: 2nd generation	1.994
	(0.569)
Immigrant: Aust born	3.017
	(0.440)
Catholic religion	0.624
	(0.101)
Anglican religion	0.637
	(0.103)
Other religion	0.569
	(0.102)
Class identification: Middle class	0.596
	(0.152)
Class identification: Working class	0.720
	(0.154)

Table 11.2 (Continued)

Left Right self placement	0.198
	(0.021)
Years of education by 2nd gen immigrant	−0.090
	(0.047)
Years of education by Aust born	−0.144
	(0.036)
R squared	0.292
Adjusted R squared	0.284
N	2,066

Notes: Dependent variable is nativism score. Reference categories are: Professional occupation; public sector; born overseas; no religion; no class identification. Standard errors are shown in brackets. *Source*: The Australian Survey of Social Attitudes 2003.

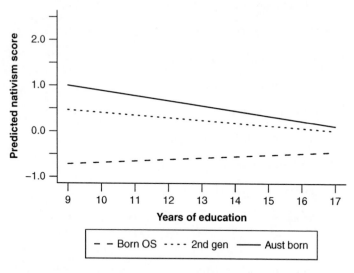

Figure 11.1 Nativism: effects of education and birthplace
Source: Based on predicated scores from nativism model.

Nativism and immigration

In the 2003 AuSSA, 36 per cent of respondents said 'the number of immigrants allowed into Australia nowadays' should be reduced rather than increased or stay the same. Is opposition to immigration driven by nativism? Is it driven by economic hardship? If economic hardship is important, is it something that drives nativism, so that nativist beliefs, far from operating independently, are largely an epiphenomenon of the way respondents register their frustrations with the day-to-day financial struggle? What of education? Since education affects nativism does it also affect, quite independently, attitudes to immigration?

Again, to observe what factors are associated with wanting to see a reduction in immigration, we fit a logistic regression model to the data. In the first instance, we look at what happens using a model without interactions, and then go on to introduce interactions into our analysis. A model with interactions allows us to test whether the association between nativism and attitudes to immigration is sensitive to the levels of other variables in the model. In particular, is this association influenced by whether a person is experiencing economic hardship, or by his or her particular level of education? We take this approach because we are interested in testing whether nativism might be a mask for economic distress or low levels of education.

The three factors that interest us the most – nativism, economic hardship, and education – all appear among the factors associated with a desire to see migrant numbers reduced, according to the first iteration of the model (see Table 11.3). Respondents who scored high on the nativism scale or who found it 'difficult to get by' on their current household income were distinctly more likely to want current immigration numbers reduced. Those with low levels of education were also more likely to want immigration reduced, but the association was not as strong. In other words, while both economic hardship and nativism influence the response to immigration, as education does, they operate separately.

Nor are these the only associations the first iteration of our modelling reveals. There were strong associations between wanting to see immigration reduced and where respondents lived, their source of news, what languages were spoken at home, and whether they classified themselves as working class. Respondents from rural areas were much keener than those from the inner city to see immigration reduced. Those who relied on sources other than the Australian Broadcasting Corporation (ABC) or the Special Broadcasting Service (SBS) for their news were much keener to see immigration reduced than those who did rely on Australia's government-owned broadcasters. Those who spoke English at home were keener than those who spoke a language other than English to see immigration reduced. And those who said they were 'working class' were keener than those who eschewed a class label to see immigration reduced. In addition, younger respondents were more likely than older respondents to want to see immigration reduced.

Table 11.3   Binomial logit model for wanting immigration reduced

	Non-interaction	Interaction
Intercept	0.976	1.079
	(0.475)	(0.481)
Age	−0.146	−0.143
	(0.036)	(0.036)
Years of education	−0.142	−0.150
	(0.027)	(0.028)
Speaks only English at home	0.510	0.521
	(0.167)	(0.168)
Nativism score	0.362	−0.164
	(0.034)	(0.190)
Hard to live on income	0.464	0.486
	(0.130)	(0.131)
Class identification: Middle class	−0.061	−0.080
	(0.204)	(0.204)
Class identification: Working class	0.247	0.225
	(0.201)	(0.201)
Source of TV news: ABC/SBS	−0.508	−0.501
	(0.143)	(0.143)
Geographical location: Outer	0.276	0.276
	(0.139)	(0.139)
Geographical location: Regional	0.044	0.030
	(0.184)	(0.184)
Geographical location: Rural	0.544	0.548
	(0.152)	(0.152)
Years of education by Nativism score		0.049
		(0.017)
Hard to live on income by Nativism score		−0.080
		(0.074)
Number of observations	2,066	2,066
AIC	2,190	2,183
Deviance	2,166	2,155

Notes: Dependent variable is agreeing with the view that the number of immigrants coming to Australia should be reduced. Reference categories are: No to speaks only English at home; no class identification; other media source for TV news; inner metropolitan location. Standard errors are shown in brackets.
Source: The Australian Survey of Social Attitudes 2003.

What happens when we turn to the second iteration of the model, the one that includes the interactions? While respondents who said they were finding it difficult to manage on their current household income were more likely to support reduced immigration, there was no interaction between nativism and economic hardship – scoring high on the nativism scale and struggling financially did not predict a level of

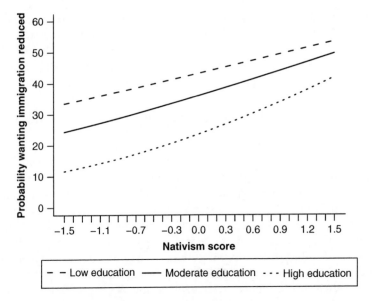

Figure 11.2 Nativism, education and reductions in immigration
Source: Based on predicated probabilities from immigration model.

opposition to immigration that was any greater than that predicted by nativism or economic hardship alone.

But there is an interaction been nativism and education. This inter-action is best understood when the data are presented in the form of a graph. As Figure 11.2 shows, not only does an increase in the nativism score see an increase in the probability of a respondent want-ing to see immigration reduced, but lower levels of formal education increase this probability.[2] For example, a person with moderate educa-tion (11 years) has a probability of wanting to see immigration reduced about 28 per cent if they score −1 on the nativism scale. When their score increases to +1, this probability jumps to 45 per cent. Another example: for a person sitting in the middle of the scale (at 0), the proba-bility of wanting to see immigration reduced climbs from 24 per cent to 36 per cent and then to 43 per cent, as their years of education drop from 15 years to 11 years to 9 years, respectively. The interac-tion effect between education and nativism is attested by the absence in the graph of parallel lines. The convergence of all three lines suggests that as people move to the more extreme nativist position, so the dif-ferential impact of education on their attitudes to immigration becomes much weaker. As a result, they begin to share a more common position, one that makes them increasingly sympathetic to reducing immigration. Nonetheless, even the set of those who combined the lowest levels of education with the highest scores on nativism was divided down the middle about wanting immigration reduced: the probability of their wanting immigration reduced was no higher than 50 per cent.

Nativism, economic hardship, and the politics of the Right

Is nativism associated with voting for the Right, whether this be broadly defined to include support for parties like the Liberal and National parties or restricted to parties of the populist radical right (Mudde, 2007, 26) like Pauline Hanson's One Nation? And where does economic hardship fit into the picture? It has been suggested that 'neo-populist parties of the right' in Europe have benefited from the economic hardship associated with economic restructuring (Betz, 1998, 7; Kitschelt, 1997/1995, 39). Is there anything similar happening in Australia? Some authors have argued that One Nation was attractive to those who were suffering economically (Denemark and Bowler, 2002) and that Pauline Hanson's protectionist pronouncements appealed to those voters (Turnbull and Wilson, 2001). However, we have suggested that economic factors explain little of One Nation's vote at its high point, 1998 (Goot and Watson, 2001; see also Gibson et al., 2002).

To explore these issues, we modelled the voting intentions of respondents to the AuSSA survey in two ways: one, without interactions (see Table 11.4a); the other, with the interaction of hardship and nativism (see Table 11.4b). Intention to vote for a party in the Senate was used as the dependent variable. We chose the Senate because many respondents lived in electorates for the House of Representatives where the range of candidates was small. The parties whose support we modelled were the parties of the Centre Right or Right – the Liberal Party, the National Party, and One Nation (both jointly and separately); the parties of the Centre or Left – the Australian Democrats and the Australian Labor Party; and others, including the Australian Shooters Party and Independents. (For evidence that this is where survey respondents themselves would have placed the parties, see Goot, 2005, 109). The background variables we used in the logistic regression models to explain party support included economic hardship (respondents who said they found it 'difficult' or 'very difficult to get by' on their 'current household income') and nativism – both on its own and to test the thesis that nativism's impact might be mediated through economic hardship. That is, we sought to establish whether nativism has a political impact, with parties of the Right mobilising the more economically disenfranchised.

Table 11.4a Multinomial logit model for voting, non-interaction specification

	Liberal	Nationals	AD	Greens	ONP	None/Other
Intercept	-0.836	-4.536	0.184	-0.105	-3.205	1.903
	(0.448)	(1.292)	(1.042)	(0.654)	(1.246)	(0.425)
Age	0.010	-0.004	-0.033	-0.022	0.003	-0.024
	(0.005)	(0.012)	(0.013)	(0.009)	(0.013)	(0.005)
Managers & administrators	0.432	1.661	-0.142	0.129	1.664	0.086
	(0.244)	(0.587)	(0.601)	(0.440)	(0.901)	(0.293)
Associate professionals	0.554	0.027	-0.022	0.300	1.378	-0.002
	(0.220)	(0.761)	(0.499)	(0.387)	(0.865)	(0.260)
Tradespersons	0.187	0.948	-0.340	0.083	1.148	0.561
	(0.262)	(0.699)	(0.702)	(0.478)	(0.891)	(0.267)
Advance clerical, sales & service	0.345	1.234	-9.946	0.477	1.068	0.215
	(0.312)	(0.708)	(0.000)	(0.572)	(1.057)	(0.363)
Intermediate clerical, sales & service	-0.075	0.420	-1.292	-0.119	1.038	-0.024
	(0.211)	(0.621)	(0.598)	(0.363)	(0.834)	(0.223)
Intermediate production & transport	-0.592	0.838	-0.613	-1.238	0.133	-0.279
	(0.325)	(0.752)	(0.830)	(0.788)	(1.062)	(0.321)
Elementary clerical, sales & service	0.333	0.489	-0.049	0.586	0.740	0.100
	(0.296)	(0.890)	(0.704)	(0.489)	(1.051)	(0.327)
Labourers	-0.139	0.409	-1.321	-0.143	1.062	-0.313
	(0.305)	(0.899)	(1.092)	(0.542)	(0.928)	(0.333)
Private sector	0.441	0.727	-0.846	0.094	1.006	0.114
	(0.149)	(0.417)	(0.378)	(0.262)	(0.492)	(0.163)
Union member	-0.920	-0.628	-0.812	-0.162	0.067	-0.630
	(0.140)	(0.341)	(0.367)	(0.258)	(0.406)	(0.153)

Table 11.4a (Continued)

	Liberal	Nationals	AD	Greens	ONP	None/Other
Hard to live on income	-0.561	-0.459	0.262	-0.088	-0.126	-0.247
	(0.174)	(0.468)	(0.415)	(0.297)	(0.436)	(0.177)
Nativism score	0.161	0.261	-0.184	-0.216	0.398	-0.007
	(0.041)	(0.110)	(0.101)	(0.071)	(0.129)	(0.043)
Class identification: Middle class	0.683	0.425	0.361	-0.646	-1.367	-0.804
	(0.321)	(0.793)	(0.789)	(0.400)	(0.612)	(0.283)
Class identification: Working class	-0.213	-0.521	0.101	-1.065	-1.292	-0.922
	(0.324)	(0.812)	(0.809)	(0.415)	(0.578)	(0.282)
Catholic religion	-0.005	1.059	-0.763	-0.952	-0.963	-0.457
	(0.182)	(0.678)	(0.469)	(0.339)	(0.527)	(0.186)
Anglican religion	0.503	1.764	-0.389	-0.486	-0.574	-0.453
	(0.186)	(0.656)	(0.475)	(0.339)	(0.497)	(0.211)
Other religion	0.365	1.840	-0.420	-0.210	-0.389	-0.117
	(0.186)	(0.654)	(0.454)	(0.305)	(0.505)	(0.194)
Source of TV news: ABC/SBS	-0.008	0.354	-0.119	1.261	-0.076	0.336
	(0.170)	(0.400)	(0.448)	(0.249)	(0.516)	(0.180)
Log-likelihood	2,246					
Deviance	4,492					
AIC	4,732					
N	2,066					

Notes: Dependent variable is voting intention in the Senate. Reference category (base) is ALP. Reference categories are: professionals; public sector; non-union member; not finding it hard to live on income; no class identification; no religion; other media source for TV news. Note that union member is defined as either current or past union member, thus allowing for retired persons. Standard errors are shown in brackets.
Source: The Australian Survey of Social Attitudes 2003.

Table 11.4b Multinomial logit model for voting, interaction specification

	Liberal	Nationals	AD	Greens	ONP	None/Other
Intercept	-0.826	-4.520	0.086	-0.069	-3.227	1.929
	(0.448)	(1.292)	(1.049)	(0.656)	(1.252)	(0.426)
Age	0.010	-0.004	-0.033	-0.022	0.002	-0.024
	(0.005)	(0.012)	(0.013)	(0.009)	(0.013)	(0.005)
Managers & administrators	0.433	1.672	-0.138	0.129	1.639	0.086
	(0.244)	(0.588)	(0.600)	(0.441)	(0.901)	(0.293)
Associate professionals	0.549	0.036	-0.006	0.293	1.310	-0.015
	(0.220)	(0.762)	(0.499)	(0.387)	(0.864)	(0.260)
Tradespersons	0.181	0.960	-0.343	0.073	1.073	0.548
	(0.262)	(0.701)	(0.706)	(0.478)	(0.889)	(0.267)
Advance clerical, sales & service	0.346	1.239	-8.562	0.482	1.042	0.219
	(0.313)	(0.708)	(0.000)	(0.572)	(1.059)	(0.363)
Intermediate clerical, sales & service	-0.081	0.431	-1.301	-0.126	0.941	-0.037
	(0.211)	(0.623)	(0.597)	(0.363)	(0.833)	(0.224)
Intermediate production & transport	-0.592	0.850	-0.648	-1.232	0.116	-0.278
	(0.325)	(0.753)	(0.832)	(0.789)	(1.060)	(0.322)
Elementary clerical, sales & service	0.328	0.490	-0.032	0.578	0.696	0.088
	(0.296)	(0.891)	(0.704)	(0.489)	(1.050)	(0.328)
Labourers	-0.148	0.417	-1.243	-0.159	1.023	-0.334
	(0.306)	(0.899)	(1.089)	(0.542)	(0.923)	(0.333)
Private sector	0.437	0.725	-0.820	0.088	0.970	0.103
	(0.149)	(0.417)	(0.377)	(0.262)	(0.492)	(0.164)
Union member	-0.922	-0.625	-0.804	-0.164	0.036	-0.634
	(0.140)	(0.341)	(0.366)	(0.258)	(0.406)	(0.153)

Table 11.4b   (Continued)

	Liberal	Nationals	AD	Greens	ONP	None/Other
Hard to live on income	-0.557	-0.548	0.440	-0.152	0.170	-0.263
	(0.178)	(0.557)	(0.437)	(0.341)	(0.464)	(0.179)
Nativism score	0.174	0.262	-0.246	-0.189	0.543	0.023
	(0.045)	(0.118)	(0.118)	(0.079)	(0.154)	(0.048)
Class identification: Middle class	0.689	0.414	0.349	-0.645	-1.293	-0.796
	(0.321)	(0.794)	(0.787)	(0.400)	(0.618)	(0.283)
Class identification: Working class	-0.205	-0.528	0.062	-1.057	-1.215	-0.906
	(0.324)	(0.814)	(0.807)	(0.416)	(0.581)	(0.282)
Catholic religion	-0.007	1.058	-0.739	-0.961	-0.988	-0.468
	(0.182)	(0.678)	(0.470)	(0.340)	(0.528)	(0.187)
Anglican religion	0.498	1.765	-0.363	-0.495	-0.633	-0.463
	(0.186)	(0.656)	(0.476)	(0.339)	(0.499)	(0.211)
Other religion	0.358	1.839	-0.388	-0.227	-0.450	-0.132
	(0.187)	(0.654)	(0.455)	(0.306)	(0.507)	(0.194)
Source of TV news: ABC/SBS	-0.007	0.355	-0.108	1.260	-0.030	0.338
	(0.170)	(0.399)	(0.448)	(0.250)	(0.516)	(0.181)
Hard to live on income by nativism	-0.054	0.048	0.238	-0.122	-0.548	-0.135
	(0.101)	(0.309)	(0.232)	(0.165)	(0.267)	(0.099)
Log-likelihood	2,242					
Deviance	4,484					
AIC	4,736					
N	2,066					

Notes: Dependent variable is voting intention in the Senate. Reference category (base) is ALP. Reference categories are: professionals; public sector; non-union member; not finding it hard to live on income; no class identification; no religion; other media source for TV news. Note that union member is defined as either current or past union member, thus allowing for retired persons. Standard errors are shown in brackets.
Source: The Australian Survey of Social Attitudes 2003.

The key finding from this modelling is that nativism is indeed associated with an increased chance of voting for parties of the Right. Liberal Party voters, National Party voters, and those who said they would have voted One Nation were all more likely than Labor voters to embrace nativist sentiments; by contrast, Greens were significantly less likely than Labor voters to be inclined towards nativism. And, except for One Nation (where the interaction made respondents less – not more – likely to support Hanson, but this effect is quite weak), there was no interaction effect for economic hardship for any of the parties. Having looked at parties of the Right separately, we also grouped them into one bloc and conducted the same kind of analysis. Our results confirmed a strong association between nativism and voting for parties of the Right.

The quite striking relationship between nativism and voting for parties of the Right (taken together) is best represented by a graph based on predicted probabilities. As Figure 11.3 shows, for someone not experiencing economic hardship, the probability of voting for parties of the Right increases from about 45 per cent to 62 per cent as one moves along the nativism scale from −1.5 to +1.5.[3] This is a large movement. A more modest shift, say from −1 to +1, sees an increase in probability from 48 per cent to 59 per cent.

Figure 11.3 also demonstrates the absence of any link between nativism and economic hardship. If on the nativism scale we compare

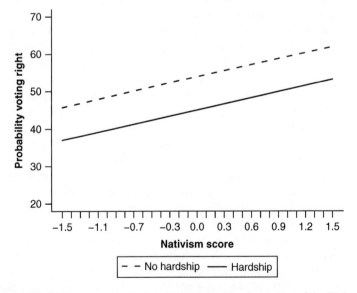

Figure 11.3 Nativism, economic hardship and voting for parties of the Right
Source: Based on predicated probabilities from voting model.

those not experiencing economic hardship with those experiencing economic hardship, the overall relationship is similar – indicated by the two upward sloping lines – with the line for those reporting hardship lower than the line for those not reporting hardship. The absence of an interaction effect is evident from the fact that the two lines are essentially parallel. (A similar survey in the United States found no relationship between the strength of nativism and sociotropic variables – respondents views not of changes in their own economic circumstances but of changes in the country's economic condition; see, Davis, 2007, 183–4).

Conclusion

Citizenship is a marker of exclusion as well as inclusion: citizenship is accorded always to some but not extended to others. That – and not the imposition of a residential requirement, competence in a language, or loyalty to a set of values – is what makes the drawing of the boundaries, whether physical or metaphorical, inherently contentious. If this were not the case, the idea of citizenship as a privilege would make no sense; nor would the idea that citizenship imposes certain burdens.

But to say the criteria for citizenship are inherently contentious is not to deny that there is widespread agreement about the qualities 'real Australians' should possess much less to imply that Australia, having gone through 'a radical period' of redefinition of its cultural institutions and conventions', is 'still a very long way from being able to define its cultural identity' (Mackay, 1993, 5), or that the very idea that there might be agreement about its 'cultural identity' or values is now 'increasingly quaint and outdated' (Ang, 2008, 234). Support for the view that real Australians have to be born in Australia or 'have Australian ancestry' may be lower in Australia than in the UK but support for the view that real Australians have to 'speak English', 'have Australian citizenship', 'feel Australian', and 'respect Australia's political institutions and law' appears to be higher (Tilley et al., 2004, 152).

According to the evidence from national surveys, while the majority of Australians believe that having Australian citizenship, speaking English, and feeling Australian are 'very important' to being 'truly Australian', and most of the rest believe it to be 'fairly important', substantial minorities believe it 'very important' that to be 'truly Australian' one has to be born in Australia, have Australian ancestry, and live mostly in Australia; indeed, majorities believe it to be at least 'fairly important' that true Australians have to be born in Australia and have Australian ancestry. Of course, there are many other characteristics that could be used to define what it is to be 'truly Australian' (O'Mara, 2008 for a select bibliography) – including the things said to constitute 'the Australian way of life' (White, 1979), to be part of our 'national character' (e.g. Hirst, 2007) or, like Vegemite (Black, 2009), to comprise an essential part of the Australian diet. But these qualities don't touch on where one was born, a core characteristic of nativism.

The support for nativism among second generation migrants suggests that nativism might be perceived – wrongly, on the evidence we have – as a dominant or hegemonic value, one to which the pressures of assimilation or integration oblige them to adjust. Why this should be so is puzzling. It is worth further research. Why support for nativism is related to religious or class identification is unclear, but an attachment to nativism may help fulfil part of a more general need for a sense of group belonging.

The connection between nativist beliefs and opposition to immigration, however, is clear (a connection already made clear by Goot and Watson, 2005, 191), though this doesn't mean that a fall in opposition to immigration is necessarily related to a fall in nativism (for the United Kingdom, see McLaren and Johnson, 2004, 179–80). Also clear is the connection between nativism and support for right-wing parties. Citizenship tests were introduced, almost certainly, with an eye to shoring up support for the Coalition in an election year – a year in which the government faced a new Labor leader and the ever-increasing prospect of defeat. Polling conducted in September 2006, when the government was officially 'considering' the introduction of such a test, and again in December 2006, after it had announced its plans, showed that support among Coalition respondents was not only wider (90 per cent in September, 93 per cent in December) than among Labor respondents (70 per cent rising to 79 per cent); it was also stronger, with many more Coalition respondents (66 per cent and 77 per cent) than Labor respondents (48 and 55 per cent) supporting a test 'strongly' (www.newspoll.com.au). However, among those inclined towards nativism, for whom the only 'true Australians' are those born here, the government's strategy is likely to have met with only limited success. Even citizenship tests more difficult for migrants to negotiate than those the Howard Government put in place may have been less welcome to those with a nativist disposition than a promise to cut immigration. For economic reasons, the government was determined not to cut immigration; indeed, it was keen to see immigration grow. Under these circumstances, citizenship tests were as far a concession towards nativism as the government was prepared to go.

Outside of Australia little work appears to have been done on the connection between nativism and support for the mainstream Right. So we cannot say whether the connection we have established between nativism and voting for right-of-centre parties like the Liberals and Nationals is part of a wider pattern. For populist radical parties of the Right, we can be much more confident. 'According to the consensus on European parties', says the foremost scholar of the non-mainstream Right, 'the main reason' for the support of parties with a 'populist radical right ideology [...] is a nativist position on the immigration issue' (Mudde, 2007, 220). This may not be the principle driver of populist radicalism in Australia, but it is clearly an important one.

Notes

1. These results are based on plugging a range of 'typical' values into the model equation, and then allowing the immigrant status and years of education to vary. The other values plugged in are the averages, or the most common categories, of the other variables (that is, aged 50, working as an intermediate clerical worker, middle class self-identification, Catholic religion, in the middle of the left right self-placement scale, private sector).
2. This graph also shows predicted probabilities and as noted before, they reflect the other values plugged into the model equation. The other values plugged in are the averages, or the most common categories, of the other variables (that is, aged 50, English-speaking background, not experiencing economic hardship, middle class, watching other than ABC or SBS, living in the outer suburbs). The nativism score and the years of education were varied to produce the data shown in the graph.
3. One should not pay too much attention to the absolute numbers here, since they reflect the other values plugged into the model equation for the purposes of prediction. Being a non-linear model (and one that contains interactions), predictions of probability are a more useful device for evaluating results than are coefficients. The other values plugged in are the averages, or the most common categories, of the other variables (that is, aged 50, working as an intermediate clerical worker, middle class self-identification, Catholic religion, other news source, non-union member, private sector). Had working-class, union member been plugged in, the absolute probabilities would have been lower, but the overall slopes and relative positions of each line would not have differed, and these are the relevant aspects in our analysis.

References

ABS (2005) 'Proportion of Australians Born Overseas Highest Since Federation' Australian Bureau of Statistics, 3412.0 – Migration, Australia, 2003–04, Media Release, 20 September. Accessed June 2008. http://www.abs.gov.au/AUSSTATS/abs@nsf/mediareleases.

Ang, I. (2008) 'Passengers on Train Australia', *Griffith Review* 19: 229–39.

Betz, H.-G. (1998) 'Introduction', in Hans-George Betz and Stefan Immerfall (eds), *The New Politics of the Right: Neo-Populist Parties and Movements in Established Democracies* (New York: St Martin's Press).

Black, S. (2009) 'And the Wankley Goes To ... Happy Little Vegemites' crikey.com. au, 9 January.

Davis, D.W. (2007) *Negative Liberty: Public Opinion and Terrorist Attacks on America* (New York: Russell Sage Foundation).

Denemark, D. and S. Bowler (2002) 'Minor Parties and Protest Votes in Australia and New Zealand: Locating Populist Politics', *Electoral Studies* 21: 47–67.

Fullilove, M. and C. Flutter (2004) *Diaspora: The World Wide Web of Australians* (Sydney: Lowy Institute).

Gibson, R., I. McAllister and T. Swenson (2002) 'The Politics of Race and Immigration in Australia: One Nation Voting in the 1988 Election', *Ethnic and Racial Studies* 25: 823–44.

Goot, M. (2005) 'Pauline Hanson's One Nation: Extreme Right, Centre Party or Extreme Left?', *Labour History* 89: 101–19.

Goot, M. and I. Watson (2001) 'One Nation's Electoral Support: Where Does it Come From, What Makes it Different, and How Does it Fit?', *Australian Journal of Politics and History* 47: 159–91.

Goot, M. and I. Watson (2005) Immigration, Multiculturalism, and Australian Identity', in Shaun Wilson et al. (eds), *Australian Social Attitudes: The First Report* (Sydney: University of New South Wales Press).

Hirst, J. (2007) *The Australians: Insiders and Outsiders on the National Character Since 1770* (Melbourne: Black Inc.)

Kitschelt, H. with A.J. McGann (1997/1995) *The Radical Right in Western Europe: A Comparative Analysis* (Ann Arbor, MI: University of Michigan Press).

McAllister, I. (1997) 'Political Culture and National Identity', in Brian Galligan, Ian McAllister and John Ravenhill (eds), *New Developments in Australian Politics* (South Melbourne: Macmillan).

Mackay, H. (1993) 'A National Identity? Wait and See', in J. Beaumont (ed.), *Where to Now? Australia's National Identity in the Nineties* (Sydney: Federation Press).

McLaren, L. and M. Johnson (2004) 'Understanding the Rising tide of Anti-immigration Sentiment', in A. Park et al. (eds) *British Social Attitudes: The 21st Report* (London: SAGE Publications).

Mudde, C. (2007) *Populist Radical Right Parties in Europe* (Cambridge: Cambridge University Press).

O'Mara, K. (2008) 'Select Bibliographies', in J.V. D'Cruz et al. (eds), *As Others See Us* (North Melbourne: Australian Scholarly Publishing).

Tilley, J., S. Exley and A. Heath (2004) 'Dimensions of British Identity', in A. Park et al. (eds), *British Social Attitudes: The 21st Report* (London: SAGE Publications).

Turnbull, N. and S. Wilson (2001) 'The Two Faces of Economic Insecurity: Reply to Goot and Watson on One Nation', *Australian Journal of Politics and History* 47: 508–11.

White, R. (1979) 'The Australian Way of Life', *Historical Studies* 73: 528–45.

12
From Earning the Privilege of Citizenship to Understanding its Responsibilities: An Update on Australian Citizenship Testing

Martina Möllering and Linda Silaghi

Introduction: The Australian citizenship test review committee

On 24 November 2007, a new Labor Government with Kevin Rudd as prime minister came into power in Australia. Within 5 months, in April 2008, the new Minister for Immigration and Citizenship, Senator Chris Evans, announced the formation of an independent Committee to review the citizenship test implemented by the Howard Government on 1 October 2007. In Chapter 9 of this book, Emily Farrell discusses the debates that surrounded the introduction of this testing regime, arguing that it was chiefly the then Government that determined the form and content of the test introduced, with other voices, such as those of community groups and experts, sidelined. To some degree, those other voices are being brought back into the debate through the Australian Citizenship Test Review Committee's consultations with the wider community. This chapter outlines the findings and recommendations of the Committee based on the report 'Moving Forward... Improving Pathways to Citizenship' (2008, henceforth 'Report'). It will also discuss the Government's response to those findings.

On 24 April 2008, The Minister for Immigration and Citizenship, Senator Chris Evans, announced that an independent Committee of seven eminent Australians was to review the citizenship test, stating that:

> The Government is committed to maintaining the citizenship test, but now that it has been in place for six months, it is timely to review it to make sure it is achieving its proper purpose as an effective

pathway for residents to become citizens [...]. The Committee will examine aspects of the content and operation of the citizenship test, including the experiences of applicants and the impact on citizenship applications, and consider ways to improve its operation and effectiveness.

(Evans, 2008a)

The brief for the Committee was thus, quite clearly, to examine the operation and effectiveness of the current testing regime with a view to amending and improving it rather than to question the existence of a formal citizenship testing regime as such, or, in the Minister's own words:

The Rudd Government believes that a citizenship test can play a valuable role in both encouraging people to find out more about our great nation as well as understanding the responsibilities and privileges which being an Australian citizen brings. [...] A test is also a useful mechanism for determining whether a person meets the general legal requirements for becoming an Australian – including whether they possess a basic knowledge of the English language. (Ibid.)

This threefold setting of objectives has been criticised, as we show in the course of this chapter, and has led to a call for a clear definition of the objectives of an Australian citizenship testing regime with clearly defined contents to be tested.

The Committee was chaired by former Department of Foreign Affairs and Trade Secretary, Richard Woolcott AC, described by senator Evans as 'a former diplomat with a long and distinguished public service career and an excellent ambassador for multicultural relations'. (Ibid.) The six other members appointed to the independent Committee were former Olympian Rechelle Hawkes; Special Broadcasting Services (SBS) director Paula Masselos; refugee advocate Julianna Nkrumah; Australia Day Council CEO Warren Pearson; former Chief of Navy, Vice Admiral Rtd Chris Ritchie AO RANR; and legal expert Professor Kim Rubenstein. The omission of inviting an expert in testing, in particular in language testing, to the review committee has been critically noted (McNamara, 2009).

The Government had planned to receive and publish the findings and recommendations of the Citizenship Test Review Committee in June 2008, however, the final document and its content, accompanied by the Government's responses to the report, was only made public in late November 2008.

The review committee's process of consultation

Based on the rationale that stakeholders and interested members of the public should be given the opportunity to contribute to the development of future policy directions (Evans, 2008a), the Australian Citizenship Test Review Committee conducted a series of extensive, cross-national consultations for a period of 6 months with a wide range of stakeholders: representatives of government and non-government organisations, business and community groups. Added to these groups of discussants, the Committee extended its enquiry towards the voices of individuals directly affected by the citizenship test, namely refugees and humanitarian entrants. A group of experts in the domain of testing, linguists, education researchers and teachers of TESOL were also consulted to share their views on the testing regime introduced in 2007. Overall, the Committee sought the input of 700 organisations and individuals in the form of written submissions. 179 submissions were received.

The key findings reached in the cross-national consultations and written submissions were unanimous and supported the vast body of criticism about the test voiced from its early stages of proposal through to its implementation in October 2007, as has been discussed in Chapter 5 by Lloyd Cox and in Chapter 9 by Emily Farrell.

Key findings of the review committee

The review Committee began its report, which it submitted in August 2008, with a list of ten key findings that served as the basis for the recommendations the Committee developed (Report, 2008, 3):

1. Citizenship is a valued and important concept and is a key factor in nation building. Its acquisition should be encouraged and facilitated by government.
2. The purpose of any citizenship test should be to assess whether a person who wants to become a citizen is conscious of the main responsibilities underpinning the Citizenship Pledge of Commitment.
3. The present test is flawed, intimidating to some and discriminatory. It needs substantial reform.

4. The legislative requirements for a 'basic knowledge of the English language' and an 'adequate knowledge of Australia and the responsibilities and privileges of Australian citizenship' require definition before a revised and more appropriate test can be established.
5. Alternative and improved education pathways to acquire citizenship need to be established for different people seeking citizenship.
6. The special situation of refugee and humanitarian entrants and other disadvantaged and vulnerable people seeking citizenship must be addressed.
7. The test questions (at present confidential) should be published in any revised test.
8. The contents of the resource book should contain relevant, clearly defined testable information.
9. The resource book should be re-written in basic English by professional educators.
10. There should be a more coordinated whole-of-government approach to civics and citizenship policy and programs.

Discussion of recommendations made by the committee

Based on its key findings, the Committee put forth a set of concrete recommendations. In the following section, we will discuss the Committee's major recommendations concerning:

- the objectives of the test
- the requirement for a basic knowledge of English
- the definition of what 'an adequate knowledge of Australia' and 'responsibilities and privileges of Australian citizenship' might mean
- the pathway system proposed by the Committee

Objectives of the citizenship test

The purpose of the test as defined by the former Government, when it proposed the introduction of the current test, was to ensure that applicants for citizenship through conferral proved their integration into the Australian community. The test was seen as an evaluation tool through which the political, social and economic participation of new citizens could be measured (*Australian Citizenship, Much More Than a Ceremony*, 2006). Criticism referring strictly to the purpose set out by the former Government centred around suspicions over whether successful integration into the Australian community could be best achieved by a compulsory test (Rimmer, 2007), whether a test could really ensure a commitment to Australia's way of life and values (Rubenstein, 2007) and whether it was a proper mechanism to address issues of national safety (Jupp, 2008).

At present the only available resource for measuring the effects of the citizenship test introduced in 2007 are the *Snapshot* reports and the *Annual Report* issued by the Department of Immigration and Citizenship. The results published in these documents do not refer to the achievement of the purpose defined for the test, but cast some light on the numeric decrease of citizenship applications, by 39.8 per cent, compared to the applications submitted in 2006–07 (DIAC, *Annual Report 2007–08*).

The submission to the Committee by the Human Rights and Equal Opportunity Commission (2008) points out that the goals set out in the 2006 Discussion Paper, *Australian Citizenship, Much More Than a Ceremony* (2006), of increasing participation in the Australian society and building social cohesion and integration are not being met. The same submission points out the confusion surrounding the current Government's vision regarding the need for keeping the citizenship test in place, and defining its new purpose. The Human Rights and Equal Opportunity Commission identified the unspecific references to the goals set forth for the implementation of the new test, consisting on the one hand of 'Encouraging people to find out more about our great nation' and 'Helping citizens understand "the responsibilities and privileges which being an Australian brings"' and on the other hand of 'Providing a mechanism for determining whether a person meets the general legal requirements for becoming an Australian and whether they possess a basic knowledge of English' (Human Rights and Equal Opportunity Commission, 2008).

Overall, submissions received by the Committee expressed the perception that the objectives of the current test are unclear to many and need to be clarified. Criticisms referred to in the submissions allude to the following:

a) The fact that the content of the resource book and the current test seem to be testing common knowledge about Australia rather than what it means to be a citizen.

b) The discrepancy between the requirement for 'basic English' only, in order to become an Australian citizen, and the perception that the current resource book and the test questions are written in English that is above the level of 'basic', therefore providing diminished access for people with low levels of English to an understanding of Australian citizenship.

Among the purposes of citizenship testing identified by participants in the consultation process were the following:

- An opportunity to understand the Pledge taken when becoming a citizen and the responsibilities and privileges of citizenship.
- An opportunity to learn more about Australia (strong focus amongst refugee groups).
- Assurance to existing citizens that new citizens understood what they were pledging.

In view of the above comments, the review Committee directed the clarification of the citizenship test's purpose and objectives towards the legislative level of the test, pointing out that the testing regime is a matter of law and should be linked directly to the legislative requirements contained in the Australian Citizenship Act 2007. In regards to the content of the test and the requirement of the applicants to demonstrate an adequate knowledge of the responsibilities and privileges of Australian citizenship, the Committee welcomed the proposition that the purpose of the citizenship test, and the subject matter of its societal knowledge component should be strongly linked to the Pledge of Commitment that applicants have to take as the last step in their trajectory of becoming citizens at a public citizenship ceremony.

The argument for adopting the Pledge of Commitment as the centrepiece of testing expresses the belief that its understanding constitutes an assurance for the general public that applicants fully adhere to the concepts covered in the Pledge, namely the responsibilities and privileges of Australian citizenship. Consequently, the new citizenship test will be based on the Pledge, which also fulfils the role of reassuring the general public about new citizens' compliance with the legislative requirements of adopting Australian citizenship.

Thus, the Committee proposed the following objectives for the citizenship test:

- To determine if a person has satisfied the legislative requirements for becoming a citizen under the Australian Citizenship Act 2007.
- To demonstrate to the general public that people applying for citizenship have satisfied the legislative requirements when making the Pledge of Commitment.

- The objectives of the citizenship test be included and made transparent in any promotional material associated with the citizenship test (Report, 2008, 16).

Defining basic knowledge of English language

The Australian Citizenship Act 2007 states that a 'basic knowledge of English language' is a requirement for obtaining citizenship through conferral, but it does not provide a legal definition of the term. Since 2007, the successful completion of the written test has been taken to prove that an applicant fulfils the language requirement stipulated by the legislation. As mentioned above, a large number of submissions[1] to the Committee have pointed to the discrepancy between the level of English described in the legislation as 'basic' on the one hand, and the translation of this requirement into the language of the test and resource book on the other hand.

The level of English used in the operation of the test exceeds the level of English referred to as 'basic' in the legislation. According to Piller and McNamara's (2007) lexical analysis, the booklet made available to assist applicants prepare for the test is written in a level of English that implies language skills higher than basic. They argue that '[...] the resource booklet *Becoming an Australian Citizen* is certainly out of the reach of a basic user of English and would present difficulties for many native speakers of English with limited education and/or limited familiarity with texts of this type' (1).

The Committee acknowledged this inconsistency between the legislation and policy of the test, but also pointed to the fact that as an advisory body, it had not been moved to amend the definition of 'basic knowledge of English' in the Australian Citizenship Act. Instead, the Committee made its recommendations on the policy side, accepting English language skills as a requirement for acquiring Australian citizenship:

> the legislative requirement for a basic knowledge of the English language (noting and supporting the current exemptions) is important for prospective citizens as it enables them to exist, be self sufficient and participate in Australian society, which are all valuable aspects of Australian citizenship.
>
> (Report, 20)

The Committee proposed that a definition of the term should be implemented that would reflect a lower threshold than that which is in operation in the current test and resource booklet. A 'basic' knowledge of the English language should be understood to mean 'a sufficient knowledge of English to be able to exist independently in the wider Australian community'. This level of knowledge is likened to level A1/A2 in the Common European Framework of Reference (for a discussion of the CEFR in the German context, see Chapter 8), for which the general descriptors read as follows:

> **A1:** Can understand and use familiar everyday expressions and very basic phrases aimed at the satisfaction of needs of a concrete type. Can introduce him/herself and others and can ask and answer questions about personal details such as where he/she lives, people he/she knows and things he/she has. Can interact in a simple way provided the other person talks slowly and clearly and is prepared to help

> **A2:** Can understand sentences and frequently used expressions related to areas of most immediate relevance (e.g. very basic personal and family information, shopping, local geography, employment). Can communicate in simple and routine tasks requiring a simple and direct exchange of information on familiar and routine matters. Can describe in simple terms aspects of his/her background, immediate environment and matters in areas of immediate need

The Committee further recommended that the level of English knowledge defined as sufficient be translated into the re-writing and development of the resources supporting applicants' preparation for the citizenship test. Although not stated as a final recommendation, the Committee also proposed involving language experts in the development of materials to ensure a fit between language level required and language used in testing and preparation materials. It also suggested that English testing be separated from other testing for citizenship, if required (see discussion of Pathways below).

Defining adequate knowledge of Australia and responsibilities and privileges of Australian citizenship

In addition to the requirement of having 'an adequate knowledge of the responsibilities and privileges of Australian Citizenship' (Nationality and Citizenship Act, 1948), the 2007 amendment to the Act added the requirement of having an 'adequate knowledge of Australia' (Australian Citizenship Amendment (Citizenship Testing) Act 2007), which, in the view of the then government, was intended to support integration and participation in Australian society, or in the words of the then Minister for Immigration and Citizenship, Kevin Andrews:[2]

> By having the knowledge and more importantly an appreciation of events that have shaped this country and the institutions that have been established as a result will help foster a nation of people with a common purpose.

In Chapter 9, Emily Farrell has critically discussed aspects of integration and belonging with regards to the new citizenship testing regime and its knowledge component. The current testing regime has also been criticised for the irrelevance of most of the information contained in the preparatory booklet and test questions made public. Linked to this criticism is the inconsistency of the resource booklet in presenting information meant to be tested. In its present form, the whole book is testable, without outlining or clearly stating the information that is most relevant for the test. The submissions received by the Committee make a clear distinction between material that would prepare prospective citizens for taking the citizenship pledge and material that provides information about Australia more generally, with a clear preference given that only material relevant to the Pledge be tested. The Committee endorsed this view, stating that material relevant to successful settlement – which some submissions considered to be relevant and therefore testable (e.g. FECCA, 2008) – should be part of an earlier process, preceding citizenship.

In order to correct the structural problem of the preparatory booklet, namely the presentation of the testable information, the Committee decided to propose a separation of the document into two sections. Section 1 should consist of the testable material referring to the civic concepts within the Pledge of Commitment, while Section 2 should contain information about Australian history, society and culture; material that will not be included in the citizenship test. The Committee recommended that in the process of re-writing both the booklet and the test, professional educators in civics and citizenship education be involved.

A set of major recommendations, which will have far-reaching consequences for a re-writing of the testing materials if implemented in full, is centred around the Committee's proposal to focus the contents of the test on the Pledge of Commitment, which Australian citizens have to make at a conferral ceremony.

The Pledge reads as follows:

> *From this time forward, (under God)*,*
> *I pledge my loyalty to Australia and its people,*
> *Whose democratic beliefs I share,*
> *Whose rights and liberties I respect,*
> *And whose laws I will uphold and obey.*
> **A person may choose whether or not to use the words 'under God'.*

Focussing on the Pledge for an operationalisation of the concepts 'adequate knowledge of Australia' and 'responsibilities and privileges of Australian citizenship', the Committee draws on three notions from the Pledge to develop a catalogue of testable material (Report, 2008, 23–4):

- Democratic beliefs
- Responsibilities and privileges of Australian citizenship
- Requirement to uphold and obey the laws of Australia

In its attempt to expand on these notions, the Committee sets out the following list of values it understands to make up an Australian democratic belief system, as well as a register of responsibilities and privileges:

Democratic Beliefs	Responsibilities and Privileges of Australian citizenship	Laws of Australia
Respect for the equal worth, dignity and freedom of the individual	Voting in federal, state and territory elections and at referendum	Understanding of system of government which creates the laws
Freedom of speech	Seeking election to Parliament	
Freedom of religion	Applying for an Australian passport and to enter Australia freely	
Freedom of association	Registering children born overseas as Australian citizens by descent	
Support for parliamentary democracy and the rule of law	Seeking full consular assistance from Australian diplomatic representatives while overseas	

(Continued)

Democratic Beliefs	Responsibilities and Privileges of Australian citizenship	Laws of Australia
Equality under the law	Seeking the full range of employment opportunities in the Australian Defence Force and the Australian Public Service	
Equality of men and women	Serving on a jury if called to do so	
Equality of opportunity	Defending Australia should the need arise (subject to the same rights and exemptions as Australian-born citizens).	
Peacefulness		
Tolerance, mutual respect and compassion for those in need.		

The Committee also sustained the belief that knowledge of the national anthem and national flag should be maintained in the new test, since they are part of the Citizenship Ceremonies where applicants are required to make the Pledge.

Further recommendations were made by the Committee in regards to the three mandatory questions, which it recommended should be abandoned – and the pass mark of the test, which it recommended should remain at 60 per cent.

Pathways to citizenship

One major issue emerging from the consultations with and submissions to the Committee is the equity and fairness of the current test (Report, 2008, 26). When looking at statistics provided by the Australian Government in its *Snapshot Report* on the Australian Citizenship Test, the group of applicants categorised as entrants in the Humanitarian program comes out as having much lower success rates in the test than applicants in the Skilled stream or Family stream. The report also highlights a decrease in number of applications for citizenship since the introduction of the test.

The July 2009 report, relating to Australian citizenship tests administered by DIAC between October 2007 and 30 June 2009, lists the success
rates for the different streams as follows:[3]

Success rates in passing Australian citizenship test

	Pass	Fail
Skill Stream	99%	1%
Family Stream	95%	5%
Humanitarian Program	84%	16%

The data show that the situation has worsened over time with the
chances of entrants in the Humanitarian Program passing the test on
their first attempt diminishing:

Attempts required to pass Australian Citizenship Test

	April 2008 Report[4]	July 2009 Report
Skill Stream	1.1	1.1
Family Stream	1.2	1.3
Humanitarian Program	1.7	1.9

The Citizenship Review Committee suggests a system of different pathways to citizenship in order to address this issue. The alternative
pathways to citizenship approach also encompasses a further objective:
aiming to correct the alienating sentiment that the current test displays
for more disadvantaged applicants. Based on the written submissions,
consultations and media reports, the Committee acknowledged that the
test introduced in 2007 is producing a sentiment of fear and inhibition
for candidates, sometimes even deterring candidates from applying for
citizenship, although for the majority of these candidates, obtaining citizenship is more than a symbolic commitment, it is a political and legal
shelter.

In order to alter 'the unduly onerous testing regime' (Report, 2008,
26) in operation at the time of the report's completion, the Committee
sought to introduce a system of citizenship education programs which
would produce an enabling, positive and welcoming process of acquiring citizenship, in which the test – and the preparation for it – would be

tailored to applicants' needs. The Committee's proposal aimed at assisting members of groups disadvantaged by the current testing regime (refugees, humanitarian entrants and some family-stream migrants), who would struggle to pass because of their particular situations, such as lacking any formal education, being illiterate in their first language or English, having limited or no experience with computers and, more importantly, having a diminished capacity to learn and retain the amount of information present in the current information booklet.

Although DIAC did implement an assistance program for disadvantaged candidates, the Committee pointed out that the services of the Assisted Test have not been extensively used. The Assisted Test is meant to help candidates by having the questions read out to them, and in the case of candidates who are computer illiterate, the operation of the computer managed by a DIAC officer. The Committee found that since the implementation of the test, the Assisted Test has been used only 314 times. The low number in the administration of the alternative test was associated with the lack of publicity about its existence as well as the stigma that it carries when compared to the Standard Test (Report, 2008, 26).

The Committee proposed three alternative pathways for obtaining citizenship that would represent a less exclusionary process of assessment, and would have consideration for the variety of literacy skills, life experiences and personal circumstances of the candidates (Report, 2008, 28).

Pathways	Pathway 1	Pathway 2A	Pathway 2B	Pathway 2C
Knowledge Level	English literacy skills	Low/lack of English language literacy		
	Sufficient oral English capacity	Literacy in another language	*Citizenship Education Program in English*	*Citizenship Education Program*
	Computer skills	Sufficient command of oral English		*(languages other than English)*
	Familiar with multiple choice tests	Not familiar with formal tests		

Preparation and Language	Self-directed and in English	Self-directed, other than English	Revised resource book Classroom-based or online learning	Teaching directed by community-based organisations, including home tutoring
Resources	Revised resource book (English)	Translated copies of the revised resource book plus additional material to be developed	From revised resource book	Material developed in multilingual multimedia formats
Test Questions	From revised resource book	From revised resource book	From revised resource book	Separate bank of questions to determine the candidate's (sufficient) knowledge of English language
Form of Testing	Computer based or paper based	Oral test in English	Ongoing competency-based assessment	Separation of testing of English language knowledge (oral interview) from societal knowledge (Certificate of Participation)

The first pathway foreseen by the Committee is designed for candidates with English literacy skills, sufficient oral English knowledge, who are educated, computer literate and familiar with multiple choice testing systems. Preparation for this tier of candidates is envisaged to be self-directed and based on the revised resource booklet. The test questions will be generated from the testable part of the booklet and candidates will sit a computer-based test, unless they lack computer skills, live in a regional area or are uncomfortable with the computer-based format of assessment, in which case a paper-based test will be available for them. Pathways 2 A, B and C would provide greater support and different assessment modes as outlined in the table above.

As a final recommendation for the process of citizenship testing, the Committee advised the government to make publicly available all the test questions and to consult with educational experts on the number of questions that would make up the pool of testable questions.

Discussion of government response

The Government response to the Australian Citizenship Test Review, released in November 2008 (henceforth "Response"), was overwhelmingly positive, accepting that most of the recommendations discussed above should be acted upon in a revision of the citizenship testing regime. The Government agreed with the objectives of the test as set out by the Committee and it supported the recommendation to consider the Pledge of Commitment as the basis of testing for new citizens and their acceptance into the Australian community. The Minister for Immigration and Citizenship considered the Pledge to be a feasible subject of assessment, since it represented the democratic beliefs, laws, rights, responsibilities and privileges of Australian citizenship (Evans, 2008b). The understanding of these concepts is considered crucial for new citizens, therefore the new test is ideally meant to mirror the commitments embedded within the Pledge.

The Government also concurred with the Committee's assessment of the mismatch of the stated language requirement as 'basic' English and the reality of the current test and resource booklet. It accepted the Committee's recommendation of defining basic English as having 'a sufficient knowledge of English to be able to exist independently in the wider Australian community' and it committed to redeveloping the resource book and test questions in plain English. It also subscribed to the idea of developing a citizenship course as an alternative pathway to citizenship for refugees and disadvantaged or vulnerable migrants, stating that this would include 'people who understand English but whose level of literacy does not allow them to undertake a formal computer-based test' (Australian Government Response, 2008, henceforth 'Response').

What it does not agree to, though, is the recommendation of the Committee to set up a pathway that provides for a citizenship education program in languages other than English for disadvantaged applicants (see Pathway 2C in the Committee's overview of recommended pathways). The Committee had recommended that for candidates participating in this pathway program, testing basic knowledge of English language be separated from testing an adequate knowledge of Australia and testing the responsibilities and privileges of Australian citizenship. The assessment relating to this pathway would have consisted of (a) a *Certificate of Participation*, proving the fulfilment of the legislative requirement to have an adequate knowledge of Australia and of the responsibilities and privileges of Australian citizenship, and (b) an oral interview in English with a citizenship referee to determine the basic knowledge of English language required. Questions for the language interview would have come from a separate bank of questions than the Standard test and would have focused on testing a level of English required from the candidate to exist independently in the wider Australian community.

Arguing that 'Migrants with better English are more successful at settling and finding employment' (Response, 2008, 4), the Government did not accept this recommendation. Here, we clearly see the limits of the consultative process. The insistence on English language skills mirrors that in other countries with citizenship testing regimes: while the required level is set lower than in, for example, Germany (A1/2 versus B1, CEFR, see Chapter 8), it is not negotiable altogether. This might be an indication of the underlying stance of the current government to hold on to a testing regime that serves its purpose not only in the attempt to 'integrate' prospective citizens, but also to assure all other citizens of the suitability of those new citizens. As Murray Goot and Ian Watson have shown in Chapter 11, based on a series of national surveys from 1995 to 2003, there is significant agreement that 'speaking English' is one of the factors that makes someone 'truly Australian', that is, in the eyes of many Australians, 'speaking English' is a necessary prerequisite for being part of the Australian nation. We might also revisit Lloyd Cox's (Chapter 5) concept of 'identity crisis' here, which he defines as the 'collective apprehension by a named population about what distinguishes it from other named populations'. In most citizenship testing regimes discussed in this book and elsewhere proficiency in the 'native language' plays a crucial role in being admitted to citizenship (most recently: Extra et al., 2009; Hogan-Brun et al., 2009).

At the time of writing, there is no clear indication of the exact content of the future test, its questions or information that will support candidates in their preparation. The recommendations made by the Committee relate to the need of ensuring coordination and consistency between testing, assessment, educational materials available and pathways implemented. The Government acknowledged the need to diversify the testing methods, to add to the existing computer-based, oral and paper-based tests, as well as competency-based assessment. It also supported the recommendation to vary the presentation format of the study material and provide additional multimedia, audio and visual learning formats both in English and community languages. The Government decided to go against the Committee's proposition to leave the pass mark of the test at 60 per cent, arguing that a 75 per cent pass limit will be introduced so as to ensure the rigour of the new citizenship test. The Committee also advised the Government to make publicly available all the test questions, advocating for diminishing the secrecy around the testable questions, but this recommendation was refused. In support of its response, the Government argued that confidentiality of the test questions will keep unaltered the integrity and rigour of the test. The Committee recognised the dynamic feature of the material that will be included in the future test and recommended the continual revision of the information to be tested. The Government supported the recommendation, agreeing upon the changing nature of citizenship and the necessity of revisiting the testable and non-testable material connected to the notion of citizenship.

Making the Pledge the centre point of the new citizenship test signifies a turn in the content of the current citizenship test. While the current version of the test stresses the importance of national values and factual knowledge about Australia, the new test, to be constructed around the Pledge of Commitment, is seen as creating a notion of citizenship driven by civic values of fundamental importance to both Australian citizens by conferral and Australian citizens by birth (Evans, 2008b). Although the adjustments proposed by the Committee and accepted by the Government intend to create a more transparent and a less discriminatory mode of testing in terms of the relevance of the information to be assessed and included in the resource booklet, the refusal to accept three major recommendations (preparation and testing in a language other than English, keeping the pass mark at 60 per cent, which is already difficult to achieve for disadvantaged applicants of citizenship, as the data show, making all test questions freely available) shows that the future citizenship testing regime will continue to have the regulatory character of the current and prior regimes where disadvantaged groups of applicants will face the most difficulties in obtaining citizenship.

Conclusion

The Report prepared by the Citizenship Review Committee suggests a substantive revision of the Citizenship Test introduced in 2007. The recommendations proposed by the Committee members recognise the flawed, intimidating and, to some groups, discriminatory nature of the current test, both in its operation and content. Departing from a view on citizenship engrained in national values, which in the current testing regime were translated into questions about Australian history and sports, the proposed reform of the test seeks to establish an approach to citizenship where membership of the nation state is expressed by adherence to laws and procedures.

In this view, The Pledge of Commitment encapsulates the responsibilities and privileges of Australian citizenship. Placing it at the core of the new citizenship test foreshadows a different understanding of the purpose of the citizenship test – focused on understanding the responsibilities of citizenship – when compared to the one established by the Howard Government in 2007, which was strongly connected to earning the privilege of being an Australian citizen. Social inclusion and cohesion for the new system of citizenship testing reflects a dynamic process based on the understanding and participation of citizenship candidates within their chosen country of residence. As opposed to the current test, the test envisaged by the review committee is meant to contain information to which citizenship adherents are able to relate directly and which they would recognise and experience in their daily lives.

The new test, based on the Pledge of Commitment, is expected to create a fairer regime of testing. Democratic beliefs and laws, rights and responsibilities of Australian citizenship are said to figure as the core content of the test; with the aim of creating a sense of belonging concomitant with participation within the political, social and economic community, based on civic responsibility. Whether the revision of the resource material and the test questions will be successful in achieving these goals remains to be seen when they become available – one indicator of their success would surely be the participation and success rates of those disadvantaged groups of applicants identified by the Australian Citizenship Review Report.

Notes

1. Coming from FECCA (Federation of Ethnic communities Councils' of Australia), Petro Georgiou, AMEP (ACT)(Adult Migrant English Program), Davidson and Court (ESL Teachers), Piller and McNamara.

2. Commonwealth, *Parliamentary Debates*, House of Representatives, 30 May 2007, in Report, 2008.
3. Australian Citizenship Test Snapshot Report, July 2009, http://www. citizenship.gov.au/_pdf/citz-test-snapshot-report-jun09.pdf, accessed 31 August 2009.
4. Australian Citizenship Test Snapshot Report, April 2008, http://www. citizenship.gov.au/_pdf/citz-test-snapshot-report-2008-april.pdf, accessed 3 May 2009.

References

Adult Migrant English Program (AMEP) (ACT) (2008) *Submission to the Australian Citizenship Review Committe*. Accessed 9 January 2009. http://www. citizenshiptestreview.gov.au/_pdf/submissions/sub103.pdf

Australian Citizenship Amendment (Citizenship Testing) Act 2007. Accessed 3 November 2008. http://www.austlii.edu.au/au/legis/cth/consol_act/ aca2007254/

Australian Government (2006) *Australian Citizenship, Much More Than a Ceremony*. Discussion paper. Accessed 12 March 2008. http://pandora. nla.gov.au/pan/64133/20061005–0000/ www.citizenship.gov.au/news/DIMA_ Citizenship_Discussion_Paper.pdf

Australian Government (2008) *Government Response to Australian Citizenship Test Review. Moving Forward…Improving pathways to Citizenship*. Accessed 3 December 2008. http://www.citizenshiptestreview.gov.au/content/ gov-response/response-to-report.htm

Council of Europe (2009) *European Language Portfolio (Levels)*. Accessed 9 January 2009. http://www.coe.int/T/DG4/Portfolio/?L=E&M=/main_pages/ levels.html

Davidson, H. and D. Court (2008) *Submission to the Australian Citizenship Review Committee*. Accessed 9 January 2009. http://www.citizenshiptestreview.gov. au/_pdf/submissions/sub016.pdf

Department of Immigration and Citizenship (DIAC) (2007) *Becoming an Australian Citizen. Resource Book*. Accessed 9 January 2009. http://www. citizenship.gov.au/test/resource-booklet/citz-booklet-full-ver.pdf

Department of Immigration and Citizenship (DIAC) (2008a) *Annual Report 2007–8*. Accessed 9 January 2009. http://www.immi.gov.au/about/reports/ annual/2007–08/html/outcome2/output2–3.htm

Department of Immigration and Citizenship (DIAC) (2008b) *Australian Citizenship Test Snapshot Report, April 2008*. Accessed 3 May 2009. http://www.citizenship.gov.au/_pdf/citz-test-snapshot-report-2008-april.pdf

Department of Immigration and Citizenship (DIAC) (2009) *Australian Citizenship Test Snapshot Report, July 2009*. Accessed 31 August 2009. http://www. citizenship.gov.au/_pdf/citz-test-snapshot-report-jun09.pdf

Evans, C. (2008a) *Independent Committee to review Citizenship Test. Media Release*. Accessed 3 December 2008. http://www.chrisevans.alp.org.au/news/ 0408/immimediarelease28–01.php

Evans, C. (2008b) *New Citizenship Test to Focus on Responsibilities and Privileges. Media Release*. Accessed 3 December 2008. http://www.chrisevans.alp.org.au/ news/1108/immimediarelease22–01.php

Extra, G., M. Spotti and P. Avermaet(eds) (2009) *Language Testing, Migration and Citizenship: Cross-National Perspectives on Integration Regimes.* London: Continuum.

Federation of Ethnic Communities Council of Australia (FECCA) (2008) *Submission to the Australian Citizenship Review Committee.* Accessed 9 January 2009. http://www.fecca.org.au/Submissions/2008/submissions_2008019.pdf

Georgiou, P. (2008) *Submission to the Australian Citizenship Review Committee.* Accessed 9 January 2009. http://www.citizenshiptestreview.gov.au/_pdf/submissions/sub039.pdf

Hogan-Brun, G., C. Mar-Molinero and P. Stevenson (eds) (2009) *Discourses on Language and Integration: Critical Perspectives on Language Testing Regimes in Europe.* Amsterdam: John Benjamins.

Human Rights and Equal Opportunity Commission (HROEC) (2008) *Submission to the Australian Citizenship Review Committee.* Accessed 9 January 2009. http://www.hreoc.gov.au/legal/submissions/2008/20080605_citizenship_test.html

Jupp, J. (2008) *Submission to the Australian Citizenship Review Committee.* Accessed 9 January 2009. http://www.citizenshiptestreview.gov.au/_pdf/submissions/sub173.pdf

McNamara, T. (2009) 'The Spectre of the Dictation Test: Language Testing for Immigration and Citizenship in Australia', in G. Extra, M. Spotti and P. Avermaet (eds), *Language Testing, Migration and Citizenship: Cross-National Perspectives on Integration Regimes.* London: Continuum.

Nationality and Citizenship Act (1948) Accessed 3 November 2008. http://www.foundingdocs.gov.au/resources/transcripts/cth13_doc_1948.pdf

Piller, I., and T. McNamara (2007) *Assessment of the Language Level of the August 2007 Draft of the Resource Booklet. Becoming an Australian Citizen.* Report prepared for the Federation of Ethnic Communities' Councils of Australia (FECCA). Curtin, ACT: FECCA.

Pledge of Commitment to Australia (2009) Accessed 29 June 2009. http://www.citizenship.gov.au/resources/ceremonies/citizenship/pledge.htm

Rimmer, S.H. (2007) *Australian Citizenship Amendment (Citizenship Testing Bill) 2007.* Accessed 27 August 2007. http://www.aph.gov.au/library/pubs/bd/2006–07/07bd188.pdf

Rubenstein, K. (2007) *Submission to Senate Legal and Constitutional Legislation Committee in its Review of the Australian Citizenship Amendment (Citizenship Testing) Bill 2007.* Accessed 27 August 2007. http://law.anu.edu.au/cipl/Expert%20Opinion/2007/Submission%20to%20Senate%20on%20Australian%20Citizenship%20Testing%20Bill%205.pdf

Afterword

Naturalisation, Rights, Duties and Waning Sovereignty

Sue Wright

> As a normative concept, citizenship is a set of rights, exercised
> by individuals who hold the rights, equal for all citizens, and
> universally distributed within a political community, as well as
> a corresponding set of institutions guaranteeing these rights.
>
> (Bauböck, 1991, 11)

This is a statist and somewhat passive definition of citizenship, the
citizen as a carrier or even recipient of rights. It presents citizenship
as guaranteeing individuals' legal safeguards within the rule-of-law and
on an equal footing with all their co-nationals. In foregrounding rights,
Bauböck of course reflects the period in which he was writing. Since
T.H. Marshall's seminal essay on the state and the citizen (1950), rights
had become the focus of discussions of citizenship, and in the 1970s and
1980s, the discourse of rights gained ground.

Marshall's work rested on two assumptions: that citizenship is a qualifying condition to gain access to rights and that citizenship is bestowed
by the nation state. These statements were legitimate in the late 1940s,
but over the six decades since then much has changed regarding the
rights of the individual, which are increasingly seen as universal rather
than national and attached to personhood rather than to citizenship
(Soysal, 1994). However, in the matter of the legal status of citizenship,
we are still acting according to the frame of Marshall's view of the world.
The state is still the means by which citizenship is conferred.

We thus have an anomaly: rights are human rights, but guarantors are
states. While the citizen will be on the inside, protected by the rights
guaranteed by the state, there will be others outside, not within this
protection. Citizenship is by definition exclusionary. Until such time as
there is a state contiguous with the world, there will always be a need

to decide who will have rights guaranteed by a particular state and who will not. The citizenship tests we have been examining are thus complex tools: they can appear a fairer and objective way of deciding who is in; they can be a gate-keeping mechanism designed to exclude the poor and illiterate or the culturally divergent.

We also have a singular omission in the tradition that links citizenship and rights. The issue of duties is not prominent in this scholarly literature. It does not regularly discuss the price of citizenship and guaranteed rights. It fails to mention what the state will ask of the citizen in return. This is a glaring omission since the cost of citizenship has often been high. In the twentieth century, nation state governments required citizens to fight for national interests as well as national defence, to be prepared to make the ultimate sacrifice of one's life for one's country. The generations from which men were conscripted in large numbers to fight in the two World Wars are a fast disappearing group. However, the narrative of defence of the nation remains strong and politicians and journalists continue to present the casualties of war as necessary sacrifice for the continued safety of the nation.[1] There are of course obvious differences where soldiers are professionals and not conscript citizen soldiers, but their involvement is still regularly presented as duty. The duty aspect of citizenship is therefore coloured by military connotations.

We rarely evoke the other ways that citizenship implies duty, for example the view of citizens' duty developed by Renan (1947 [1882]). He held that citizenship is a daily plebiscite, a daily renewing of the agreement to uphold the values of the state. However, this aspect of national duty is salient in naturalisation and particularly evident in the new citizenship tests. In the tests there is an attempt to define values and then seek adherence to them.

Opponents of Marshall had argued that too much insistence on rights makes for a passive, receptive citizenship (Stråth, 2003). It was likely that there would be a backlash in which the questions of restricting who should have these rights and how they should pay for them in duties would return to the centre stage. Citizenship tests can perhaps be seen as a small part of this backlash.

The authors in this book have shown in great detail how the issues of rights versus duties and insiders versus outsiders and newcomers played out in Australia. In the first part, Andrew Buck, Charlotte Frew, Alison Holland, Ian Tregenza and Lloyd Cox give a historical overview of the legal frames and the dominant discourses. Australian citizenship was a long time in gestation, and when the Nationality and Citizenship Act was finally passed in 1948, the legal status of becoming an Australian remained intricately linked to British subjecthood, and the cultural context in which this could happen was coloured by the colonial legacy. Buck and Frew explore the exclusionary nature of immigration in the decades immediately after the Second World War and discuss how the British Isles continued to be the provenance of many immigrants. Contemporary discourses of nation-building promoted the idea that a harmonious and unified state was more easily achieved when the cultural homogeneity of the group was maintained. This conviction found expression in the White Australia policies of the 1950s and 1960s.

Holland, Tregenza and Cox consider how, in the late twentieth century, the belief spread among certain sectors of the political class that the ideal of the homogeneous nation had come to term and that a democratic state could function with a certain degree of tolerance for cultural diversity. In the early 1970s, the Whitlam Government introduced multicultural policies and amended the Nationality and Citizenship Act. The aim of policy under Prime Ministers Fraser, Hawke and Keating was to open access and improve equity. This was recognition that political rights have to be translated into civil and social rights if citizenship is to be meaningful, in the way that Marshall (1950) had argued.

Marshall's account of the competition among interest groups as each seeks to define civil and social rights in terms favourable to its own side is a useful frame for understanding the Australian situation.[2] Holland's essay tracks the move to multiculturalism and the intense unease this caused in parts of the population. Although the government was always restrained in its policy, and multicultural structures aimed for a celebration of diversity within an old-style commitment to the nation state, the position was radical enough to create fear among those who had been socialised into the 'one nation' model. Howard's victory in the 1996 election can be attributed in part to the fact that the multiculturalists were not able to persuade opponents that they too might benefit from a multicultural environment. The conservative viewpoint was strengthened by world events, and in the new security environment of the 2000s, the Australian Right was able to refloat the ideal of cultural cohesion as sensible and justified. The citizenship test of linguistic and cultural knowledge appealed as a possible strategy for making explicit the values that newcomers were expected to adopt. However, as Cox demonstrates, the question of testing Australian values was fraught with problems: some values are so 'universal' that it is hard to claim them as a requirement to become an Australian; values that could conceivably be claimed as particular to Australia are likely to be seen as subjective and arbitrary; all values are difficult to test. The chapters by Farrell and

Möllering and Silaghi document the ethical objections to testing as well as the questions raised about the efficacy of the tests. We hear the views of those taking the tests as well as the policy makers.

Tregenza and Mackenzie focus on different facets of the duties issue. Tregenza's essay provides us with a historical frame, taking us back to the genesis of the idea of virtuous citizenship and its elaboration in the Anglo-Saxon world. Mackenzie provides an analysis of how present-day philosophers disagree about 'the capacities and virtues necessary for active citizenship, and about the proper role of the state in their development and exercise' (this volume: pages 191–192). Goot and Watson provide empirical evidence which suggests complex and unexpected patterns of identification which challenge the simple (simplistic?) assumptions of the test makers. Slade, Möllering and Hargreaves provide comparison and context demonstrating how Australian policy is part of a worldwide trend.

This book underscored for me the complexity of the citizenship issue and confirmed my belief that it is absolutely essential to have interdisciplinary perspective to begin to grasp the full extent of that complexity. The authors also caused me to revisit a question that has been nagging ever since I started to be interested in the citizenship test issue: Why at this precise point in time are so many states requiring would-be citizens to pass entrance tests? This was one of the questions that we grappled with in the symposium held to present and discuss the contributions to this book. Christina Slade (this volume) agrees with the suggestion that the sheer scale of migration in Europe may be at the root of that continent's turn to testing. Newcomers have arrived in unprecedented numbers in this last half century. It is tempting to view the current interest in citizenship testing in Europe as reaction to diversity and the manifestation of a continued desire to maintain a culturally cohesive community. The majority of European nation state governments and elites still subscribe to the 'one language, one nation and one territory' ideal[3] and have always been enthusiastic nation builders, and so maybe we should see the new enthusiasm for testing as just a new phase of the nation building process. Opponents to the tests deconstruct them in this way, categorising testing as a hegemonic and assimilationist response to late twentieth-century migration (e.g. Blackledge, 2008; Extra et al., 2009; Hogan-Brun et al., 2009).

But, could there also be a deeper structural reason for the flurry of tests? Could the turn to testing be indicative of more than the traditional concern that newcomers be incorporated into the nation? Could the tests be interpreted as a desire to nation-build in a situation where the power and reach of the nation state have become less secure? We have to be wary here because, to paraphrase Mark Twain, to report the death of the nation state would be an exaggeration. The nation state survives; new nation states have come into being in the recent past and old nation states have consolidated their power. But, on the other hand, the concept of the independent sovereign state whose frontiers are impermeable is clearly disappearing in some parts of the world, and in all parts of the world the defining characteristics of the nation state are under attack.

There is no uncontested set of criteria for these defining characteristics[4] but most would accept that the nation state classically has some or all of the following attributes: a defined territory with stable borders; a national government which is the sole law giver and law enforcer for its citizens; a domestic market usually protected by quotas and tariffs from foreign competition; a national defence force, sometimes staffed through conscription; a population that identifies with the state through the complex influence of national media, a national education system, a standardised national language and the elaboration of national symbols and icons. Now, to examine any of these characteristics is to reveal the extent to which the nation state system is changing.

First, the territorial integrity of the nation state is routinely challenged in a way that did not happen in the past.[5] This is particularly true in Europe, where devolution and independence have been on the rise (Harty and Murphy, 2005). Admittedly this is not the case for Australia but nonetheless there has been change. While the territory as container may not be altered, its contents are undergoing transformation. The UN's Demographic Yearbook shows how many of us move from state to state. Australia, recorded as having a population of 17,892,423 with 4,047,807 foreign born and 616,840 of unknown provenance in the period 1995–2004, is a state of immigration hugely affected by these migration flows.

Second, the nation state is no longer the sole guarantor of rights (Castles and Davidson, 2000; Risse and Sikkink, 1999). Soysal (1994) argues that global human rights hollow out the substance of national citizenship by decoupling rights from membership of the nation. The process may be more advanced in Europe where there are now regional courts of justice to hear cases where citizens challenge their state.[6] In other parts of the world, this is not yet the case. The International Court of Justice in The Hague may only adjudicate disputes among states. The interesting question here is whether the challenge to state sovereignty in matters of law will spread and increase.

Third, where the free market has been adopted (or imposed), much economic activity has become transnational, outside the control of the individual nation state. Not only is the state less able to protect its national industries, but also it has little influence on large transnational corporations or international markets for capital, commodities, service and futures.[7]

Fourth, national defence once meant the capacity to remain sovereign. National security required the necessary material resources and manpower to act alone to defend national interests when and wherever necessary. The events of the first decade of the century show that some states maintain this capacity. The proliferation of nuclear capability illustrates this. But many states do not aspire to military independence and thus enter into alliances or trust in the UN[8] to mobilise members' forces to counter aggression.

Fifth, for many people, the imagined society to which they belong is no longer exclusively the nation. According to Anderson's (1983) analysis, the national media are one of the key elements in the construction of an imagined national community. This is no longer the case in so far as the national media are only one of many sources of influence and information. Those who have the language repertoires and who can afford the hardware necessary enter the flows and exchanges of the global Information Society. Powerful technologies permit real-time communication and almost limitless access to information from all parts of the world. The Internet generation forms its opinions under a much wider range of influences than its parents or grandparents'.

It would be possible to continue.[9] For each defining attribute of the nation state, one can find examples where it no longer applies to all states or is weakened. Thus the frame that made us respond strongly to the trials and tribulations of our co-nationals is weaker than in the past. The national solidarity that permits the taxation burdens of the welfare state and the willingness to die to defend the national group are disappearing. Will we continue to accept that we should support fellow nationals? Why should we accept responsibility for the national group and not for the supra-national group? In the changing situation, the answers to these questions are not at all clear.

Looking at the naturalisation issue from this perspective seems to provide various insights. The requirement that newcomers demonstrate their willingness to jump through citizenship test hoops before gaining citizenship may be in direct relationship with the state's diminishing control of the defining variables which make it a nation state. It may well be that the post-national situation into which we seem to be slowly slipping is the very trigger for these nation building endeavours. Can tests be seen as part of a profound desire to shore up a system that is changing? To continue to require new citizens to be coached as if they were joining the homogenous monolithic nation state system of the past seems to be an exercise of nation state power simply because naturalisation is an area where the nation does still have sovereign power.

Coming to the issue from a number of different disciplinary traditions, the contributors have found different historical, legal, social, philosophical and economic data that explain why citizenship has become a subject of concern in Australia in the early twenty-first century. It is interesting that, considering there are so many different starting points, there is one consistent message from every paper: each contributor reveals the lack of consensus about the citizenship issue. Beck, Frew and Holland have documented the wide gulf among political parties on policy. Tregenza and Cox have shown how difficult it is to identify national core values, perhaps more difficult than it was in the past. Farrell, Möllering and Silaghi and Mackenzie document the dispute among those concerned with devising and conducting the test. Goot and Watson provide empirical evidence to profile the supporters of the anti-multicultural, nativist view and find that there are anomalies. What these papers tell us is that there is no agreement on how Australians want to define membership of the nation and how they want to regulate acquisition of citizenship. The three comparative chapters that look at other states reflect similar lack of consensus elsewhere.

And along with lack of consensus we have heightened interest in the area. Tregenza discerned three periods in which citizenship was much studied and discussed: the period of Idealist thought in the 30 years before the First World War, the spread of the idea of the welfare state following the Second World War, and the multicultural debate of the late twentieth century. We could speculate that we are now in, and that this book forms part of, a fourth wave of heightened interest in citizenship. Today our interest is driven by the changes happening in a globalising world. How will we organise citizenship if we move outside the nation state as a framework for action.[10] As Kostakopoulou (2008) has argued, we are trying to reconcile twenty-first-century challenges with nineteenth-century models.

Marshall saw citizenship as a process which had three stages. In the 'civil' stage, citizens gained the rights necessary for individual freedom. In the political stage, citizens gained the rights necessary to participate in the exercise of political power. In the social stage, citizens gained the rights to a modicum of economic rights and security, to share the social heritage and to live the life of a civilised being. Maybe this analysis can admit a fourth element. In the 'global' stage, how can we continue to guarantee citizenship rights we have acquired? Should we be listening to those like Somers (2008) who argue that the growing authority of the global market is distorting the meaning of citizenship?[11] Preoccupation with the integration of newcomers and the imposition of citizenship tests seems to be a sidetrack from the key issue of guaranteeing rights in a situation where the state is losing control and no other guarantor is yet in place.

To believe that it is worthwhile to induct new citizens into the nation by testing presupposes a situation where the nation state provides the structure for the political, economic and social worlds. This is the crux of the matter: whether we are still in a situation where it makes sense to persist with nation-building or whether the movement and mixing of peoples, the cosmopolitan nature of many societies and the reconfiguration of political and economic power make this endeavour anachronistic and ultimately futile. On the one hand, citizenship has proved to be one of the bastions of the nation state system and an area in which national governments have retained power. On the other hand, citizenship has been instantiated in the nation state system (Dobson, 2006) and this system of political organisation appears to be changing. How will citizenship remain unchanged? All enquiry in this area does need to take the *longue durée* perspective and be informed by a consideration of how the national may be becoming the post-national. Together the contributors to this book do this, providing a historically anchored, interdisciplinary examination of the citizenship issue in Australia.

Notes

1. For a discussion of patriotism and the call to fight for one's country, see Primoratz and Pavković (2007).
2. Giddens (1982) suggests that Marshall underplays the struggle; none of the three sets of citizen rights was achieved without challenge and confrontation.
3. Although there have been some minor concessions and/or some granting of autonomy to autochthonous minority groups, a linguistically and culturally cohesive state is still the aim of most governments, as their national education systems demonstrate.
4. See Özkirimli (2000) for a discussion of the extent of the disagreement.
5. Ewin (2003) discusses the assumption of the territorial integrity of the state, and the acceptance that 'we cannot rightly divide up territories that the

state has a right to'. He notes that there are now those who challenge state integrity as nothing more than 'another form of property worship'.

6. Individuals may apply to the European Court of Justice if they feel their state is contravening the rights guaranteed by EU treaties and legislation and to the European Court of Human Rights set up by the Council of Europe if they feel that their state is contravening or not defending their universal human rights.

7. Transnational Corporations will move out of states if the latter try to enforce unwanted employment, environmental or tax laws. The extent of the power of TNCs whose turnover is of a greater magnitude than the GNP of some small states has long been noted as a cause for concern. The international financial markets also escape the control of national governments. Traders were relatively unfettered by national constraints in the boom years of the 2000s as they moved capital from market to market. It was only in the crises of 2008 and 2009 that companies remembered that they were national enterprises as they turned to the state for help in difficult times.

8. This is a somewhat risky position in this era of change. While it is difficult to envisage a situation where there would not be reaction to invasion, it is clear that not all contraventions of state sovereignty will receive equal treatment from a UN dominated by the present Security Council.

9. For a full discussion of this, see, for example, Held (1996) who argues that there are seven sources of political power and that five of these are now relocated partially at least to levels above or below the national; Stråth and Skinner (2003) who claim that contemporary states do less than they used to do, and have more rivals that have usurped their power; and Castles and Davidson (2000) who contend that globalisation has eroded the power of the nation state.

10. In these remarks I am aware that my European experience is an influence. Commentators with other experience do not seem so convinced. American scholars often argue against post-nationalism in a very muscular way. See, for example, Rudolph (2005).

11. In fairness to Bauböck whose 1991 work I used to exemplify the view of that era, we should note that he is another who has recognised the present challenge and is currently researching nested and transitional aspects of citizenship.

References

Anderson, B. (1983) *Imagined Communities* (London: Verso).

Bauböck, R. (1991) *Immigration and the Boundaries of Citizenship*. Research Paper 280. Accessed October 2009. http://www.ihs.ac.at/publications/ihsfo/fo280.pdf

Blackledge, A.J. (2008) 'Liberalism, discrimination and the law: Language testing for citizenship in Britain', in G. Rings and A. Ife (eds), *Neo-colonial Mentalities in Contemporary Europe? Language and Discourse in the Construction of Identities* (Cambridge Scholars Publishing).

Bulmer, M. and A. Rees (1996) *Citizenship Today: The Contemporary Relevance of T. H. Marshall* (London: UCL Press).

Castles, S. and A. Davidson (2000) *Citizenship and Migration* (Basingstoke: Palgrave Macmillan).

Dobson, L. (2006) *Supranational Citizenship* (Manchester: Manchester Uni. Press).

Ewin, R. (2003) 'Peoples and Political Obligation' *Macquarie Law Journal* 3: 13–28.

Extra, G., M. Spotti and P. Avermaet (eds) (2009) *Language Testing, Migration and Citizenship: Cross-National Perspectives on Integration Regimes* (London: Continuum).

Giddens, A. (1982) *Profiles and Critiques in Social Theory* (London: Macmillan).

Harty, S. and M. Murphy (2005) *In Defence of Multinational Citizenship* (Cardiff: University of Wales Press).

Held, D. (1996) *Democracy and the Global Order: From the Modern State to Cosmopolitan Governance* (Palo Alto, CA: Stanford University Press).

Hogan-Brun, G., C. Mar-Molinero and P. Stevenson (eds) (2009) *Discourses on Language and Integration: Critical Perspectives on Language Testing Regimes in Europe* (Amsterdam: John Benjamins).

Kostakopoulou, D. (2008) *The Future Governance of Citizenship* (Cambridge: Cambridge University Press).

Marshall, T.H. (1950) *Citizenship and Social Class and Other Essays* (Cambridge: Cambridge University Press).

Özkirimli, U. (2000) *Theories of Nationalism: A Critical Introduction* (Basingstoke: Palgrave Macmillan).

Primoratz, I. and A. Pavković (2007) *Patriotism* (Aldershot: Ashgate).

Renan, E. (1947 [1882]) Qu'est-ce qu'une nation? *Discours et conférences, Oeuvres completes*. Vol. 1 Paris.

Risse, T. and K. Sikkink (1999) 'The socialization of international human rights norms into domestic practice', in R. Risse, S. Ropp and K. Sikkink (eds), *The Power of Human Rights Norms and Domestic Change* (Cambridge: Cambridge University Press): 1–38.

Roche, M. (1992) *Rethinking Citizenship* (Cambridge: Polity Press).

Rudolph, C. (2005) 'Sovereignty and Territorial Borders in a Global Age' *International Studies Review* 7 (1): 1–20.

Stråth, B. (2003) 'The state and its critics: Is there a post modern challenge?', in Q. Skinner and B. Stråth (eds), *States and Citizens: History, Theory, Prospects* (Cambridge: Cambridge University Press): 167–191.

Stråth B. and Q. Skinner (2003) 'Introduction', in Q. Skinner and B. Stråth (eds), *States and Citizens: History, Theory, Prospects* (Cambridge: Cambridge University Press): 1–11.

Somers, M. (2008) *Genealogies of Citizenship* (Cambridge: Cambridge University Press).

Soysal, Y. (1994) *Limits of Citizenship: Migrants and Postnational Membership in Europe* (Chicago, IL: University of Chicago Press).

United Nations *Demographic Yearbook. Volume 3 – International Migration Characteristics: Native and Foreign-Born Population*. Accessed October 2009. http://unstats.un.org/unsd/Demographic/products/dyb/dybcens.htm#MIGR

Index